EYES OF THE NIGHT

EYES OF THE NIGHT

THE AIR DEFENCE OF NORTH-WESTERN ENGLAND 1940–1943

Joe Bamford & Ron Collier

Pen & Sword
AVIATION

First published in
Great Britain in 2005
By Pen & Sword Aviation
An imprint of Pen and Sword Books Ltd
47 Church Street
Barnsley
South Yorkshire
S70 2AS
England

Copyright © Joe Bamford & Ron Collier, 2005

ISBN 1 84415 296 0

The right of Joe Bamford & Ron Collier to be identified as the Authors of this Work has been
asserted by them in accordance with the Copyright, Designs and Patents Act 1988.

A CIP record for this book is available from the British Library.

All rights reserved. No part of this book may be reproduced or transmitted in any form or by any
means, electronic or mechanical including photocopying, recording or by any information storage
and retrieval system, without permission from the Publisher in writing.

Typeset in the UK by Mac Style, Nafferton, E. Yorkshire.
Printed and bound in the UK by CPI UK.

Pen & Sword Books Ltd incorporates the imprints of Pen & Sword Aviation, Pen & Sword
Maritime, Pen & Sword Military, Wharncliffe Local History, Pen & Sword Select, Pen & Sword
Military Classics and Leo Cooper.

For a complete list of Pen & Sword titles please contact
Pen & Sword Books Limited
47 Church Street, Barnsley, South Yorkshire, S70 2AS, England
E-mail: enquiries@pen-and-sword.co.uk
Website: www.pen-and-sword.co.uk

Contents

Foreword

This book is the result of extensive research by aviation archaeologist and *Dark Peaks* author Ron Collier. Many years ago Ron made contact with a number of wartime pilots, some of whom passed away a long time ago. Their anecdotes and recollections of the war form part of what is a unique story about Britain's night defences in the north-west during the period 1940–3. My contribution has been to follow up Ron's research and establish fresh contacts with former 9 Group personnal.

Eyes of the Night is primarily the story of 9 Group, Royal Air Force Fighter Command, which was specifically formed for the protection of Liverpool and Manchester during its 'darkest' hour. It gives a detailed account of the air defence organization which was built up to protect north-west England but it is especially concerned with the Royal Air Force's night-fighter operations. The story includes accounts of combats which took place around the region and tells of the fate of Allied and German aircrew who were involved in such actions.

What is different about this book is that it also contains details of those incidents involving pilots and airmen who were killed or injured on non-operational flights. While 9 Group's squadrons lost only a handful of aircrew to enemy action, a large number were killed during training. They are generally the 'forgotten ones' but the authors recognize their courage and contributions to the night air-war.

Many of those who died were young New Zealanders who had travelled halfway around the world to fight for their 'Mother Country' and the Empire. Because of the lack of equipment and outdated training methods, a significant number were killed even before they got the chance to take part in operations. This book documents the triumphs and the tragedies of 9 Group and it is dedicated to all those who were killed, regardless of the circumstances.

The authors owe a great deal to Russell Brown, Brian Wild, Eric Raybould, John MacDonald, Dave Sanderson, Tom Smith, Stan Walker, Clem Lea, Norman Hurst, Tony Harratt, Graham Berry and Edwin Booth of Booth's Supermarkets. Without their contributions and enthusiasm this book would never have been possible and a period of RAF history might have been forgotten. Others who have supported the project and donated additional material include aviation historians and authors Harry Holmes and Frank Cheesman. We also appreciate the support and help given by Mr Peter Turner and John Williams of the Manston Spitfire & Hurricane Memorial Building.

Thanks also to Derek Pratt and Michael Grant for permission to use some of their diagrams of 9 Group. There are probably many others not named here who have been involved at some stage or other and I sincerely apologize to anyone I have not mentioned.

Joe Bamford

CHAPTER ONE

Provisions for Air Defence: 1936–40

In 1939, when Britain declared war on Germany, most people failed to realize just how unprepared the air defences were in the regions outside London. The north-west of England was particularly badly organized and on Merseyside there were serious shortages of all kinds of vital equipment. Local politicians were well aware of the situation and a number of councillors had repeatedly warned the Government about the poor air-defence situation.

Open criticism included an article written by the Editor of the *Liverpolitan* magazine in May 1938, who claimed that not a single air-raid siren existed in the city. The reason for that, he said, was that the Government had refused to authorize a particular type or make. There were other shortfalls as well; of the 2,500 air-raid wardens required, fewer than 1,200 had been enrolled. Only half of those had received any training and in the event of an air attack the situation would be bleak.

The Editor also claimed that there were only four heavy anti-aircraft (AA) guns in Liverpool capable of hitting a target at 21,000 ft. The 1937 Air Defence Plan for the distribution of heavy AA allocated just forty guns to the defence of the whole of Merseyside. That was a huge shortfall compared to the fifty-six allocated to Manchester and the eighty to Birmingham and Coventry, and just a fraction of the 224 distributed around London. Setbacks in production and modifications to the 3.7 and 4.5 in guns caused lengthy delays in their allocation.

Both Liverpool and Manchester came under the control of the 4th AA Division which was part of the 2nd AA Corps that also covered the North Midlands. On the outbreak of war the 4th AA Division had just ninety-two heavy and twenty-six light AA guns to protect some of the country's most heavily industrialized areas. Despite the earlier estimates of 1937, by June 1940 Liverpool had just sixteen heavy 4.5 in AA guns, supported by twenty-four 3.7 in guns, of which all but four were mobile. Manchester also had sixteen 4.5 in guns but a smaller number of 3.7 in guns, which were all static.

Apart from the shortage of armaments and manpower, Liverpool and Manchester remained vulnerable because they were not covered by the radar (RDF) network. While there were nineteen radar stations down the east coast of Britain there was not a single operational site north of Strumble Head in South Wales. There were a number of experimental stations under development on the Isle of Man and others at various locations along the coast of North Wales. Officially titled Air Ministry Experimental Stations (AMES), the sites on the Isle of Man at Bride (AMES No. 62) and Scarlett (AMES No. 63) would not be declared fully operational for another year.

The one concession to technology was that some AA units in Liverpool, such as 33 AA Brigade, were equipped with gun laying (GL) radar Mk 1. GL radar was capable of detecting targets at a range of 17 miles and the data it received was fed through to the predictors which guided the guns. The equipment may have been instrumental in the destruction of a Dornier 17 which was claimed by 33 Brigade on the night of 23/24 July.

The cover given by GL sets in the north-west was quite limited and in most areas AA units had to rely on mobile sound locators operated by the army's Acoustics Corps. In most cases the sound locators proved to be quite useless because they were designed to detect the sound made by a large force of bombers. The sound made by the approach of a single raider or a small force of enemy bombers could not normally be detected.

At night the powerful searchlights of AA Command scanned the dark sky to illuminate enemy aircraft so that their silhouettes could be identified. Despite being trained in aircraft recognition its personnel were not the best qualified in that role; it was the men of the Royal Observer Corps (ROC) who were the real experts. Its organization was one aspect of the defences that worked well, and it was an exception to the chaos found in other parts of the air-defence system.

A network of ROC posts was set up throughout the region, along the west coast and on high ground, where observers had a clear all-round view. Most observer posts consisted of nothing more than a sandbagged bunker equipped with an instrument to calculate the height and range of aircraft, and a telephone connected to headquarters (HQ). Despite working in primitive conditions, observations made by the ROC often provided the only information about where an enemy raid could be expected. Its observers passed on details about the position, direction and numbers of aircraft to their local HQ, and the information was given to Fighter Command. During the early days a large number of reports, concerning both enemy and friendly aircraft, originated from the ROC.

As early as 29 November 1939, Adolf Hitler had issued a directive which identified Liverpool and Manchester as key targets of decisive importance to the *Luftwaffe*, recognizing the strategic value of their industrial output and the ports which were linked via the Manchester Ship Canal. This vital waterway was high on the *Luftwaffe*'s list of priority targets, and from the first days of the war they regularly carried out aerial reconnaissance sorties along its length.

A German map – GB 463c (Irlam 5) – dated October 1939 displayed a section of the Manchester Ship Canal running through Irlam towards the Partington coal basin. There is no doubt as to what the intended target was; Irlam Lock is clearly outlined with a thick black line. What is different about this map is that it was not produced from an aerial photograph but a map which was almost certainly copied from a library book or other publication. The fact that the *Luftwaffe* was forced to take such measures suggests that its bombing campaign in the north-west was not as well planned as it might first have appeared.

If there were any deficiencies in the *Luftwaffe*'s intelligence reports concerning the north-west, however, it soon made up for them and most areas of the region were well reconnoitred. The reservoir in Heaton Park, north Manchester was overflown and photographed on 4 October 1939 by a German reconnaissance aircraft. The photograph was centred on the boating lake but it also covered the outlying areas of Prestwich. Remarkably it features the position of a heavy gun battery located in the park (H 15) with the word 'Flak'. This was a significant observation considering events in Heaton Park at

Luftwaffe aerial photograph of Heaton Park, Manchester, taken October 1939. Courtesy of Ken Hamlet

the height of the 'Christmas Blitz' and the fact that the following year it became an important RAF unit in the form of the Aircrew Despatch Centre.

Liverpool was threatened for the first time on 25 June 1940 when enemy aircraft flew over the city but for some reason failed to drop their bombs. Heavy cloud obscured the ground and it is thought that the bombers overshot their objective because they were operating at the extreme range of the Knickebein VHF radio beam which guided crews to their targets. By the end of July the *Luftwaffe* had overcome these technical problems and

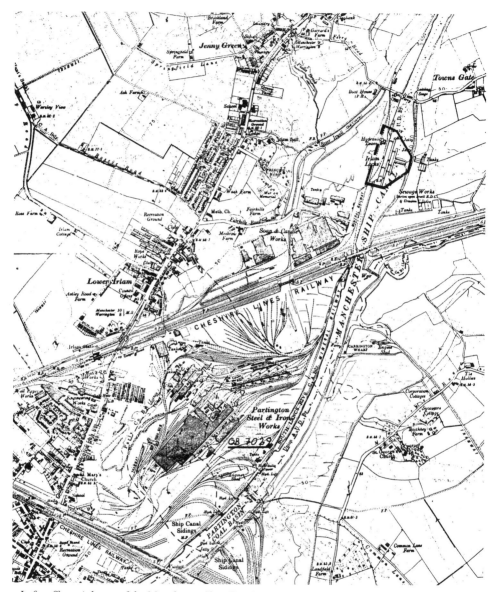

Luftwaffe aerial map of the Manchester Ship Canal, Irlam Locks. Dated October 1939 but made up from a map. Courtesy of Norman Jones

the introduction of a more powerful radio beam meant that the bombing became more accurate as Liverpool and Manchester came into its range.

During the early part of its offensive the *Luftwaffe* did not just drop bombs. Sometimes crews distributed propaganda material in a last-ditch attempt to win over the British public. On 8 August a bundle of leaflets was dropped over Salford which contained details of Hitler's speech to the Reichstag on 19 July. One of them struck a policeman on the head as he was standing guard outside the Salford Civil Defence Centre, but it caused him no permanent harm. Not surprisingly, the leaflet, which was appropriately titled, 'A Last Appeal To Reason', failed to convince local people about Hitler's intentions and his commitment to a peaceful solution.

After the events of the First World War it was generally accepted that the use of AA gunnery was subordinate to the use of fighter aircraft. During the first year of the war the north-west of England was under the control of 12 Group, Royal Air Force Fighter Command. Both Liverpool and Manchester were in the Kirton-in-Lindsey Sector, sandwiched between the Church Fenton and Digby Sectors. No. 12 Group was responsible for defending most of northern England from the Scottish border to the Midlands and across to East Anglia. With its HQ at Watnall in Nottinghamshire it was overstretched and most of its airfields were a long way from the industrial centres of Liverpool and Manchester.

With the exception of the RAF airfields at Hawarden, Tern Hill and Sealand, the majority of permanent stations were situated to the east of the Pennines in Yorkshire. The 12 Group sector stations at Church Fenton and Kirton-in-Lindsey were heavily committed to the defence of Humberside and the east coast. Problems with communications and delays in response times meant that any air cover that its squadrons provided for Merseyside or Manchester was often too little too late.

Liverpool's Speke Airport was taken over by the RAF and a number of night tactical-exercises were held there in the months leading up to the war. During one such action, in June 1939, Cobber Kain of 73 Squadron, who went on to become the first ace pilot of the war crashed, and was lucky to escape unharmed. Such incidents highlighted the dangers of night-flying even for those pilots with exceptional ability.

There was one new RAF airfield in the region at Cranage, which was sometimes used by single-engined fighters, although many pilots considered it a dangerous place to land because it had been built on land which had a high water table and the grass runways were often very muddy. RAF Cranage, or Byley as it was known to the locals, was situated in the Cheshire Gap 18 miles south of Manchester.

The airfield had been built in 1939 by John Mowlem Constructors and handed over to the RAF in June 1940. With its eight Bellman and four smaller blister hangars, Cranage's original role was to have been an aircraft storage facility and a relief landing ground for No. 5 Flying Training School (FTS) at Sealand. A Ministry of Aircraft Production factory which assembled Wellington bombers was sited just a few hundred yards away and a large number of them were stored there. In November 1940, 2 Air Navigation School (ANS) moved in and regular RAF staff who were posted in soon discovered that Cranage was not in any sense a traditional RAF station and it had few home comforts!

RAF Hawarden, 3 miles to the south of Chester, was the site of another shadow aircraft factory which manufactured Wellington bombers. It also acted as a relief landing ground for RAF Sealand and housed a number of service units including 48 Maintenance Unit (MU) and 7 Operational Training Unit (OTU). Operating as part of 10 Group, it was one of only three establishments which specialized in training pilots to fly the Spitfire. The unit was commanded by the forward-thinking Wing Commander Hallings-Pott. He was very much aware of the lack of fighter cover in the north-west region and he was in a position to do something about it.

No. 7 OTU had twenty-five Spitfire Mk 1s and 14 Hurricane Mk 1s on strength, plus a number of Miles Masters. Most of the instructors were experienced pilots, and some had already gained considerable experience during the evacuation of France. From the pool of instructors Hallings-Pott formed a Battle Flight, and he ensured that there were always three Spitfires on the flight line, fully armed and ready to go. The unit had exchanged Spitfires Is equipped with Browning .303 guns for others that were fitted with Hispano Suiza 20 mm cannon and the Battle Flight proved to be a powerful fighting force.

CHAPTER TWO

The Enemy at the Door: August 1940

During the evening of 13 August there were several incidents in the Peak District which suggested that the Germans might be about to launch a parachute assault in the area. At 2310 No. 2 machine-gun post at the RAF's 28 MU on Harpur Hill reported an aircraft circling overhead. The droning noise continued for over fifteen minutes but nothing could be seen through the dense cloud. On the ground, some 1½ miles way, lights were observed flashing as if someone was trying to signal to the aircraft's crew.

At 0228 the following morning, 14 August, No. 3 machine-gun post reported another aircraft passing low overhead. Some time later a civilian transport driver who was reporting for duty told a guard that he had just been stopped by the police. He said that after checking his identity the police officer had told him that three enemy parachutists had been caught and arrested in the area. The officer in charge of 28 MU's defences was immediately informed and when he checked with Police HQ at Chapel-en-le-Frith, the driver's story was confirmed.

Up until August 1940 the majority of RAF personnel had not been properly trained in the use of firearms, and units were often defended by ill-equipped local army units. In an emergency it might have taken up to twelve hours for reinforcements to arrive at Harpur Hill and so the situation must have seemed quite bleak. The officer in command took no chances: personnel at the machine-gun post were doubled and all the remaining personnel held in reserve in case of an attack by enemy forces.

On the same night there were several other unconfirmed reports of empty parachutes, flares and radio equipment being dropped at various locations around the Peak District. It has been claimed that this was part of a 'hoax' invasion, about which Lord Haw-Haw boasted during his broadcast the following evening. It is not known whether the Germans captured in the Peak District were paratroopers or spies, but it is quite likely that they were fifth columnists dropped to cause chaos in Britain's backyard.

At 28 MU on Harpur Hill, all the high ground which overlooked the unit was searched and despite the fact that nothing was found, guard posts remained doubled up. Enemy aircraft were regularly heard passing low over Harpur Hill, but because its defences mainly consisted of small arms, there was nothing much anyone could do. However during the evening of the 14th one enemy aircraft made the mistake of flying low over RAF Hawarden near Chester. Its German crew presented themselves as the perfect target and they were about to encounter a number of fighter pilots who did not want to miss such an opportunity.

After hearing the unsynchronized and distinctive sound of enemy aircraft engines, Wing Commander Hallings-Pott abandoned his beer in the officers' mess. He and Squadron Leader McLean ran to the waiting Spitfires, where they were joined by another officer, Pilot Officer Peter Ayerst who had served in France with 73 Squadron. The three airmen quickly strapped themselves in, took off and climbed out in the direction of the Welsh border and RAF Sealand.

During the course of the day the *Luftwaffe* dispatched three He 111s to attack RAF Sealand. The first one dropped a number of incendiaries from just 1,000 ft, but they missed their target. The second, flown by *Oberleutnant* Artur Weisemann, bombed the sergeants' mess and caused a lot of damage and a single fatality. As the Spitfires approached Sealand, the He 111 was making its second pass across the airfield. Weisemann was an experienced pilot and as soon as his crew became aware of their presence, he immediately tried to make good his escape.

He pushed the throttles open and turned towards the coast, and although he temporarily shook off the Spitfires, the aircraft's position was betrayed by puffs of black smoke from an AA battery at Hawarden. The pilots of the Battle Flight spotted the smoke and Hallings-Pott led them straight into the attack – with immediate results. The He 111's starboard engine began to show signs of fire. McLean followed up with a second attack and he also claimed to have scored a number of hits on the enemy machine. The outcome of the combat was not immediately clear because the He 111 then flew into some low cloud and completely disappeared. Hallings-Pott and his fellow pilots were, however, convinced that the enemy aircraft had been badly damaged.

Back at Hawarden and in the absence of any night-flying facilities the 7 OTU pilots had to land in the dark, aided only by the headlights of a motor car. Despite the hazardous conditions, soon after landing McLean took off again in hot pursuit of the third He 111, which flew low above Sealand. He did not make any contact with the enemy aircraft but on his return he was given the good news that the Heinkel he had attacked earlier with Hallings-Pott had crashed. After the starboard engine was damaged it had seized up and *Oberleutnant* Weisemann was forced to fly very low while he looked for somewhere to make a crash landing. He crossed a golf course, skimmed across the River Dee and flew under some power lines, but after clipping a 10 ft high hedge he was forced make a belly landing on farmland near Saltney.

Oberleutnant Weisemann's four-man crew consisted of: *Feldwebel* Heinrich Rodder, observer; *Feldwebel* Hans Kocky; wireless operator; *Unteroffizier* Walter Schaum, flight mechanic; and *Unteroffizier* Gustav Ullmann, air gunner. All escaped serious injury, and after jumping out of the wreckage they tried to set fire to the Heinkel with a flare. They were soon captured by Corporal Anderton and his platoon from the local Home Guard unit but not before the fire had got a hold and totally destroyed the Heinkel.

Despite their actions the German airmen were well treated and taken to nearby Border House Farm, where they were offered something to eat and drink by the farmer's wife, Mrs Jones. She gave the airmen tea and biscuits but they were very suspicious and only ate them after she had sampled some first. The atmosphere was quite tense, and *Oberleutnant* Weisemann had ordered his crew not to say anything to anyone about the details of their mission. By the time the Germans departed under escort, their attitude had softened a little and Weisemann gave Mrs Jones' daughter some chocolates. He also gave

Mrs Jones a 10 Reichmark note – with a German invasion expected at any moment, she suspected that it might have been his way of warning her of what was to come.

As was the usual practice, the victors were soon at the crash site; Wing Commander Hallings-Pott arrived on the scene within ten minutes to inspect the wreckage and scavenge for a trophy. Intelligence sources later discovered that the aircraft, coded 1G + FS, was from III/KG 27 based at Rennes in France. A propeller boss was recovered from the wreckage and put on display at the main entrance of the officers' mess at Hawarden.

In the Peak District a high state of alert was maintained at 28 MU until 0900 hours on the 15th when the guard levels were returned to normal. There were more reports of enemy aircraft flying low and circling the area between 0645 and 0656 on Saturday, 17 August and on the 21st the *Ormskirk Advertiser* claimed that during the early hours of the 17th at least twenty parachutes had been dropped by enemy aircraft over the north-west.

A Flight of 264 Squadron Defiants – representative of those that were at Ringway at the end of August 1940. The units temporary presence marked the first organised attempt to combat the Luftwaffe's attacks on the north-west.

The Home Guard was given the job of rounding them up and taking them to special collection centres. It was later claimed that many of them went astray and were turned into wedding dresses and petticoats by innovative women.

The authorities were so concerned about the situation that forty-six airmen were despatched from 9 Recruiting Centre at Blackpool to 28 MU. Despite the fact that the situation was still causing concern, they were posted back to Blackpool almost as soon as they arrived. Over the next few days there were further sightings of lights flashing on the Ashbourne Road and both the police and an armed party of airmen searched the area but nothing was ever found.

Both air and ground defences remained on high alert but despite the interventions of 7 OTU's Battle Flight at Hawarden, the region's fighter cover remained poor. In August a number of day-fighter units were detached to RAF Ringway but most of them were only Category C units. (Category A squadrons were normally made up of experienced pilots, Category B were a mixture of experienced and newly qualified pilots and Category C were mainly inexperienced pilots with a few seasoned airmen to make up numbers.)

One of the first units to provide organized fighter cover in the Manchester area was A Flight of 264 Squadron, which was attached to RAF Ringway at the end of August 1940. Based at Kirton-in-Lindsey in Lincolnshire, it was equipped with the two-seat Boulton & Paul Defiant. The type had just been taken out of front-line service after it had proved to be too vulnerable during the Battle of Britain. At Ringway its crews had few opportunities to intercept enemy aircraft but they kept the men of 487 AA Battery on their toes, practising dive bombing, which allowed them to calibrate their guns. At the beginning of September the Defiants left Ringway and returned to Kirton-in-Linsdsey, where 264 Squadron converted to a night-fighting role.

After the fall of France the *Luftwaffe* changed its tactics and enemy aircraft began to approach the north-west of England in a different way. Instead of flying over the heavily defended south coast, or crossing the equally dangerous east coast, they began to infiltrate the west coast. Enemy aircraft from the IV, V, and VIII *Fliegkorps* of *Luftlotte* 3 flew along the Welsh coast, up St George's Channel and across Cardigan Bay. They did not follow a direct course to their targets and they could not use the Knickebein radio beam. There were, however, adaquate visual references to guide the crews to their targets, including Great Orme's Head, the Point Of Ayr and the estuary of the River Mersey.

No. 12 Group did not have either the facilities or the equipment to extend its already overstretched chain of command. In August 1940 a bold decision was made: following the formation of 10 Group on 31 May, another new group was established in Fighter Command, in the form of 9 Group. From the very beginning it suffered from a shortage of manpower and equipment, and the complex organization took several months to become fully operational.

CHAPTER THREE

9 Group: September 1940

No. 9 Group RAF Fighter Command was officially formed at Preston on 9 August 1940, but it was September before its organization began to fall into place. It was established specifically for the defence of the north-west of England and the North Midlands and its HQ was at Barton Hall. The eighteenth-century building, situated 3 miles north of Preston off the A6, had been the long-standing home of the Booth family. When the Hall was requisitioned in June 1940, John Booth and his family went to live at Bellsfield House in Bowness.

The estate on which Barton Hall was located has an interesting history going back to the thirteenth century, when the land was owned by the Barton family. They owned the land for several centuries but in 1846 it was purchased by Charles Roger Jacson, the son of a mill owner from Preston. There were many changes over the years and the original

Photograph of Barton Hall which was probably taken from a painting. The origins of Barton Hall go back to the 12th Century when the land was owned by the Barton family. The original Barton Hall was turned into a farmhouse and the mansion house, called Barton Lodge, was renamed Barton Hall. It was built around 1786 and over the centuries, the property and surrounding land had a number of owners, but by the 19th Century the Jacson family were in residence and they owned the hall until 1899. Courtesy of Tass Cotton

Barton Hall Preston. Staff Bonus day 1930 when it was the home of the Booth family, who then ran a grocery business but now own a supermarket chain in the north. In the centre is John Booth, who purchased Barton Hall in 1910, but had probably rented it for a number of years before that.
Courtesy of Edwin & Graham Booth & Booths' Supermarkets.

Barton Hall was turned into a farm house, while the building which had previously been known as Barton Lodge became the new Barton Hall. When Charles Jacson died in 1893 the estate was split up and soon afterwards it became the home of the Booth family. The occupation by the RAF was to prove an interesting period for Barton Hall and years later it was to become one of the most important sites involved with British aviation.

Initially 9 Group HQ, which was also known as RAF Preston, had an establishment of thirty-one officers and 145 airmen. They were under the command of Air Vice-Marshal Wilfred Ashton McClaughry, DSO, MC, DFC. McClaughry was a veteran of the First World War, during which he had served with distinction as the commanding officer of 4 Squadron, Australian Flying Corps. He was the oldest son of James and Charlotte, of Adelaide, and his brother, Edgar James, was also a distinguished airman who had reached the rank of air vice-marshal.

Unlike his contemporaries, such as Air Vice-Marshal Keith Park, the Air Officer Commanding (AOC) of 11 Group and Air Vice-Marshal Leigh-Mallory at 12 Group, McClaughry was not well known. Prior to being posted to 9 Group, he had been the

Director of Training at the Air Ministry and he was promoted to the rank of air vice-marshal on taking up his appointment at Barton Hall. While a number of senior officers were posted in from 12 Group HQ at Watnall, others arrived from a variety of different backgrounds.

Group Captain Charles Ley King, MC, DFC, arrived from HQ Technical Command to take up the post of senior air staff officer of 9 Group. He was another veteran of the First World War who had served in 139 Squadron and was awarded the DFC for action on 31 August 1918. Group Captain C.W. Hill, who was posted in from HQ Flying Training Command, had flown with 14 Squadron and as a young lieutenant had been shot down and taken prisoner in May 1916. Between them, the AOC and his staff had a lot of experience but there was a need for younger and more dynamic officers who were able to look at things from a fresh perspective.

Squadron Leader John Oliver William Oliver, DSO, DFC, was posted in on 9 August and on 1 September he was promoted to the rank of acting wing commander. This 30-year-old officer had trained at the Central Flying School and he was awarded a permanent commission in July 1931. 'Doggie' Oliver, as he was known, had served with distinction in 43 and 55 Squadrons and was credited with three enemy aircraft destroyed. On 13 May, while serving with 85 Squadron, he was shot down over France and fired upon by Belgian troops as he fell to earth. He survived his ordeal and returned to England that same afternoon. He was subsequently responsible for the safe return of large numbers of aircraft and aircrew from France.

A group portrait of officers from 4 Squadron Australian Flying Corps at Clairmarais on 10 June 1918. The future A.O.C of 9 Group, Major Wilfred Ashton McClaughry, D.S.O., M.C., D.F.C., is fourth from the right on the front row. His younger brother, Captain Edgar James McCloughry, D.S.O., D.F.C, is on his left. Courtesy of the Australian War Memorial

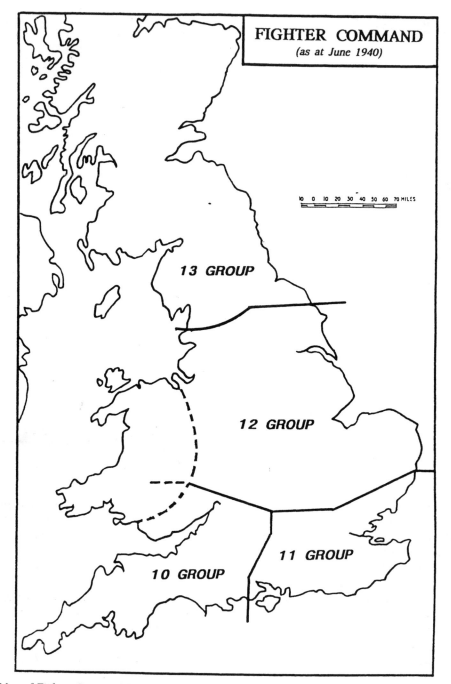

Map of Fighter Command Sectors (12 group) in the north-west region in June 1940, before the formation of 9 Group. Courtesy of Derek Pratt and Michael Grant

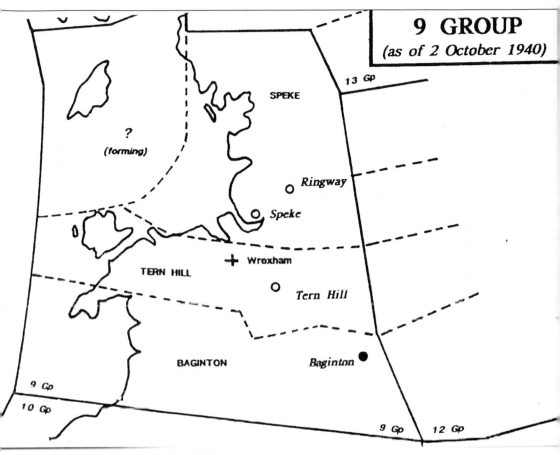

Map of 9 Group Sectors October 1940. Courtesy of Derek Pratt and Michael Grant

Oliver would play an important role in helping to get 9 Group operational but to begin with it lacked even the most basic methods of communication and telephone links. On 9 September, McClaughry, attended a meeting with Air Commodore Goodman of the ROC and Colonel W.T. Dodds of the 4th AA Division at Barton Hall. The meeting was held even before McClaughry had taken up his command, as he was not officially posted to 9 Group until 16 September.

The officers met representatives from the General Post Office (GPO), who were trying to arrange a timescale for the installation of telephone lines and other equipment. One of the most vital communication systems was the Defence Teleprinter Network which had been established by the GPO in 1938. They said it would take at least two months to fulfil the full scale of 9 Group's communication requirements, McClaughry was frustrated at the delay which would prevent 9 Group from becoming fully operational.

The GPO was, however, willing to provide a number of telephone lines within three weeks, including two to the AA Command HQ at Chester. Priority for connection was also given to another three lines to RAF Sector Control and another two to Fighter Command HQ at Bentley Priory. The GPO representatives pointed out that provision had already been made to connect ROC 5 Group HQ at Lancaster, and Squadron Leader Passmore confirmed that two other lines to 12 Group HQ at Watnall were operational.

Former Aircraftswoman Barbara Foden, a Special Duties Operations clerk was posted to Barton Hall a few months after it opened. One of her most vivid memories was of the Operations Room floor, which was covered with bright green rubber tiles. The surface was very difficult to clean but in typical RAF fashion it had been mopped regularly. Such a task was often given to airwomen who complained about their duties and those who were out of favour.

In the centre of the main Operations Room she said there was a large table approximately 20 ft long and 12 ft wide with a detailed map of the United Kingdom superimposed upon it. The table was slanted slightly towards a glass-fronted balcony, known as the 'Goldfish Bowl'. It was the sanctum of senior officers, who observed what was going on from above. The balcony ran the whole length of the room and below it were other glass offices which overlooked the table. They were staffed by a variety of experts including weather men and officers from the 4th AA Division.

It was the job of the filter plotters in the Filter Room to check with other sectors, groups and airfields about the movements and identification of aircraft. Only when an aircraft had been identified was it was plotted on the Operations Room and given a letter and number to match its role. Aircraft from Coastal Command, Training Command and Fighter Command were prefixed with the letters 'C', 'T' and 'F' respectively. Those aircraft which could not be identified were marked with an 'X' and they often presented the biggest problem.

The Operations Room monitored the movements not only of aircraft but also of outbound convoys from Liverpool. Each convoy was represented on the table by a piece of red plastic shaped like a boat and former Aircraftswoman Foden remembered a particularly embarrassing incident involving a Women's Auxiliary Air Force (WAAF) corporal. She was giving a running commentary to some VIPs in the Goldfish Bowl and keeping them informed on the movement of two convoys with troopships.

The convoys were called Funnel and Bucket, and as the corporal progressed with her commentary she became increasingly agitated. Then she got the names muddled which caused her to blush and burst into tears. Her mistake and distress caused the VIPs to grab their binoculars to check the names of the convoys. The corporal's error rejuvenated some of those on duty and even some of the officers in the Goldfish Bowl had a good laugh about it.

The AA Operations Room had a complement of eight army officers who worked under a senior liaison officer holding the rank of major. There were also three captains and four subalterns on duty, and their main purpose was to pass on details of aircraft movements to the gun operation rooms of the 4th AA Division at Chester. Chester was the main HQ of 4th AA Division and its commanding officer was Major General Cadell.

No. 9 Group staff faced many other problems during the early days. In a period of uncertainty it was short of both of aircraft and pilots. The group's first unit was an anti-aircraft co-operation flight, which arrived at RAF Wrexham on 7 August. The establishment of four pilots and seven unarmed aircraft hardly resembled a fighting force, however, and 9 Group had to wait for several months before it received its first fighter aircraft.

Because of the shortage of experienced fighter pilots, pilot training was reduced from six months to four weeks the day after 9 Group was formed. On 16 August it was cut to just two weeks, with the priority being to keep squadrons operating in the south fully manned. As result of these and other restrictions, 9 Group did not receive a sufficient number of trained pilots to form a squadron until October.

Some of the new squadrons formed in 9 Group were made up of Poles, Czechs and other foreign nationals, many of whom were stationed at RAF Weeton, 9 miles north-west of Preston near Blackpool. Weeton had opened in May 1940 as No. 8 School of Technical Training for parachute packers, metal workers and mechanical transport. In the same month the Polish Training Centre moved from Eastchurch to Blackpool and between 1 and 3 July thirty-one officers and 754 airmen of the Polish Air Force arrived at Weeton after being evacuated from France. Another 358 arrived just a few days later and Blackpool was to become a major centre for processing and training Polish airmen.

The decision to allow foreign nationals to fly operationally was a controversial one but it was necessitated by the shortage of trained RAF pilots. Some foreign pilots went to a lot of trouble to get to England and a small number of them even escaped after being captured. One was Stanislaw Wandzila, who was interned in Romania but then escaped and travelled overland to France via Syria. He was then given the job of evacuating some ground crew and they all eventually sailed to Britain from Argeles near the Spanish border. His party reached England on 24 June and eventually became part of 308 (City of Krakow) Squadron.

Technically, 308 Squadron (Polish) was 9 Group's first fighter unit; it was formed at the Polish Training Centre in Blackpool on 9 September 1940. As it turned out its commissioning was just a formality, and it did not receive a single aircraft for several months. Because of a shortage of aircraft and other problems, it was overtaken in the process of being declared operational by a unit made up Czech airmen.

Initially 9 Group's command was broken down into four sectors each one based around an airfield which controlled its operations. The first sector stations were created at Speke, Tern Hill, Baginton and Jurby on the Isle of Man. By the outbreak of war Speke, near Liverpool, was the second busiest airport in Britain and it was to play a vital part in 9 Group's operations. RAF Speke was commanded by Squadron Leader McMorgan. Following the RAF's dispersal policy the 9 Group Sector Control was based in a local school. Later staff occupied some of the lower rooms in the control tower.

Unlike some civil airports which were pressed into service, Tern Hill was a traditional RAF station which had first opened during the First World War. After being closed down it was reactivated in January 1936 and occupied by 10 FTS and 4 Aircraft Storage Unit (ASU). It was a large airfield with four C-type hangars and two D-types, but in 1940 it only had grass runways. Although the land it was built on had been drained, the airfield was still very wet and flooded regularly during the winter months.

The first night fighters to operate in 9 Group were a section of 29 Squadron Blenheims which had arrived at Tern Hill in August. The detachment was only on loan from 12 Group and it was detailed to provide one aircraft at immediate readiness and another two at fifteen minutes' readiness. No. 29 Squadron crews operated along a number of patrol lines, one of the first of which was the Mersey Blue, that covered the approaches to the River Mersey.

Under 9 Group it was superseded by the Holt Patrol Line which was routed along a series of datum points and towns. The patrols took the Blenheims on a south-westerly – north-easterly track, across Middlewich and Holt, between Liverpool and Manchester. The patrols were operated to protect the various approaches that the enemy used to attack Liverpool and Manchester but they proved to be no deterrent.

CHAPTER FOUR

Action in the Air:
7 OTU and 64 Squadron

Despite the increase in enemy activity, by the end of September 9 Group was barely operational and its staff continued to rely upon lodger units to provide air cover. No. 7 OTU's Battle Flight at Hawarden was still an essential part of the air defences and on 7 September another of its pilots was in action.

Information was passed on from an ROC post in the Wirral about an enemy aircraft which was operating in the area. Sergeant Lionel Pilkington, DFM, an experienced pilot who had flown in France with 73 Squadron was instructing a pupil when he heard the news over the radio (R/T). He immediately ordered his pupil to return to Hawarden and then climbed above Hoylake to 20,000 ft, the estimated height reported by the ROC.

Very soon he observed a twin-engined enemy aircraft, which he immediately identified as a Ju 88. Once he got within range he fired several short bursts, and chased it down to

Sergeant Lionel Pilkington, (on the left) Instructor at 7 O.T.U. Hawarden. Formerly of 73 Squadron and in the company of two other members of the unit, Flight Lieutenant Lovett (centre) and Flying Officer 'Fanny' Orton. Courtesy of Sqn Ldr Chris Goss & Goss/Rauchbach Archives

5,000 ft, before closing to within 100–150 yards and opening fire again. The Ju 88 disappeared into a thick bank of cloud but when he saw it again Pilkington noticed that its port engine had been hit and was trailing a steady stream of white smoke. Pilkington quickly opened fired again but after only three rounds his port cannon jammed. Fortunately the starboard cannon continued to work and he fired another fifty-seven rounds in the general direction of the Ju 88.

Pilkington's Spitfire was hit by some return fire but he managed to land safely at Hawarden, where he soon learned that the Ju 88 had crash landed in the Clywedog Valley near Machynlleth. *Leutnant* Bohle and his crew from III/KG 54 survived the impact and were taken prisoner. Sadly Sergeant Pilkington did not survive the war; after being commissioned and promoted to flight lieutenant, he was killed on 20 September 1941, while in the service of 111 Squadron.

On 17 September, British intelligence sources intercepted a German radio signal which indicated that Hitler had postponed Operation Sealion. As the threat of invasion receded and the Battle of Britain came to an end, night bombing raids on towns and cities in the north-west became more frequent. There were three raids on Liverpool that day and during the afternoon the first attack on the Rootes aircraft factory at Speke proved that the *Luftwaffe* knew what it was looking for.

There were developments on the day-fighter front at RAF Ringway. The Spitfires of 64 Squadron's B Flight replaced 264 Squadron's Defiants at the beginning of September. Throughout that month it flew what amounted to the first regular standing patrols of the region. Each operation consisted of two or three Spitfires flying sorties for up to one-hour; on some days as many as twenty-four such sorties were flown. Typically, the Spitfires did not operate much after sunset and by 2000 on most nights operational flying had normally ceased.

The words 'No contact made' featured almost as a matter of routine in the operational records of 64 Squadron but on 18 September its luck changed. Flying Officer Taylor took off at 1850 in company with a second Spitfire. They were ordered to join up with another two aircraft, which had taken off five minutes earlier. Few details are available but it is believed that Taylor spotted and attacked a Dornier in the area of Birkenhead. The 64 Squadron Operational Records Book (ORB) (RAF Form 540) duly credited him: '1 Do

Wreckage of Ju 88 shot down by Sergeant Pilkington on 7 September 1940, resting on a Welsh Mountain side. Courtesy of Sqn Ldr Chris Goss & Goss/Rauchbach Archives

215 probably destroyed by F/O Taylor.' Taylor was only airborne for fifteen minutes and he landed at 2005 after losing contact with the other Spitfires. It is possible that his Dornier was credited to another unit and at least one publication claims that it was destroyed by an aircraft from 41 Squadron.

There were numerous sightings of Dorniers in the region on that day and three Spitfires from 7 OTU's Battle Flight took off from Hawarden at 1930 after reports from the ROC that enemy aircraft were massing near Liverpool. Squadron Leader McLean engaged a Do 17 in combat at 16,000 ft and later reported that he had probably killed the rear gunner and damaged the bomber badly enough to make it lose height.

Sergeant Armitage, also of 7 OTU, reported a combat with a JU 88 which he claimed to have damaged before being forced to return to base with engine trouble. Meanwhile Flying Officer Brotchie saw what he identified as a Do 215 below him over Liverpool being fired upon by the AA guns. He was told over the R/T that the 'bandit' was at 8,000 ft, but then before he could intercept it, the aircraft flew away towards Hawarden. Soon afterwards he spotted two enemy aircraft at 20,000 ft, some distance apart; while Squadron Leader McLean went after one of them, Brotchie chased the other.

Levelling out at 20,000 ft Brotchie followed the Dornier along the Welsh coast and sat on its tail but then the crew spotted him and it suddenly dived away. He followed it down and gave it a long burst of fire while the German tail gunner returned only one short burst. At 4,000 ft Brotchie claimed that the Dornier was descending almost vertically and while he was levelling out he noticed it crash into the sea off Anglesey. There had been no sign of a fire and Brotchie concluded that the pilot had either been killed or had lost control during his attempt to escape. This was the last time that the instructor pilots of 7 OTU were involved in combat air operations.

There were a number of other combats around the same time and a flight of Spitfires from 611 Squadron based at Tern Hill were in action on 21 September. Pilot Officer Adams pursued a Dornier 17 and shot it down over Denbighshire. Three of the aircraft's crew were captured but *Unteroffizier* Pelzer was killed and buried with full military honours at Pwlheli on the Lleyn Peninsula.

A major development took place the following day when 9 Group's first two radar stations on the Isle of Man were declared operational. The Advanced Chain Home (ACH) stations at Bride and Scarlett were part of a temporary system based in wooden huts. The aerials and mast were much shorter than those in the permanent Chain Home system and the stations would not become fully operational until the following year. ACH only gave a limited radar coverage; and its weakness was that it gave no indication of the height of an enemy aircraft.

As the *Luftwaffe* turned increasingly to the use of night bombing the authorities in the north-west became more frustrated by the situation. A number of officials made their feelings known at a meeting of the Emergency Committee of Manchester City Council on 3 October. Complaints were made about the absence of any effective fighter cover during air raids and the inadequacy of AA provisions.

It was resolved by those present that the Town Clerk would write and make representations to the Regional Commissioner, Mr Hartley Shawcross, requesting further reinforcements. Unknown to the Emergency Committee, 9 Group's first fighter squadron had been declared operational just the day before and its arrival was warmly welcomed by the people of Liverpool.

CHAPTER FIVE

312 Squadron: October 1940

The defences of the City of Liverpool were boosted not just by a detachment but by a complete squadron based at RAF Speke. After being formed at Duxford in August 1940, 312 (Czech) Squadron was transferred to Speke in September and at the end of the month it was working up to becoming operational. Ironically it was commissioned at a time when the greatest need was for night-fighter units.

Under the command of Squadron Leader Tyson, the squadron's pilots took a while to achieve that status but the delay was no reflection of the quality of their flying ability. The unit waited a considerable time for the allocation of its aircraft and pilots had to struggle with various mechanical and structural problems to keep them airworthy. On 10 September, L1544, a Hurricane flown by Sergeant Keprt, caught fire and crashed near Cambridge. Such incidents were quite common but not all the pilots were as lucky as Keprt, who later transferred to a night-fighter unit.

Many of the mechanical problems were caused by the fact that 312 Squadron was equipped with what were effectively the oldest Hurricanes in RAF service. Several of them were survivors of the first production batch and the unit was plagued by continual engine failures and hydraulic leaks. The pilots persevered throughout Setpember and on 8 October they proved that they were worthy of their operational status.

There were several attempts to destroy the Rootes aircraft factory at Speke and on 8 October a single Ju 88 from KGr 806 took off from its base at Caen to bomb the site. Loaded with four 250 kg bombs it flew along the Welsh coast and headed east across Cardigan Bay, making land in North Wales to pick up the line of the River Mersey estuary. As it crossed the coast the enemy aircraft was seen by duty staff at an ROC post and information was passed down the line.

At Speke three Hurricanes of 312 Squadron's Yellow Section were scrambled and took-off just as the Ju 88 was on the final stages of its bombing run. Flight Lieutenant Gillam took off in L2575 at 1609, followed by Pilot Officer Vasatko in L1926, but the pilot of L1807, Sergeant Stehlik experienced some problems and was delayed for several minutes. He had engine trouble but he did not intend to miss out on the action and persevered until he cleared the problem.

The delay actually put him into a favourable position because as he became airborne the Ju 88 flew right in front of him, passing very low above the gun butts. Stehlik did not hesitate, and opened fire even before he had retracted the wheels of his Hurricane. His sudden appearance must have taken the German crew by surprise, and although he did not immediately shoot it down, his attack probably contributed to the ultimate fate of the Junkers.

Despite Stehlik's attack it continued on its course but its crew stood little chance of getting away from the Hurricanes as they formed up to attack. The chase was on, but determined to escape, one of the *Luftwaffe* crew returned fire from the rear position hitting and slightly damaging all three Hurricanes. Taking turns to make attacks on the low-flying aircraft, the RAF fighters made a number of hits and *Leutnant* Schegel, the observer, was shot in the head and killed instantly. The pilot, *Oberleutnant* Helmuth Bruckmann, had no choice but to make a crash landing. The Ju 88 slid down onto some land owned by Lever Brothers and during the impact the port engine was torn from its mountings. It had taken the 312 Squadron pilots just eleven minutes to claim their first victim.

The Ju 88 crashed near an AA gun site and some soldiers were amongst the first on the scene to take the three remaining crew prisoners. The wireless operator, *Unteroffizier* Helmuth Weth was wounded in his hand and was taken to Clatteridge Hospital. The Ju 88 was coded M7 + DK and the letter 'D', which identified the aircraft within its *staffel*, was painted bright red. An initial survey revealed that two bombs remained in its racks and investigators were suddenly surprised by a very loud bang. To everyone's relief however, it was not the bombs that had gone off but a self-inflating dinghy which exploded out of its storage position in the fuselage. After it had been fully examined by intelligence officers the Junkers was put on public display at St George's Hall in Liverpool.

The squadron's victory celebrations were spoiled two days later when a Hurricane burst into flames while on a test flight, with fatal results. Everything appeared normal as Sergeant Otta Hanzlicek flew over the River Mersey at the controls of L1547 near Ellesmere Port. As he banked around to return to Speke he experienced some vibration and found the Hurricane increasingly difficult to control. Eyewitnesses on the ground said the engine's rpm sounded wrong for the speed that the Hurricane was flying. Hanzlicek was unable to keep the aircraft straight and level, but although he struggled to save the aircraft he was eventually forced to abandon it and bale out. Possibly because he was overcome by smoke and fumes, or because the aircraft was too low for his parachute to open properly, Hanzlicek fell straight down into the River Mersey. The Hurricane was then seen to do a complete roll before it crashed on some mud flats just off the shore, close to Speke.

L1547 had been built in 1937 and it was the first Hurricane to enter RAF service so its loss was a blow to the squadron, and to Fighter Command. The body of 29-year-old Sergeant Hanzlicek was washed ashore along the banks of the river over a week later. He was buried with full military honours in Liverpool's West Derby Cemetery, where his body lies in Section 11, Grave 392.

On the unlucky 13th the squadron's fortunes declined even further when a number of its pilots were involved in an unfortunate incident after they wrongly identified some friendly aircraft. Two Blenheims from 29 Squadron were flying off the coast of North Wales near Point Ayre in fading light during the early evening when they were attacked by a section of 312 Squadron Hurricanes. Blenheim L6637, flown by Sergeant Robert Stevens crashed straight into the sea and he was killed instantly, together with his wireless operator, Sergeant Oswald Sly and his gunner, Aircraftsman Arthur Jackson.

The crew of the second Blenheim, K7135, were able to keep it airborne long enough to return to Tern Hill and make a safe landing. A board of inquiry was held on 16 October at Speke, with Group Captain Hill as its president and Squadron Leader Peter Townsend and Flight Lieutenant Lavers as its members. Although its findings were never made public, it is understood that one of its recommendations was that IFF (Identification Friend or Foe) systems should be installed in all aircraft immediately. The incident was thought to have been the result of mistaken identity, with the Blenheims assumed to be Ju 88s. It was also alleged that some of the pilots were a bit 'gung ho' and over confident after their recent success.

Of the three airmen who were killed, only the body of 29-year-old Aircraftsman Arthur Jackson was ever found and he was buried at Mexborough Cemetery in Grave 542. Sergeant Robert Edward Stevens is commemorated on Panel 19 at the Runnymede Memorial. Sergeant Oswald Kenneth Sly, formerly of Weston Super Mare, is also commemorated at Runnymede on Panel 19.

On the morning of 16 October an enemy aircraft penetrated the airfield defences at Tern Hill. At 0720 hours a single Ju 88 dropped four 250 kg bombs along with a clump of incendiaries, killing a number of service personnel. The bombs badly damaged one of the hangars, which was full of aircraft including K7135, the Blenheim which had survived the attack by 312 Squadron Hurricanes three days earlier. It was destroyed, along with twenty other aircraft. The only consolation was that many of them were non-operational types such as Oxfords and Harvards.

The following day another raider, a Dornier 17 Z-3, crashed on the hills above Denbigh in North Wales. Although the full details of its destruction are not known, it is possible that it was hit by AA fire over Liverpool. One of only twenty versions of the long-range photo reconniassance Dornier built and coded 7T + LL, it was from KGr. 606 based at Brest. Crewed by *Kriegsmarine* officers, it was only one of a small number of enemy aircraft which had taken off on a day when most of the *Luftwaffe* stayed on the ground. The pilot was *Leutnant* Heinz Havemann and the other members of his crew were *Unteroffiziers* Gerhard Socknitz and Karl Holscher and *Gefreiter* Rudi Fahrmann. The four officers had the distinction of being the first Germans to be buried in Hawarden cemetery.

CHAPTER SIX

Andreas and Cranage:
Battling with Administration

In October the 9 Group Sector Operations HQ on the Isle of Man was nearing completion in a new wing of Ramsey Grammar School. This was to control the Jurby Sector, named after the airfield in the north-west of the Isle of Man. When the new RAF airfield at Andreas became operational in 1941, the 9 Group Sector was renamed the Andreas Sector.

A description of Fighter Command's Operations Room at Ramsey by a former sector controller is similar to the one of Barton Hall given earlier by Barbara Foden. It contained a waist-high table which sloped down slightly at the front, covered with a map of Britain detailing each sector of 9 Group. On the table was what was known as the 'master plot', made up of aircraft positions given by distant RDF stations combined with filtered plots from Preston.

Overlooking the centre of the table sat the sector controller on a raised dais. His job was to make decisions about everything laid out before him. He had a microphone beside him and was able to talk to pilots on any channel, including the common sector frequency of Command Guard. Every word spoken by pilots or the controller was logged by operators who worked in four radio cabins behind the controller. At the side of the Controller sat his specialist assistants who co-ordinated with Air Sea Rescue, AA Command and Royal Navy HQ at Douglas.

The 9 Group sector Control Room at Ramsey was a substantial site. It had a signals centre with a telephone exchange with direct lines to the mainland and routed all over the world. It also housed a huge communications network with a number of teleprinter and radio cabins. There was a cypher office from which WAAF officers controlled all the secret codes and cypher machines, and distributed all the secret material. Just in case the complex was bombed it was duplicated by another site just up the road at the Regaby crossroads. Its facilities remained unoccupied but in an emergency they could have been operational within minutes.

Back on the mainland at Barton Hall there were further developments. On 19 October a number of new telephone lines were finally connected. Twenty WAAF clerks and a number of other personnel arrived to work in the the operations centre, which remained only a temporary facility. Amongst the new arrivals was the Sector Controller, Sergeant Frank Cheesman. He was sent to Barton Hall to gain further experience after completing his course at Leighton Buzzard and a brief posting to 13 Group HQ at Kenton Bar, Newcastle.

At Preston Sergeant Cheesman found accommodation and messing facilities a very mixed affair; he was billeted on a small housing estate in Broughton. With the exception of a small number of RAF Police, nobody lived on the Barton Hall site; everyone was driven in and out by RAF transport. The house where Sergeant Cheesman lived had been stripped and partioned off with bunk beds in every room. The bowling club in Broughton was used as the airmen's mess, while the Willows Café became the sergeants' mess.

The WAAFs were accommodated in a hostel, which was a large country residence known as Broughton House, where they also had their own mess. There was plenty of entertainment; in the early days most of it was in Preston, although eventually dances and concerts were organized locally. On the night of 7 November Al Ross and his band were the main attraction in the town; it was a good night to be out because there was little activity by the *Luftwaffe*.

Such relief was rare and in October the *Luftwaffe* bombed Liverpool on no less than fifteen occasions, sometimes harassing the defences as many as three times in twenty-four hours. After being operational for three months, not only did 9 Group have no effective night-fighter squadron, but it still had to be agreed where any such unit would be based.

On 9 November Wing Commander Oliver submitted a report to Air Vice-Marshal McClaughry about the possibility of using Cranage as a base for a permanent night-fighter squadron. He was aware that there were many problems to overcome, not the least of which was the fact that 9 Group had yet to be allocated such a unit. It was the first of two reports that he wrote about Cranage and one of the main points he addressed concerned the dispersal of aircraft. His interest in the subject had been raised by a survey of the airfield which suggested that a stick of four bombs dropped from any direction at normal height could cause devastating damage to aircraft parked there.

When Hawarden was bombed on the night of 14 November, Wing Commander Oliver's worst fears about the dispersal and storage of aircraft at Cranage were realized. The attack happened at 2005 when a lone raider dropped two bombs, one of which fell through the roof of K hangar while the second hit J hangar on No. 1 site. Both were packed with aircraft and a number of brand new Wellington bombers were destroyed, along with other types such as Blenheims and Hurricanes. Fortunately the majority of them were older aircraft used for training purposes and there were no serious casualties except for one dead rat!

Wing Commander R.J. Cooper the Station Commander at Cranage was involved in the discussions, and he was given the responsibility for organizing the dispersal programme. Another major concern of Oliver's was that of aircraft identification and ensuring that the pilots of any night-fighter unit avoided 'friendly fire' incidents with Cranage's resident Air Navigation School Ansons. The ANS devoted one-third of each course to night-flying training and it was resolved that some system must be developed to prevent incidents such as that involving the 29 Squadron Blenheim and 312 Squadron.

A second document prepared by Wing Commander Oliver a few days later dealt mainly with problems of accommodation and the logistics of maintaining a night-fighter squadron at Cranage. With over 200 pilots and 1,000 other personnel already crammed into the confines of the airfield, it was suggested that a separate camp be set up on the E site. It was estimated that a night-fighter unit would comprise twenty pilots, fifteen NCOs and 190 airmen, which would be divided into administrative and operational echelons. Wing Commander Cooper pointed out that there was a property about a mile to the east of the airfield which could accommodate up to seventy airmen. It was thought that pilots, armourers and mechanics should live in the immediate area of the dispersals, where tented accommodation would be available until Laing huts could be erected.

At the end of November, 9 Group's Order of Battle was made up of the thirteen Hurricanes of 312 Squadron and another ten belonging to 306 (Polish) Squadron based at Tern Hill. This unit had formed at Church Fenton at the end of August and was declared operational on 8 November. It was listed in 9 Group records as a another 'lodger unit'.

Another meeting was held at Cranage on 23 November between Pilot Officer Anderson, a section commander in 29 Squadron and Wing Commander Oliver. They discussed temporary arrangements which could be made to plug the gap in the night air defences until the arrival of a permanent unit. A proposal was made to move the section of Blenheims from Tern Hill to Cranage and it was agreed that operational flights would start at the beginning of December. Wing Commander Oliver believed that Fighter Command had arranged for 85 Squadron, which he had previously commanded, to join 9 Group. On 23 October it had flown north to Kirton-in-Lindsey where its pilots prepared to begin training for its new role, but it was about to move again to Gravesend.

At Cranage the flight-safety measures which had previously been discussed were put into action and strict conditions imposed upon the crews of the ANS. It was planned that its Ansons would be fitted with formation lights and IFF equipment but staff pilots were ordered not to fly above 5,000 ft. No. 9 Group sector stations were to be informed about the routes of all training flights.

Before any operational unit could be housed at Cranage, however, a number of other matters had to be resolved, and one of the most urgent being the supply and storage of aviation fuel.

Wing Commander Cooper secured the use of an 8,000 gallon tank which had been meant for use as a storage facility by Cranage's motor transport (MT) section. Another major problem was that there was no regular supply of 100 octane aviation fuel at Cranage; that would have to be requisitioned. It was anticipated that future requirements would be as much as 1,000 gal every twenty-four hours and other supplies needed to be found. There was no equipment to refuel the aircraft at the dispersals and an immediate request was issued for four 450 gal mobile tankers. As regards armaments and ammunition, the station armoury only held what was used for ground defence. The supply and storage of all types of ammunition likely to be used by fighter aircraft on operations was made a priority.

In anticipation of the arrival of a permanent fighter squadron, the requirement for further telephone lines and communications equipment was set out. Two further tie lines were required to connect the Operations Room at Cranage with the Speke Sector and another direct line from the Operations Room at Preston to the main switchboard. More telephone lines were needed to connect the Operations Room with the flight dispersals and section offices, which everyone hoped would be occupied and put to good use in the very near future.

CHAPTER SEVEN

Wing Commander Oliver and 307 Squadron: November 1940

On 24 November, the day after his meeting with Pilot Officer Anderson at Cranage, Wing Commander Oliver visited 308 Squadron at Baginton, but he was not impressed with what saw or heard. Because of the bad weather and a shortage of instructors, Squadron Leader Scott, the commanding officer (CO), had forecast that 308 Squadron would not be operational before the spring at the earliest. After receiving this dismal news Oliver decided to accompany some pilots on a training flight; that experience changed his opinion of them.

Soon after take-off he and Sergeants Grudzinski and Parafinski noticed some smoke over Coventry and decided to investigate. An aircraft was spotted in the distance but there was a question over its identity, so the wing commander exercised caution. Grudzinski had to break off because he had no oxygen but Sergeant Parafinski had already identified the Ju 88 and eagerly began his pursuit.

Just as Parafinski was delivering his quarter attack, Wing Commander Oliver joined in and went into a steep dive, from which he nearly failed to recover. For a few seconds he blacked out but fortunately he recovered quite quickly and managed to land at Baginton. As a result of Parafinski's attack one of the Ju 88's engine's caught fire and it burst into flames before crashing near Gloucester. The unit's first victory, was later confirmed as Ju 88, 4U + HL, and credited to Sergeant Parafinski. His actions and the experience of Wing Commander Oliver contributed to 308 Squadron being declared fully operational in December.

This was a period of rapid developments. On 1 December 9 Group took over responsibility for the Holt Patrol Line from 12 Group. The next day 9 Group's operations room at Barton Hall finally became operational at night, some three and half months after the start of the heavy night attacks on Liverpool. To coincide with the group being operational at night the Holt Patrol Line was moved further north, taking it above Tabley Brook, Eddisbury, Stapleford Hall and Aldford. This was done because the searchlight carpet was extended to the area of the old patrol line and the modifications demanded that crews flew closer than ever to the Gun-Defended Areas (GDAs) of Liverpool and Manchester.

On 3 December an important meeting took place at Barton Hall to discuss 9 Group's air-defence plans. Amongst those who joined the AOC were Lieutenant-General Grove of the 2nd AA Corps and Major Cadill of the 4th AA Division. Plans for 'Operation Layers' were discussed, as were proposals to move a night-fighter unit to Cranage on a permanent basis. Such developments required the co-operation of the AA Corps and in anticipation of further progress, all parties were urged to work together.

Although Wing Commander Oliver had been given assurances that 85 Squadron would be transferred to 9 Group on 28 November, Fighter Command had other plans. The unit had suffered heavy losses in the south and on 3 September its CO, Squadron Leader Peter Townsend, was wounded, while some of its other most experienced pilots had been killed. On the day that had been set for 85 Squadron to join 9 Group it was still stationed at Gravesend equipped with Hurricanes.

It did later start to convert to the night-fighting role and in January 1941 it was equipped with a small number of Defiants. Possibly because of its reputation during the Battle of Britain, the Defiant was not very popular amongst pilots and they were only ever used on three sorties. No. 85 Squadron continued to fly Hurricanes until March and the squadron then converted to the Douglas Havocs fitted with AI Mk IV radar.

The reasons why 85 Squadron failed to join 9 Group are not known and the only clues are references which suggest that its pilots found the Hurricane and Defiant unsuitable for night operations. Whatever the reason the result was that 9 Group was left without an effective night-fighter squadron at a time when it needed one most. The failure of Fighter Command to allocate a night-fighter squadron for the defence of the north-west region was a significant factor in the *Luftwaffe*'s air superiority during the Christmas blitz.

No. 307 Lowski (Polish) Squadron was formed in 9 Group in early September, when a number of pilots were posted to the Instructions and Translation Unit on Lytham Road, Blackpool. On 5 September the Polish pilots were posted to Kirton-in-Lindsey where the squadron was to be equipped with Boulton & Paul Defiants. It had been intimated that the unit would receive Hurricanes and the Defiants were a bit of a shock! Not very many of the Poles wanted to be night-fighter pilots and even fewer wanted to fly the two-seat Defiant.

One reason was that pilots did not like the idea of 'chauffeuring' air gunners around, most of whom were complete strangers to them. The relationship was made even more difficult when some air gunners were arrogant enough to claim that they should be the captain and tried to tell their pilots what to do! Within a short while most pilots were desperate to return to single-seat fighters and the squadron commander, Squadron Leader Pietraszkiewicz was bombarded with requests for transfers. He was not a happy man either and he also put in a transfer request for himself at the same time.

The requests were officially put to Wing Commander Hardy on 15 September and a few days later the issue was raised again during a visit of the AOC, Air Vice-Marshal Trafford Leigh-Mallory. Leigh-Mallory flew in from Watnall for a formal inspection of Kirton-in-Lindsey but a long conference was held about the operational state of 307 Squadron. Amongst those present were Squadron Leader Tomlinson, the unit's RAF commanding officer under the dual command system and Squadron Leader Pietraszkiewicz. The majority of the Polish airmen and officers spoke little English and Flying Officer Virpsha acted as the official translator. The eventual outcome was that the AOC reluctantly agreed to transfer all the disaffected pilots to day-fighter units immediately, subject to the agreement of the Polish authorities.

In the meantime, on 17 September, 307 Squadron was allocated its own aircraft and amongst the first to arrive was Defiant N1671. It was coded EW–D for Dog and allocated to A Flight. It was to survive the war and eventually become an exhibit in the RAF

Museum. The arrival of the Defiants did not change the pilots' minds about them, as the authorities might have expected. On 21 September Pietraszkiewicz flew to Northolt and visited the Polish Inspectorate at the Rubens Hotel; permission for the pilots to transfer was granted.

It seems strange that of the two squadrons assigned to 9 Group in the night-fighting role, one went elsewhere and the other struggled to become operational in any capacity. Both 85 Squadron and 307 Squadron were at Kirton-in-Lindsey at the same time and although there is no dispute about the fact that the Polish pilots disliked the Defiant, their motivation might be questioned. The possibility remains that their objections were 'echoing' those of their RAF colleagues in 85 Squadron and it was originally its pilots who did not want to become 'chauffeurs' to air gunners.

In effect 307 Squadron was torn apart by the reluctance of its pilots and gunners to fly the Defiant and work together as a crew, but despite its bad start, a core of older and generally more experienced pilots remained with it. Most of them were former airline pilots, instructors and test pilots who had a vast amount of experience on different types of aircraft. To them night flying was not a problem but the majority struggled with the English language and that in itself was a hazard. During the day R/T transmissions were normally kept to a minimum, but at night it was often necessary for pilots to follow detailed instructions from a controller. The inability of a pilot to understand information about height, a course to steer or a clearance was a danger to all those in the air.

In November 307 Squadron moved to Jurby on the Isle of Man, but its pilots experienced a number of difficulties with the conditions on the airfield and especially the length of the runway. On 11 November both the CO, Squadron Leader Tomlinson, and Flight Lieutenant Donovan ran into a hedge while landing at night. The incidents provoked more arguments about whether Jurby was suitable for a fighter squadron or night-flying training. It was originally a grass airfield built in 1938 by Gerrards of Swinton, Manchester, and it was handed over to the RAF in 1939. Although provision had been made for a single tarmac runway 3,600 ft long and 50 yards wide, work did not begin on it until 1940. As a result 307 Squadron pilots were forced to use an area of grass which had been set aside from the areas under construction. There were continual complaints that the landing area was too short and that the approach to the runway was too steep and unsafe.

While 307 Squadron continued with its night-flying training its crews flew on convoy patrols over the Irish Sea and gained valuable operational experience. However, the squadron faced yet another crisis when Fighter Command posted out some of its most experienced pilots because of heavy losses in the south of England. This second major crisis badly disrupted the night-training programme and badly affected morale but the unit was finally declared operational on 8 December.

On 10 December a section of the Squadron was sent on detachment to Cranage and joined a number of 312 Squadron pilots for night-flying training. None of the crews saw any action and their low morale and failure to progress began to frustrate 9 Group staff officers at Barton Hall. On the 12th the squadron was ordered into the air by a controller at 9 Group. Pilot Officer Alexandrewicz with Sergeant Lydke were airborne between 1425 and 1600 but encountered no enemy aircraft.

Things were not made any better by other events. On the 18th, Sergeant Dukszte was at the controls of N1671 when it was fired upon by a ship sailing in a convoy which it was supposed to be protecting. Because of such incompetence, as well as bad maintenance and inexperience the accident rate began to soar. Within a month 307 Squadron's strength was reduced from fourteen Defiants to just nine on 23 December and the accident rate continued to increase.

Night-flying training progressed slowly; on 21 December the squadron completed sixteen and a half hours by day and none at night. The lack of practice was to take its toll. On 23 December Sergeants Szablowski and Brode crashed N1541. The incident happened at night while Szablowski was trying to land at Jurby after returning from a late evening convoy patrol. Both survived but were seriously injured and taken to Ramsey Cottage Hospital.

Within a month 307 Squadron was on the move to the mainland but the Isle of Man remained a vital part of 9 Group's operations. As the Polish unit was preparing to leave, the Andreas Sector Control Room at Ramsey was just becoming operational.

CHAPTER EIGHT

29 Squadron at Cranage: December 1940

At the beginning of December the section of 29 Squadron Blenheims on loan from 12 Group was moved from Tern Hill to Cranage in an attempt provide better night-time fighter cover. The detachment of two Blenheims was accompanied by seven senior NCOs, two corporals and nineteen airmen. It arrived at Cranage on 1 December and the crews were ordered to be at a state of readiness half an hour before sunset.

Pilot Officer Don Anderson was the officer in charge of the section, and his experience of events at Cranage was typical of the things which plagued Fighter Command in 1940. He claimed that poor organization and the failure of equipment prevented pilots from making any serious attempts to intercept enemy aircraft. The few basic radio navigation aids available were totally unreliable and they were often controlled by inexperienced and badly trained personnel.

There were other problems as well because various groups of the RAF service organization had an input into operational requirements. The 29 Squadron detachment was under the command of 9 Group but during operations its crews came under the direct control of the Speke Sector Controller. Control of the Speke and Tern Hill Sectors had only recently been handed over from 12 Group and it still exercised a great deal of influence over events.

The units which operated aircraft equipped with airbourne interception (AI) radar in Fighter Command performed their tasks in a variety of different ways. Crews in some groups performed controlled interceptions over land or sea in co-operation with RDF

Pilot Officer Don Anderson of 29 Squadron at Wattisham 1940. He was the pilot of a Blenheim which crashed at Glossop in December 1940 and was blamed for the accident, which was almost certainly not his fault. Anderson flew some of the first patrols over the north-west which were badly organised and no real threat to the Luftwaffe.

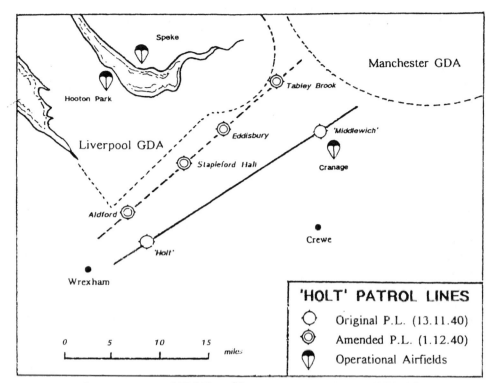

Diagram explaining positions of 'Holt' Patrol Lines. Courtesy of Derek Pratt and Michael Grant

units or the ROC. Others flew along fixed patrol lines under the guidance of a controller. Because of the lack of technology that is how 29 Squadron crews operated in 9 Group.

Pilot Officer Anderson considered himself to be a typical pilot of his generation. He had learned to fly at 11 Flight Training School (FTS), Shawbury, before moving on to 5 OTU at Aston Down. He was posted to 29 Squadron on 8 July 1940 and his first duties involved ferrying Blenheims from Wellinglore to St Athan, where they were fitted with AI radar and converted to night fighters. The radar was developed in 1940 and it gave the operator the range and bearing of other aircraft in the immediate vicinity, but with a range of just 2 miles the Mk III sets were not very efficient. The Mk IV, with a range of 3.78 miles, was gradually introduced into service, but the sets were only being fitted into aircraft such as the Beaufighter during production.

The conversions involved making alterations to the interior to accommodate the electronic gadgetry and most aircraft had their turrets removed. An armament pack of four Browning machine-guns was fitted under the fuselage and the bomb bay was used to store ammunition. During the summer months Anderson flew a number of Blenheims down to St Athan. On 28 July he ferried L6712, L6603 on the 31st, L1324 on 12 August, L1169 on the 22nd and L1503 on 20 September.

It was during one of these trips that he saw the Short Stirling, the RAF's new giant four-engined heavy bomber, for the first time. Flying Officer Anderson said it towered above all the other aircraft in the hangar and after seeing it he felt quite vulnerable, flying such a relatively small aircraft like the Blenheim.

After the events of 12 September he had even more reason to feel vulnerable, as his aircraft was attacked by a *Luftwaffe* intruder. That night he was operating out of Kirton-in-Lindsey, but he had landed at Hibaldstow and just taken off again when he was caught by a German night fighter. Anderson said that the aircraft just appeared out of nowhere and its deadly cannon smashed into his Blenehim before it vanished into some cloud. He freely admitted that he froze at the controls, as the terrifying noise and devastation caused him to forget all his training. A substantial amount of damage was done to the starboard wing and the AI radar was hit and put out of action.

Rather miraculously neither Anderson nor the radio operator were physically harmed, but they were both in state of shock. Enemy aircraft from *Luftwaffe* unit NJG2 were operating in the area and its crews claimed several victims in September. *Leutanant* Hermann claimed to have shot down a Blenheim on the night of the 6th/7th and *Feldwebel* Sommer claimed another on the night of the 9th/10th. Anderson could so easily have become the third casualty.

Even before he flew his first operation from Cranage, Anderson was involved in an unfortunate accident, which he claimed marred the rest of his service career. On 1 December, the date set for patrols to begin, he flew Sergeant Skillen and some equipment from Tern Hill to Cranage. That afternoon at 1520 he took off again on his own, having reluctantly agreed to do a homing test, which had previously proved unsuccessful.

The test involved various VHF and HF radio systems but after this flight Anderson noted in his log book, 'What a headache!' It is unclear exactly which type of homing system he was testing but the fact that he had carried out the test with HF radio suggests that it could have been the Pip Squeak system, which dated back to 1932. It involved up to three HF/DF stations tracking an aircraft, as its radio automatically transmitted a signal for fourteen seconds out of every minute.

The position of each aircraft was fixed every minute as the signal was transmitted but the pilot had an override switch in case he needed to use the radio during the transmission period. Pip Squeak could only handle four aircraft at a time and a clock face in the sector control room informed the controller which aircraft was transmitting. No. 9 Group used Pip Squeak to control aircraft flying on patrols over Liverpool Bay and it was still in use during the spring of 1941.

The fact that Anderson already knew what problems could be associated with homing co-operation flights did not prevent him being called upon to do more tests the next day. The second exercise went better but Anderson was not impressed and further problems during the trials prompted him to write 'Homing Test – No good' in his log book.

At 1610 on 3 December he took off again to repeat the previous afternoon's exercise. To begin with things went better than expected. The weather conditions were forecast as $^{10}/_{10}$ cloud with the base at 1,500 ft, and Anderson noticed that the homing signal was much stronger outside the cloud. There was a temptation to try and maintain visual conditions but his orders were to make the test as realistic as possible. So with everything seemingly working fine he flew into the nearest cloud bank and put his faith in the system.

As his aircraft entered the turbulent cloudy conditions, Anderson suddenly lost complete radio contact with the homing operator at Cranage. The Blenheim was engulfed in thick, swirling cloud as Anderson made repeated attempts to contact Speke Sector on another channel, but all he heard was static. Daylight was rapidly disappearing and he knew he would have to act fast if he was to make a safe landing. He found it difficult to work out an exact course because his calculations had taken into account figures passed on to him during the homing procedures. However he had a strong gut feeling that he was still over the Pennines.

He did not have a lot of time to assess all his options, but he knew that if he had drifted just a short distance to the west there was more than a possibility that he could have ended up in a premature 'watery' grave in the Irish Sea. However, he had a strong feeling that he had drifted to the east and with the fuel running low he began to look for somewhere to land. The prospect of a forced landing in the hills of the Peak District was not something that he looked forward to, but he thought it would be better than ditching in the sea. As he strained his eyes to see through the windscreen, his confidence lifted when he caught sight of a large reservoir through a small gap in the cloud. Moments later he spotted a long, narrow field and immediately made a decision to land there before it disappeared from view.

He lowered the undercarriage. As he made his final approach the night was already setting, but he could see well enough to make a very bumpy landing. He immediately experienced great difficulty in controlling the Blenheim and the brakes failed to stop it gathering momentum. He managed to slow the aircraft down and he was feeling quite pleased with himself as he came to the end of his landing run. Then suddenly, before he could react, the Blenheim had ran over the edge of the field and the wheels dipped down into a drain, which tipped the aircraft over. He later described what happened as an 'unreal sensation' as the Blenheim's tail rose slowly through the air in an arc, before all movement stopped.

It was deadly silent as he hung upside down in a precarious position, held only by the straps of his Sutton harness. He could not remember whether he turned off the fuel cocks and his only thoughts were of getting out before the Blenheim caught fire. The normal exit above the cockpit was blocked by the ground but he struggled out of his straps and managed to clamber out of the emergency door on the underside of the wing. He was about to jump down when he discovered that part of his boot was caught in the engine cowling. Fortunately he managed to release it, but he fell heavily to the ground in the process and then the realization of what had happened slowly sunk in.

As Anderson took stock of the situation he looked around the field, taking in his surroundings. Checking his watch he saw that the time was 1730. He had been airborne for an hour and twenty minutes and he knew that the tanks of the Blenheim were practically empty. Within minutes the local policeman arrived on the scene and told Pilot Officer Anderson that he had landed at a place known locally as Woolly Flats, on the outskirts of Glossop.

With the help of the policeman Anderson rang Cranage to report the incident and got a very frosty response from the duty officer. He was told that no transport was available. Nothing could be done until morning and he would have to remain with the aircraft. As the Blenheim was fitted with AI radar Anderson knew that it would have to be guarded overnight. Fortunately the local policeman assured Anderson that he would make all the necessary arrangements. Later that evening, he took Anderson back to his own home, where he was able to get a good night's sleep in a comfortable armchair. Early the following morning the RAF transport turned up and Anderson returned to Cranage to face the music.

Knowing that a board of inquiry would be set up to investigate the circumstances of the accident, Anderson went over things in his mind. He was certain that the homing operator had given him the wrong course, which had put his aircraft on a reciprocal heading. Instead of flying south-west towards Cranage, Anderson had been instructed to fly on a north-easterly course, which explained why he had ended up over the Peak District.

Having accumulated 250 hours' flying experience, fifty-four of them on night flying, Anderson had already proved that his skills were above average. With the exception of the incident when he had been attacked by a night fighter, he had always remained calm under pressure. On 26 August the propeller fitted to the starboard engine had fallen off during a night flying exercise, but against the odds, he had made a safe landing. Such things went through Anderson's mind and after returning to Cranage there were no attempts to ground him. He believed that because of his previous experiences any inquiry would exonerate him, especially as he understood that the Blenheim had not been badly damaged. The board of inquiry was not due to report until the new year, and meanwhile Anderson carried on flying.

On 11 December he finally flew his first patrol in Blenheim L1292 with Sergeant Price as his radio operator. They took off at 2100 and flew a 2¼-hour patrol around the coast

A message from Manchester City Police's Crime Information Room about a flashing light in Heaton Park, dated 22.12.40, timed at 11.20 p.m. Courtesy Manchester Police Museum

[2708]

MANCHESTER CITY POLICE

CRIME INFORMATION ROOM

RECORD OF MESSAGE RECEIVED—~~DESPATCHED~~

Date..........22.12.40..............Time..........11.20 p.m.

From—~~Txxx~~..........Lieut. Webb, Heaton Park Gun Station, Sheepfoot Lane...........

About 45 mins ago two of my men saw a person flashing a light in Heaton Park, about ½ mile N.W. of the White Heather Camp in Heaton Park. They gave chase but the person ran away. I have myself seen the light.

Phoned Willert St. Station who stated that information respecting this light had already been received and two men had been dispatched to investigate the matter.

Copy to Assistant Chief Constable, Det. Superintendent, R.O.
          & "B"

                                            WK.

Officer

and sea approaches to Liverpool. There was no enemy activity and nothing of any significance happened although Anderson was told to carry out what he thought at the time was a strange order. He was instructed to fly down the Welsh border and look for lights on the ground, or any obvious infringements of the Blackout. It seems likely that this was connected with the lights that had been seen around the Peak District and suspected fifth-columnist activity.

He did not see any unusual lights but just a few weeks later there was another incident in Manchester involving exactly the type of activity that he had been told to look out for. On Sunday, 22 December, at 2235, two police constables on duty in Heaton Park spotted a man behaving in a strange way, flashing a light towards the sky. Heaton Park Gun Station on Sheepfoot Lane was notified and Lieutenant Webb arrived on the scene in time to see the light for himself. The two constables gave chase through the White Heather Camp where the culprit had last been seen but they failed to catch him. Wilbert Street Police Station had already received a number of calls about the light and more policemen were sent to the scene but they also failed to find the culprit. The matter was never resolved but it was suspected that an IRA sympathizer was responsible.

Back at Cranage, the daily routine for the short period of time that 29 Squadron was there included ferrying aircraft and crews to Tern Hill and flying on air test. The day after he flew his first patrol Anderson flew on a weather test over the Irish Sea with Corporal Phillips. The next couple of days he spent ferrying airmen, and it was not until 16 December that he flew on his second operational sortie. He took off at 2100 in the same aircraft, but with Sergeant Freeman as his radio operator.

There was some enemy activity around Manchester that night, and the Ancoats district was bombed and several people were killed. Stockport was being bombed at about the time Anderson was becoming airborne and one person was killed. Anderson was ordered by a controller to investigate an unidentified radar contact known as an 'X raid'. He was happy to respond as it was one of the only bits of excitement he ever had while he was at Cranage.

The sector controller told him to climb to 21,000 ft in pursuit of a suspected enemy aircraft that was in the vicinty. Anderson said that the Blenheim wallowed all over the sky and he struggled to get it to climb in the freezing conditions. Eventually he reached his assigned height but by that time the 'X raid' contact had long disappeared. Anderson was just happy to descend again and thaw out after a sortie which lasted an hour and a quarter. That was effectively the last operational sortie that he flew from Cranage. On the afternoon of the 19th he returned to Digby and waited to hear the outcome of the inquiry into his accident.

At the beginning of 1941 he had his first experience of flying a Beaufighter and on 8 January he flew with Flight Lieutenant 'Guy' Gibson in R2094. He stood behind him, observing his every move and trying to remember the correct drill and procedure. It was the only experience that he had before he was expected to fly the aircraft on his own twenty minutes later but it went well.

It was on 18 January 1941 that he finally heard that he was to be severely reprimanded and his log book endorsed by the AOC 12 Group. The wording of the endorsement made it clear to all who read it that he had been found guilty of a serious error of judgement, which resulted in the loss of the Blenheim.

The Air Officer Commanding No 12 Group has minded that an entry shall be made in P/O Anderson's log book to the effect that the accident in which he was involved on 3.12.40 causing serious damage to Blenheim L1792, was due to an error of judgement on his part as pilot.

Ian. R. Parker. W/Cdr.
18/1/41
(Authority 12 Group letter Ref. 12 G/521/588/P1)

Every time he was posted to a new unit, his squadron commander would examine his log book and learn of the endorsement, so the blot on his record would be carried around with him.

When Anderson heard about the action, he was shocked; he considered the AOC's decision to be harsh and inappropriate. On the day of the incident he had been briefed to give the homing station some practical experience and to make it as realistic as possible. The Form 700 flight authorization had been signed for that specific purpose and everything had gone well until he flew into $^{10}/_{10}$ cloud and lost radio contact with Cranage. By the time he realized what had happened darkness was falling and his fuel endurance did not allow him the luxury of finding his own way back. An immediate landing was the only solution.

Blenheim K7172 had started its service life on 8 February 1938 with 61 Squadron but the aircraft was handed over to 19 MU on 15 November 1939, before being passed on to 32 MU in 1940. It first appeared on the strength of 29 Squadron on 6 June 1940, but after the forced landing at Glossop, it was struck off charge. That was possibly because of its age and condition, but Anderson felt he had been heavily penalized for damaging an aircraft which was already approaching the end of its useful service life.

On reflection many years later, Anderson said that 29 Squadron's sorties from Tern Hill and Cranage served no real purpose. Having made the arrangments with Wing Commander Oliver for the move to Cranage, Anderson claimed that 29 Squadron was sent there as a token gesture to appease the authorities in Liverpol and Manchester. He claimed that everyone knew that the Blenheim's crews stood very little chance of intercepting enemy aircraft. Very few pilots had faith in the AI Mk III or RDF and co-operation between pilots and special operators was not always what it should have been.

Anderson remained on 29 Squadron for nearly another year, but in October 1941 he was posted overseas to 89 Squadron in Egypt, where his bad luck continued. He was taken off flying duties because he was affected by the hot and dusty climate and medically downgraded. He returned to flying briefly in 1942 but he was then posted as a fighter controller on board HMS *Ulster*, where he remained throughout the rest of the war.

He was discharged as a Flight Lieutenant in 1946 and he joined a company of solicitors dealing in affairs of probate. The incident at Glossop in 1940 was never far from his mind and in 1977 he visited Woolly Flats to exorcise the ghost the of the past. It was only the second time he had been to Glossop but it was the last and in January 2000 he died at his home at Epping.

It was in the months leading up to his death that Don Anderson imparted much of the information contained in this chapter. He said that he always wanted people to know how bad things were during the first years of the war. His experiences may not have been typical but a number of other pilots have expressed similar feelings about what was going on during this period, and Anderson's story is not unique.

CHAPTER NINE

96 Squadron: Experience in Action

96 Squadron was formed at Cranage on 18 December 1940 with five Hurricanes which had arrived from Shoreham nine days earlier. The aircraft and their pilots had previously been part of 422 Flight and the fledgeling unit was under the temporary command of Flight Lieutenant James Gilberts Sanders, DFC. The other four pilots from 422 Flight were Flying Officer Verity, Flying Officer Rabone, Sergeant Scott and Sergeant Hampshire.

Flight Lieutenant Sanders had been appointed as the CO of 422 Flight in October, but he was to take no part in 96 Squadron's operations. Soon after arriving at Cranage he was posted to 255 Squadron at Kirton-in-Lindsey as a flight commander. Wing Commander Ronald Gustave Kellett, DSO, DFC, VM, an officer of character with a reputation for bravado, was appointed as 96 Squadron's CO.

Kellett had already experienced some of the difficulties of being a commanding officer, having only recently relinquished the command of 303 (Polish) Squadron. The son of a colliery owner from Chester-le-Street in Durham, he had joined the Auxiliary Air Force in 1933 and served with 600 Squadron (City of London). In May 1940 he was posted to 249 Squadron as a flight commander. In July 1940 he was appointed as the CO of 303 Squadron at Northolt, and by 31 October he had claimed five enemy aircraft destroyed. In 96 Squadron, as in 303 Squadron, Kellett proved to be a squadron commander who led by example.

Most of the those who joined 96 Squadron from 422 Flight were seasoned pilots. One such a man was Sergeant Hampshire, who had joined the RAF in 1930 as an apprentice at Halton, before starting his flying training in 1937. By the time he joined 422 Flight he had already destroyed three enemy aircraft and damaged several more. Sergeant Scott had flown on operations with 43 Squadron, before joining 422 Flight but he had yet to open his account.

Flying Officer Victor Bosanquet Strachan Verity was one of two experienced New Zealanders in the squadron. No. 9 Group had a large number of 'Kiwis' amongst its ranks, a total of approximately 5,000 New Zealanders served as fighter pilots in the RAF, which was a significant contribution from a population of only 1.4 million. A number of those who joined 96 Squadron had taken part in the Battle of Britain, and their skills were an important contribution to the night air war in the north-west.

William Joseph Jordan, the New Zealand High Commissioner to Britain from 1936 to 1951, made it his business to meet as many of his fellow countrymen serving in the RAF and he was well known for his hospitality. What many airmen and servicemen might not

Line up of airmen from New Zealand with the High Commissioner for Britain 1936–51, William Joseph Jordan (centre front row). Flying Officers Verity (third from right front row) and Rabone (fourth from right front row) from 96 Squadron are on the front row with the latter's dog, 'Skita'. 9 Group had a considerable number of New Zealanders amongst its ranks.

have known about the high Commissioner was that he had actually been born in Ramsgate, Kent. The son of a fishing smack skipper, he was educated at St. Lukes in Ramsgate and later worked as a postman and served in the Metropolitan Police, before emigrating to New Zealand in 1904. In 1907 he became the first Secretary to the New Zealand Labour Party and in 1932 he became its President. Jordan was a remarkable man and served as the Member of Parliament for Manukau from 1922 until 1936 and in 1938 he became President of the Council of the League of Nations. Having served with the New Zealand forces in France during the First World War, the High Commissioner had experienced the problems that his countrymen faced while being a long way from home, and he was always keen to help them.

Born at Timaru in November 1918, Victor Verity attended Timaru Boys' High School between 1932 and 1934, before leaving to work on his father's farm. He sailed to England on 1 February 1939 and in May he was awarded a short-service commission by the RAF. He trained on Magisters at Sutton Bridge and Ansons at Hullavington before being posted to 229 Squadron equipped with Blenheims, at Digby in November 1940. When it converted to Hurricanes in March 1940 Verity gained his first experience of flying a modern fighter.

In May 1940 he was one of three pilots who were attached to 615 Squadron in France and on the 20th he destroyed his first enemy aircraft. After the combat his Hurricane was attacked by a number of Bf 110s and he had to make a forced landing in France. On his return to England his claim of destroying two Heinkels and damaging another was subsequently changed by an intelligence officer to a single Heinkel damaged. Some time later Verity met Pilot Officer Pemberton, who had been flying on the same patrol but 5,000 ft beneath him. Pemberton confirmed that he had seen the two Heinkels crash and some time later the RAF intelligence authorities at the Air Ministry credited the New Zealander with their destruction.

On 31 May, during the evacuation of Dunkirk, Verity shot down an Bf 110, although during the pursuit he was also shot down for the second time and he baled out over the English Channel. He was quickly picked up from the sea by a paddle steamer whose captain had witnessed the action. Soon after he landed back in England he met Lord Trenchard and they talked about the future of Fighter Command. Trenchard told Verity that he wished he was fifty years younger, but expressed concern that Fighter Commmand might not hold out until September, when production of fighter aircraft would increase. Verity told Trenchard that large numbers of Hurricanes had been delivered to airfields in France with no pilots or ground crew and they had to be destroyed because there was no way of getting them back to England.

Flying Officer Victor Verity, D.F.C. Verity was one of the founding members of 96 Squadron, who gained considerable experience of night-fighting while with 422 Flight at Shoreham. Verity was responsible for taking 96 Squadron into battle in May 1941 after he rang the A.O.C. of 9 Group late at night and demanded that they should be allowed to get airborne.

Verity rejoined his unit at Biggin Hill and at the end of June 229 Squadron moved north to Wittering. There he was amazed to discover that he was still officially listed as missing, and that the authorities believed him to have been killed in action on 1 June! The mistake was caused because the Air Ministry failed to cable records that he had rejoined his unit and it caused his family a lot of unnecessary concern.

In September 229 Squadron moved to Northolt and Verity was given the responsibility of looking after a Hurricane which was the personal aircraft of the AOC of 11 Group, fellow New Zealander Air Vice-Marshal Keith Parks. Verity's relationship with Parks and other high ranking officers he met gave him confidence and the ability to talk frankly on issues that others considered too delicate to discuss.

In October Verity joined 422 Flight, based at Shoreham in Sussex, where it was part of the experimental Night Interception Unit. Under the overall command of Wing Commander Chamberlain its task was to evaluate the Hurricane in the night-fighting role and develop new tactics for night-fighter operations. Verity claimed that the main reason he volunteered for night-fighter duties was because of the overwhelming hospitality he had received from the British public. In some places people had given him free food and drink and taxi drivers often had regularly refused to take any money from him. After a while he began to feel guilty and felt that he should give something back. 'Pay back' began almost straight away; on 6 November he damaged a Ju 88 which dropped its bombs into the sea and escaped. On the night of 13 November 1940, he destroyed a Ju 88 while operating under radar control and by the time 96 Squadron was formed, his tally was five enemy aircraft destroyed.

The other experienced pilot from New Zealand was Flying Officer Paul Rabone, who had joined the Royal New Zealand Air Force in 1938. He had sailed to England on the same ship as Verity in February 1939, but their paths were not to cross again until the end of 1940. Rabone was attached to 88 Squadron at Boscombe Down, which was equipped with Fairey Battles. It flew to France in early September 1939. During a raid on Maastricht Rabone's aircraft was so badly damaged that he and his crew were forced to bale out. They landed behind enemy lines but after dressing in civilian clothing they joined a refugee column and walked to the coast.

After rejoining the squadron Rabone was shot down for a second time during an attack on some bridges over the River Seine but he again evaded capture. The Squadron withdrew from France on 15 June in such a hurry that Rabone was forced to leave his flying log-book and other personal possessions behind.

In July he was posted to 19 OTU at Kinloss as an instructor on Whitleys and promoted to the rank of flying officer. The following month he volunteered to join Fighter Command and was transferred to 145 Squadron at Drem for operational training. It was equipped with Hurricanes and operated in the Turnhouse Sector of 13 Group in Scotland.

At the beginning of October 145 Squadron moved south to Tangmere and on the 11th, during an operational patrol, he experienced his first combat. His formation was attacked by fifty Me 109s over the Solent, but Rabone, flying in Hurricane V7838, gained some valuable experience. The following day he destroyed his first enemy aircraft, an Me 109, and damaged another in the same combat. It was a good beginning and on 18 October he was posted to 422 Flight at Shoreham to train and develop night-fighter tactics. On 6 November he claimed his third Bf 109 in a combat some 20 miles south of Tangmere and after attaining exceptional results in Night Visual Capacity Test, he joined 96 Squadron.

On its formation Verity claimed that 96 Squadron was an unhappy bunch of pilots, because while there were those like himself who had volunteered for night-fighter duties, some had been forced into the move. There were also other reasons for some to feel unhappy, just before the squadron had been formed eight experienced pilots had been lost in one night. They had been ordered to fly a routine patrol, during what Verity described as the worst flying weather he had ever encountered in England.

This experience lowered the morale of 422 Flight pilots and as a concession they were given the privilege of being able to refuse to fly at night if the weather conditions were unsuitable. Verity thought this decision totally undermined the authority of the flight commanders and the CO. At Cranage things began to improve but it took time for attitudes to change and for pilots to gain confidence in their night-flying abilities.

In late December 96 Squadron was boosted by the arrival of a number of additional personnel, including some more officers who already had significant combat experience. Flight Lieutenant Raphael, DFC, was a Canadian who had served with 77 Squadron. On the night of 18/19 May he had been wounded when his Whitley bomber came under attack from an Me 110. He was forced to ditch into the North Sea but after four hours he and his crew were rescued by a Royal Navy launch. Soon afterwards he transferred to Fighter Command and joined 43 Squadron, which was equipped with Hurricanes, at Drem. On his arrival at Cranage he was appointed as the A Flight commander.

Other newcomers were Flying Officer Hill who was also from 43 Squadron, Flying Officer Marrow from 54 Squadron and Flying Officer Petty from 605 Squadron. Flying Officer Pelham, formerly of 229 Squadron, was one of the most experienced pilots, with a number of enemy aircraft destroyed, and he was detached from HQ 9 Group at Barton Hall for intelligence purposes. He was the intelligence officer responsible for reducing Flying Officer Verity's claim of two Heinkels in May 1940 to one damaged, and the two officers did not get on.

Other pilots included Sergeant Rauls, who had destroyed a Ju 88 and had been credited with damaging another one. One of the most promising senior NCO pilots was 22-year-old Sergeant Robin McNair, who had been born in Rio de Janeiro, but educated at Gaveney House, Hampstead, and Douai School, Reading. He joined the RAF Volunteer Reserve in February 1939 and learned to fly at 4 Elementary Flying School (EFS) Brough in Yorkshire on the Blackburn B-2. He was initially posted to 3 Squadron at Wick, but later transferred to 249 Squadron and flew Hurricanes from North Weald. He was one of the few married airmen in the squadron and he was to achieve great things and rise rapidly through the ranks.

That the Hawker Hurricane could be used as a night fighter was a great tribute to its designer, Sydney Camm No. 96 Squadron was equipped with versions of the Mk 1, fitted with Rolls-Royce Merlin III engines. Not all the Hurricanes from 422 Flight were retained in 96 squadron; V6863 was handed over to 43 Group in Maintenance Command on 22 December. But as some Hurricanes departed others flew in from maintenance units and the unit's strength soon rose to nine aircraft.

CHAPTER TEN

First Action for 96 Squadron: December 1940

On 21 December A Flight of 96 Squadron sent a section on detachment to Squires Gate, with the aim of giving the region more effective and wider night-time air cover. Flying Officer Rabone was appointed as temporary flight commander of the four Hurricanes and the support crews.

By this time the strength of 96 Squadron had increased to thirteen Hurricanes, including the four detached to Squires Gate. The squadron's pilots did not have much time to familiarize themselves with the region before they tasted their first action. On the night of 22/23 December, the third night of the Christmas Blitz, Flying Officer Rabone was on patrol in Hurricane V6887 when he observed an enemy aircraft flying between Formby and Liverpool at 14,000 ft. He was initially attracted by the glow of the engine exhaust and he estimated that its speed was approximately 170 mph.

Positioning himself some 50 yards behind the enemy aircraft and some 25 ft beneath it, he approached cautiously before opening fire into its belly. It immediately dived steeply in front of Rabone's Hurricane but he maintained contact and managed to fire another two short bursts. He then noticed that the whole aircraft seemed to be glowing and as he passed over it a cloud of black smoke appeared and the windscreen of his Hurricane was heavily smeared with oil.

After it dived away Rabone never saw the aircraft again. Although he failed to make a positive identification he thought it was either a Dornier or a Heinkel. He claimed it as a 'probable' and he was later credited with what amounted to 96 Squadron's first 'kill'. There is no confirmation, but KGr. 606 reported the loss of a Dornier on the night of 21/22 December, whose crew had been assigned to bomb Liverpool. It is possible that there was some confusion in the records and the Dornier could have been the aircraft claimed by Rabone.

No wreckage, or oil patches were found in the sea to confirm Rabone's claim but six months later a sliding roof, thought to be from a Ju 88, was washed up. The perspex framework was discovered south of the River Ribble near St Annes on 27 June 1941. It could have been from any of a number of German aircraft brought down in the area. As the 96 Squadron diary later noted, 'The sea was reluctant to give up its treasures.'

On 28 December Rabone's success was followed by tragedy when Pilot Officer Leslie Sharp's Hurricane, serial number P3899, crashed into the sea during a night training exercise. The incident happened just a mile off the coast of Blackpool and the aircraft was last seen heading south before it suddenly and inexplicably dived into the sea. Other 96

Squadron pilots were quickly on the scene, including Flying Officer Rabone, and flares were dropped to create artificial light and aid the rescue of the pilot.

Despite the Lytham life boat being launched and an extensive search of the area from the sea and air, however, Pilot Officer Sharp was not found. The K-type one-man rubber dinghy was not issued until the summer of 1941 and all that an airmen had to rely on if he ended up in the sea was his Mae West. His body was recovered the following day after it had been washed up on the beach near Starr Gate.

Although he was a seasoned pilot, Pilot Officer Sharp had relatively little experience of night flying and that fact alone probably cost him his life. The 23-year-old officer had previously served with 111 Squadron and flown Hurricanes in the Kenley Sector of 11 Group, during the Battle of Britain. He was the son of Mark and Annie Sharp of Belfast. He was later buried in Carnmoney Jewish Cemetery in Belfast, where his body lies in Grave 4 on Line 1.

CHAPTER ELEVEN

Fighter Nights 1941: Build-up at Cranage

A number of changes were made to the patrol lines on 29 December when the Holt Patrol Line became the Yellow Patrol Line. The old line, from Tabley Brook through Eddisbury, Stapleford and Aldford remained as part of the new patrol line but a new 'dog leg' was added, running from Tabley Brook at 90 degrees to the old line, heading south-east

Diagram of 'Yellow' Patrol Lines. Courtesy of Derek Pratt and Michael Grant

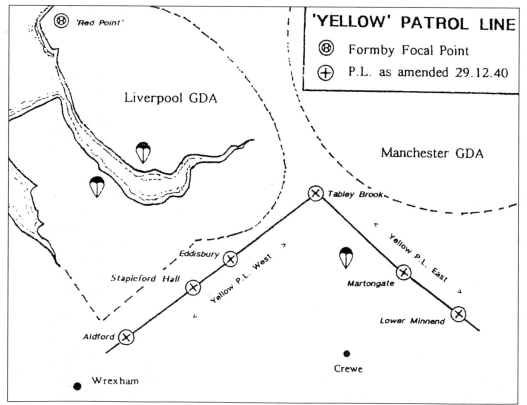

through Martongate and Lower Minnend. The new patrol line effectively formed an arrow head between the two GDAs of Liverpool and Manchester, covering the approaches to both cities from the south.

On the final day of 1940, a directive code named Operation Layers was issued, which laid down the guidelines as to how the cats' eyes night-fighter squadrons in 9 Group would operate. On the nights when the *Luftwaffe*'s objective could be clearly identified, the night fighters would take off and fly at set heights above the area which had been predicted as the main target. Unless they received other orders, pilots were to operate above 14,000 ft to give them a 2,000 ft safety level between their aircraft and the height at which the AA shells exploded.

The system of 'layers' patrols or 'fighter nights' as they were also known, was not new, such operations had been carried out in the south earlier in the year. They had been abandoned because the AA Commander, Frederick Pile had complained about the uncertainty they caused. On some occasions the guns were ordered to stop firing when night fighters were overhead and he argued that it was better for the AA gun post to be certain that all aircraft in their zone were enemy aircraft.

Air Vice-Marshal McClaughry was responsible for developing the operational technique in 9 Group and he worked very closely with the 4th AA Division commander, General Cadell. McClaughry was a veteran of such tactics; during the First World War he had been part of an elite night-bombing squadron. In 1917 he had flown on numerous raids over enemy territory at night with 100 Squadron in flimsy FE2ds. More than anyone, he understood the dangers and of night flying in a hostile environment and he was instrumental in designing a system of beacons in the north-west, similar to those that pilots had used in France during that period.

Although technology and aircraft design had improved drastically since the First World War, the principles of night-fighting in many ways remained the same. A number of the tactics drawn up in 1940 were reminiscent of those used in 1918, including standing patrols and the old recipe of using searchlights and a 'pilot's eyeball' to search for enemy aircraft beneath him. If all went well enemy aircraft were silhouetted against the backdrop of the searchlights and fires on the ground, so that they could be seen more easily by prowling night fighters.

The layers patrols developed into what were called Shortshrift Operations, and each one normally involved a minimum of twelve single-engined night fighters. They still operated at heights above 14,000 ft, which remained the safety altitude over the AA barrage; aircraft flew at intervals of 1,000 ft above that. Flying so close to one another pilots had to ensure that they had the correct barometric pressure set on their altimeters. Each operation normally lasted an hour, and on some occasions the AA guns stopped firing so that the night fighters could enter the danger area to search for enemy bombers with the aid of the searchlights. No. 96 Squadron's motto, translated from the Latin, meant 'We stalk by night', and that is exactly what its crews did.

Not every sortie involved layers operations. On most nights, when the weather allowed, the Defiant crews flew on routine patrols. When 96 Squadron moved into Cranage Wing Commander Kellett was promised a perimeter track and two properly laid-out runways. The work was never carried out and his pilots had to put up with an improvised steel planking runway, which was often rutted and covered in mud. Sometimes it rose up in front of aircraft taking off like a bow wave, and pilots were worried that it might hit the propeller and cause a bad accident.

Kellett had to make do with what he had. One good thing came out of the airfield's natural environment. Cranage was surrounded by woodland and Kellett noticed a thick coppice of silver birch trees near the boundary. They were scheduled to be cut down but the CO thought the area would make an excellent camouflaged dispersal. Kellett saved the trees and 96 Squadron moved its Hurricanes into an area which provided safer cover that any fighter pen could.

Lighting and approach aids were very primitive; in effect there were no approach lights, only hooded 'goose-neck' flares, which were laid out in a path on either side of the runway and hooded to prevent them from being seen from the air by German aircrew. That made it extremely difficult for 96 Squadron pilots to see them as well, of course, and to get their aircraft lined up for landing. Clearance to land was given by an Aldis signal lamp; the operator flashed a 'green' for permission to land and a 'red' to hold off and go around again.

Cranage's limited facilities had to be shared with students of the ANS flying Ansons and Oxfords, which made conditions more hazardous. It was quite rare for an operational squadron of any kind to be based on the same airfield as a training unit. Such circumstances did nothing to improve the morale of those pilots who were still trying to get used to the rigours of night flying.

To help pilots find Cranage when the Pundit beacon was switched off at night, a makeshift homing aid was devised in the form of a VHF/DF loop aerial. It was fitted into a van which was positioned in a field adjacent to the airfield and it was normally operated by an inexperienced locally trained airman who was only able to give a pilot a QDM (a magnetic bearing), the rest was up to the pilot. Although the system was unreliable, it was the only one available and aircrew learned to depend upon the guidance given by its humble operator. On nights when the squadron was active on operations there were often large numbers of aircraft, all trying to land at once, which put tremendous pressure on the operator in the van and on the pilots, who were sometimes desperate to land. However, there were few accidents that could be attributed to that factor.

Just to add to the dangers, at the end of December bomb disposal experts were called from Hucknall and discovered a number of unexploded 50 kg bombs on the airfield. It was decided, however, that the bombs were safe, owing to the nature of the soil and the wet ground. Three days later, on 27 December, ordnance experts were called in from Sealand when further suspect devices were found on the airfield. It was discovered that they were not bombs but unexploded AA shells. Because of the nature of the ground they were also considered safe and left in place.

In the New Year 96 Squadron continued to build up its state of operational readiness and crews were regularly sent on short detachments to Speke, Tern Hill and Wrexham. On 1 January a 'Jacob's ladder' layers exercise was held above Liverpool but the unit's eight Hurricanes returned early due to bad weather. January was a quiet month; the highlight for Flying Officer Rabone came when he was ordered to shoot down a drifting barrage balloon. It provided some target practice and he sent it down in flames some 10 miles south of Manchester.

On 16 January HRH the Duke of Kent visited Cranage and inspected the dining halls. He was pleased with the conditions that he found, but those airmen who were living in the very cold and cramped conditions were not as impressed. On some parts of the airfield no running hot water was available and huge tureens were hung over fires to provide a limited supply for washing and shaving. Accommodation was so overcrowded that some airmen had to sleep in Byley Church, while many others were billeted a long way from the airfield.

The day after the Duke of Kent's visit, Flight Lieutenant Payne arrived at Cranage to instruct 96 Squadron pilots in landing techniques. His services were requested after a series of minor accidents while pilots were trying to get used to landing at night. Pilot Officer Lauder was involved in a landing accident with a Hurricane on the 11th and the following evening Sergeant Kneath damaged another in similar circumstances.

Then, just as the new boys were getting used to handling the Hurricane the type was about to be phased out of regular operational service. No. 96 Squadron was re-equipping with the two-seater Defiant, which many claimed was a lot more difficult to handle than a Hurricane and generally more likely to cause its pilot problems.

CHAPTER TWELVE

Reorganization and
Searchlight Homing: 1941

In the New Year 9 Group's defences were totally reorganized with the aim of making its night-fighter operations more efficient. The 11th AA Division was formed with three brigades to lighten to load on the 4th Division, and they formed part of the defences of Crewe and the Midlands. Units also supported the powerful new defences which were set up around Liverpool and Manchester.

The rings of steel which surrounded the cities were their GDAs. The origins of such schemes stemmed from defence plans made in 1935. In the north-west the GDAs [Gun Defended Area] were manned mainly by the 4th AA Division with units of 33 Brigade in Liverpool and 44 Brigade in Manchester. Each brigade had two regiments of heavy AA guns and searchlights, with light AA in support. By the end of 1940 Liverpool had amassed a total of eighty heavy AA guns, while Manchester still only had forty. The two GDAs were totally independent of one another and there was only a narrow gap between them to facilitate the transit of aircraft.

In February 1941, major changes were made to the pattern of patrol lines flown by night-fighter crews. A new system was introduced which was far more complex than what had previously existed. The Yellow Patrol Line was scrapped and replaced by thirteen separate patrols spread throughout 9 Group's sectors. Seven of the new lines were connected and formed a circle around the GDAs of Manchester and Liverpool.

Every patrol line was given a name. At the south-western end of the Liverpool GDA was George South, which ran across Liverpool Bay in a north-easterly direction. Running clockwise from that was George North and then Wool South, the most northerly patrol line. Following on from that were Cotton North, Cotton East and then Cotton South, which ran across the top of the Crewe GDA and it connected up with George South.

In between each patrol line, at the beginning and at the end, were electric flares or Tilly lamps, which were known officially as focal points. These were McClaughry's beacons which were similar to the 'lighthouses' which had been used to guide pilots during the First World War, and the system was reminiscent of another age. They were used to guide pilots. They could also orbit them while on patrol to wait for instructions, or to hand over to another crew.

There was a separate patrol, known as the Bar Patrol, around the estuary of the River Mersey, which was an extension to the seaward side of George South. The purpose of the Bar Patrol was to prevent enemy aircraft dropping mines in Liverpool Bay. No more than four aircraft could operate on it at any one time because of its close proximity to the

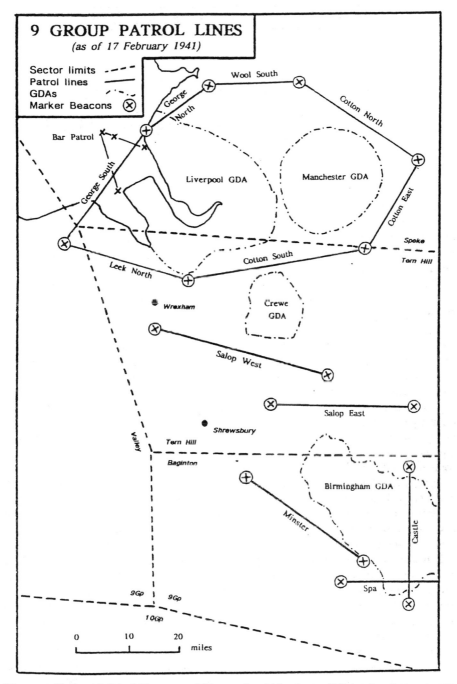

9 GROUP PATROL LINES
(as of 17 February 1941)

Sector limits
Patrol lines
GDAs
Marker Beacons ⊗

Wool South

George North

Cotton North

Bar Patrol

George South

Liverpool GDA

Manchester GDA

Cotton East

Speke

Tern Hill

Leek North

Cotton South

Wrexham

Crewe GDA

Salop West

Salop East

Shrewsbury

Tern Hill

Valley

Baginton

Birmingham GDA

Castle

Minster

Spa

9 Gp | 9 Gp
10 Gp

0   10   20   miles

Diagram of 9 Group's Patrol Lines around Liverpool and Manchester G.D.A.s. (Dated February 1941)
Courtesy of Derek Pratt and Michael Grant

Liverpool GDA and the fact that the Pip Squeak control system could not handle more than that number. When the 9 Group controller decided to fly the Bar Patrol Line he had to inform the Flag Officer Liverpool so that the Royal Navy and other elements of the defences did not engage the night fighters.

The exact positions of most focal points on the patrol lines are not known, but whereas the patrol lines were just theoretical courses subject to wind and drift, the beacons at the focal points were fixed points on the ground. They were controlled by AA Command but manned by ancillary organizations and units which were attached to the searchlight batteries.

One man's recollections from the period detailed not only the location of one particular focal point but how the organization concerned worked. Gunner John Hamer was from Eccles in Manchester, near Barton Airport where he had spent many happy hours before the war. He joined the army in 1937 and trained as a driver and mechanic with the Territorials. On the outbreak of war he was attached to a mobile searchlight battery. He travelled all over the country but at the beginning of December 1940 he and the unit were moved from Bristol to Edale in Derbyshire. At the time he thought that it was the most unlikely location for a searchlight battery that he had come across because it was totally isolated and surrounded by high ground.

The unit was located in the Hope Valley close to Coopers Farm. Accommodation for the troops was very basic and came in the form of wooden huts formerly used by the LDV.

(Land Defence Volunteers) It was very bleak and cold, and there were nothing to do, but very soon that changed and a number of large electric flares arrived. John said that they looked like large Chinese lanterns and nobody had seen anything like them before. Not even the senior NCOs knew about them, and, it was some days after their delivery that AA HQ at Whaley Bridge sent orders on what should be done with them.

The orders were very precise: the lights were to be set up on an exact compass bearing and form an isosceles triangle with the base running from east to west and the apex pointing north. To begin with nobody on the battery knew

Gunner John Hamer at his searchlight battery in Edale with a Lister diesel generator on the back of a lorry which provided power for Focal Point (Marker Beacon) called 'Cotton East'. The beacon was one of a number of visual Focal Points around Liverpool and Manchester which marked the boundaries of the patrol lines.

what they were for and when they were tested for the first time the strange, 'eerie' glow attracted the attention of the local population. Rumours quickly spread about their purpose and various theories were put forward. Many people believed that the lights were some kind of decoy to attract the attention of the *Luftwaffe*.

John's main job was to maintain and operate a Lister mobile diesel generator which sat on a flat-back lorry and provided electrical power for the beacon. During the night he had to run the generator for ten minutes in every hour to ensure that it was serviceable and prevent it from freezing up. That meant that he had to leave the comfort of his warm bed and run up a hill and then walk back down again in the freezing cold. To get back to bed just a little bit faster John made a toboggan which he dragged up the hill behind him. After running the generator he sledged back to his hut and saved several minutes' sleeping time every night.

The focal point was situated at the south-easterly point of the main patrol area around Liverpool and Manchester, and it was called Cotton East. It was at the eastern end of the Cotton South Patrol Line and the southern end of the 'Cotton East' line. It also exactly marked the geographical boundary between the Speke Sector and the Tern Hill Sector, which lay to the south.

Those who worked on the searchlight unit at Edale were never told the true purpose of the beacon but most men were aware that every time the order 'Lights Cotton East' was received from AA HQ at Whaley Bridge, the sound of aircraft was heard overhead. Their presence nearly always coincided with air raids and a lot of air activity in general. The fact that the beacon was a visual reference point on the patrol line where night fighters congregated overhead was a secret, but John and his colleagues eventually worked it out for themselves.

The parent mobile searchlight unit at Edale, of which the searchlight marker beacon was a part, was equipped with American-built Sperry 150 cm reflector lights, and John often worked on them as part of his secondary duties. It mainly involved searchlight homing, a procedure set up to guide pilots who were lost to the nearest airfield. There were many reasons why aircrew became lost, but lack of experience amongst pilots and navigators was a common cause. Also, during air raids radio blackouts were enforced and the sudden loss of communications could sometimes cause even the most experienced airmen to become lost.

The normal searchlight homing procedure required that a pilot who was lost to fly around in a circuit and fire off the colour of the day from a Very pistol or flash it with an Aldis lamp. In November 1940 all RAF aircraft except flying boats were fitted with coloured bulbs for that purpose. Unless a pilot was unlucky and he was in a searchlight blackout zone such as that running down the Welsh border, sooner or later someone would see the lights or flares.

When an aircraft was observed taking such action the nearest air defence centre (in this case Whaley Bridge) was notified and the information passed on to 9 Group HQ and the local sector station. If the duty officer was convinced that the aircraft was friendly the local HQ ordered the nearest searchlight battery to carry out the homing procedure. The master searchlight was then positioned vertically and switched on so that it shone straight up into the sky. Very slowly its elevation was decreased so that its bright beam hung in the air at an angle of about 30 degrees, pointing like a 'finger of light' towards the nearest RAF airfield. On the airfield rockets would be fired to attract the attention of the pilot and if no enemy aircraft were in the vicinty the flare path was lit so that he could make a safe landing.

In most cases a duty officer at the designated airfield had to authorize such action but permission was rarely refused because it might have meant the aircraft flying a considerable distance. John recalled that the battery at Edale received a number of congratulatory messages from pilots and crews who had been saved by their actions.

Nobody realized at the time that the searchlight homing technique was the basis for the introduction of flying control in the RAF. Over the next few years it was introduced generally and saved the lives of thousands of airmen.

John Hamer remained with his unit until the May Blitz but wartime secrecy meant that he did not learn the full truth about the role he played in the night air war until many years later. His was the typical story of a small cog in a big wheel but his part in the night air war was vital nevertheless.

The searchlight batteries were an important element of the defences and particularly the small number of units which were equipped with GL. The technology provided some of the earliest radar information in the north-west region. Gun laying – elevation finding (GL Mk 1 E/F) became available in November 1940 but by the spring of 1941 only a limited number of sets had been allocated to the 4th AA Division.

Information about the height at which the *Luftwaffe* was operating was crucial to the night-fighter unit but AA Command considered it to be confidential and normally kept it within their organization. Eventually pressure was put upon General Pile to allow the information to be passed on to RAF sector controllers. In 9 Group, up to early 1941, there was no other source of such information and co-operation between the AA batteries and the RAF was not all it should have been. It was just one of the problems which had to be resolved, because as spring approached the prospects of another night-fighter unit joining 9 Group, seemed more remote than ever.

CHAPTER THIRTEEN

307 Squadron: January 1941

Fighter Command's plans to provide 9 Group with a second cat's eyes unit to support 96 Squadron were continually set back for a variety of reasons. To fill the gap, Fighter Command sent sections of day-fighter squadrons to train alongside existing night-fighter crews, but it was only a temporary measure. Although 307 Squadron was originally selected as 9 Group's first night-fighter squadron it remained on the Isle of Man.

It was still equipped with the Boulton & Paul Defiant, which had caused so much controversy when the unit had been formed the previous year. It was an all-metal fighter planned as a replacement for the Hawker Demon in 1935, and it was powered by a Rolls Royce Merlin III engine. It was built at Pendeford, Wolverhampton, and had flown for the first time in August 1937 but underwent many changes before entering RAF service in December 1939.

The aircraft's unique design incorporated a Boulton & Paul type A Mk IID turret situated behind the pilot's seat and equipped with four Browning .303 machine-guns. The Defiant carried 600 rounds of ammunition per gun. Without the turret it was similar in design to the Hurricane but it had no forward-firing guns and a smaller wing area, which gave it a higher landing speed.

The Defiant had its critics. Some squadron commanders thought that it was a death trap and there is no doubt that some features of its design and technology left a lot to be desired. There were some airmen, however, who praised it, amongst them a number of 264 Squadron pilots and gunners. They claimed that it was the tactics handed down from Fighter Command that were at fault, and that the Defiant could have been used more successfully.

The unforeseen circumstances concerning the Defiant seriously delayed 307 Squadron's progress towards fulfilling its night-fighting role, and while it awaited orders to return to the mainland, crews continued to fly on convoy patrols. On 9 January 9 Group sent a detachment of the squadron to Squires Gate. The advance party consisted of four senior NCOs and sixteen other ranks. They were flown there during the morning by a Handley Page Harrow, which had been assigned to carry heavier pieces of ground equipment.

During the evening a section of five Defiants left Jurby: N3401, N3435, N3391, N1809 and N3315. They did not all land without incident; N3315, with Flying Officer Smok at the controls, ran into a ditch while making a night landing.

The squadron did not waste time and at 2345 the first aircraft, N3401, piloted by Sergeant Joda accompanied by Sergeant Gandurski, took off on patrol. Just over an hour later, however, something went seriously wrong. The weather closed in, with fog reducing visibility over the coast to less than 600 yards. To add to the problems the Pundit beacon at Squires Gate, which flashed the airfield's identification in Morse code, suddenly stopped working. Radio contact was lost and when Joda failed to return within the time of his aircraft's fuel endurance the Defiant was posted as 'missing'. Within a short while a report was received from an ROC post saying that an aircraft had been spotted in the sea, upside down and half submerged off Fairbourne Beach at Barmouth. It was later positively identified as the missing Defiant, but the authorities never found out the cause of the accident.

Because of the tides and currents it was not until three days later that the bodies of the two Polish airmen were recovered from the wreckage. As a mark of respect a section of Defiants from 307 Squadron from Jurby performed a flypast to salute the two airmen when they were buried at Blackpool's Layton Cemetery on 15 January. The pilot, 25-year-old Sergeant Antoni Joda was buried in Section BB, Grave 339. His air gunner, Wiktor Gandurski, was the same age as his pilot and although he only held the Polish rank of airman, he was awarded the rank of sergeant by the RAF. He was also buried in Section BB, in Grave 441.

On 10 January 307 Squadron was officially notified by 9 Group HQ at Preston that it was to move to Squires Gate in the immediate future. The change was generally welcomed but what most people failed to understand was that it was case of 'out of the frying pan and into the fire'. They were moving from one half-built airfield to another; there were three concrete runway at Squires Gate – 08/26, 14/32 and 02/20 – but in early 1941 they and the surrounding perimeter track were still under construction and the airfield was effectively a building site.

In preparation for the move 307 Squadron's Defiants were fitted with VHF radios to replace the unworkable HF sets and IFF equipment was also installed. The work was carried out at various RAF MUs and the modifications to each aircraft took approximately two months to complete. N1671 was one of the first aircraft to be modified and it flew out to 6 MU at Brize Norton on 14 January. Over the next few days the squadron strength was boosted by the arrival of two new aircraft when N3390 and N3336 were delivered from 10 MU.

On 23 January and in exceptionally poor weather conditions, a section of Defiants from Jurby attempted to reach Squires Gate, but only a single aircraft, N1769, landed without incident. Two pilots had to make forced landings in a field near Ormskirk and while N3439, was later flown out, N3320, was badly damaged. Both airmen escaped without serious injury. On the same day a party of six officers, twelve senior NCOs and a hundred other ranks left Jurby by road and sea, to make the short crossing from Douglas to Liverpool.

Bad weather slowed down the move and on the 26th Handley Page Harrows arrived from Doncaster to airlift some of the heavier ground equipment. Although loading was completed in less than two hours at 1330, the prevailing weather conditions caused the postponement of the flights. The following day the Harrows proceeded to Squires Gate and they were followed by another six of the squadron's Defiants, with N3432, N3314, N3402, N3336, N3339 and N1616, which arrived without any problems. To celebrate its arrival at Blackpool and to promote War Weapons Week, 307 Squadron put on a demonstration flight above Preston.

The next day a couple of Fairey Battles which were used for training landed at Squires Gate and the move was finally completed on 1 February with the help of another two Harrows carrying the last of the ground equipment. Amongst the last Defiants to arrive were N1545, N1643 and N1686, and despite bad weather, training flights began almost immediately. On 6 February the unit completed twenty-hours and twenty minutes of day flying and thirteen hours and five minutes of night flying. With the unit's arrival at Squires Gate, 96 Squadron's A Flight detachment returned to Cranage.

On the night of 15 February enemy aircraft dropped a number of flares over Squires Gate and although 307 Squadron were ordered into the air, the crews failed to make any contact with them. The following night two crews were ordered to patrol over Formby Point on the George North Patrol Line, but the atmosphere was tense and some pilots argued that the weather was too bad to operate. The Defiants eventually took off at 0030 but soon returned and were forced to land in poor visibility. The airmen complained bitterly that they should not have been forced to fly in such appalling conditions. Things were made worse when Pilot Officer Alexandrowicz's Defiant collided with a steamroller on landing; fortunately there were no serious injuries. Squires Gate airfield was littered with contractors' vehicles and it was the first of many such accidents.

On 17 February Sergeant Kazimiekz Bochenski was allegedly carrying out unauthorized low-level aerobatics when his Defiant, N3314, crashed at Fox Lane Ends, Wrea Green. Both Bochenski and his air gunner, Sergeant Kazimerz Frackiewicz were killed instantly. The two airmen were buried at Blackpool Cemetery on 21 February; 41-year-old Sergeant Bochenski in Section BB, Grave 442. The 24-year-old Sergeant Frackiewicz Section BB, Grave 440.

At 0445 on 25 February there was another collision on the ground between Defiant N3375 which was taking off and a petrol bowser. The crew were uninjured but the accident resulted in the death of the driver of the petrol bowser, AC1 Short.

Although Aircraftsman 1st Class William Walter Short was serving on a Polish unit like many others he was actually British and his family came from Bromley-by-Bow in London. The 21-year-old airman, the son of George and Lizzie Short was buried in Manor Park Cemetery Essex where he is buried in Grave 14.

Division Farm was situated between runways 26 and 02 and it had a right of way which passed close to the end of the runway. It has been claimed that it was used regularly as a short cut and that caused a number of accidents.

Two replacement Defiants were flown in during the first few days of March. N1729 from 24 MU at Tern Hill and N1559 from 27 MU at Shawbury.

On 1 March, five of 307 Squadron's crew flew to Speke to take part in a liaison visit to broaden the knowledge of its mainly Polish crews. The airmen were shown around the 9 Group Sector Operations Room in the control tower and it was explained to them how the various elements of the defences worked and how staff co-ordinated with other sectors.

One officer who did not participate was Flying Officer John Millar Ritchie, the 307 Squadron gunnery leader, who was posted out to 96 Squadron at Cranage the same day. Ritchie, who had served with 141 Squadron, was amongst a number of experienced airmen pilfered from 307 Squadron and such action further weakened the morale of the unit.

As other night-fighter squadrons were formed and the RAF built up its forces for a spring offensive, so the need for trained airmen to fly them increased. For the second time in just a few months, 307 Squadron was affected by the loss of experienced personnel. With the posting out of more pilots and air gunners to other units its training programme suffered yet another setback at a crucial time. Despite everything the remaining crews continued to improve their night-flying skills and in March the squadron began to participate in Shortshrift operations.

Within a short while all of 307 Squadron's Defiants were fitted with TR1133 VHF sets to replace the ageing TR9 HF boxes. The TR9 had been designed for short-range transmissions over land, while the TR1133 had a greater range of up to 140 miles at a height of 10,000 ft and it facilitated much better communications during patrols and interceptions.

On the night of 12/13 March 307 Squadron's training and persistence was rewarded when one of its crew intercepted and damaged an He 111, in what was effectively the unit's first combat. Sergeant Janowiak, with his gunner Sergeant Kale, took off from Squires Gate at 2150 hours in N3739 and they encountered the Heinkel over Ruthin soon afterwards. Flying at heights between 17,000 and 22,000 ft they were one of five 307 Squadron crews which took part in a Shortshrift operation between 2200 and 2300. Kale fired a three-second burst and observed a number of rounds enter the cockpit of the intruder, but the results were inconclusive and they were credited with a 'probable'.

To add to the excitement, on 14 March the first American-built Liberator, AM259, landed at Squires Gate from Gander after a flight of nine hours and forty-five minutes. Soon after its arrival there was an air raid and it was very slightly damaged by shrapnel from some of the bombs that fell close by. It remained at Squires gate for several days before it was flown to Hatfield to be inspected by Air Ministry officials. It was eventually given a civil registration, G-AGCD and handed over to BOAC, and it worked on the Return Ferry Service throughout the war.

Just after midnight on the night of 14/15 March, another 307 Squadron crew was involved in combat with an enemy aircraft. It happened after the squadron had been ordered to provide five Defiants for the second Shortshrift operation of the night. The unit was not operating alone; it was supported by three Hurricanes from 229 Squadron whose pilots were training alongside the Polish squadron. At 0050 Flying Officer Leandowski in N3439 spotted an He 111 in the vicinity of Formby at 20,000 ft. His air gunner, Sergeant Niewolski, managed to get in a one second burst from a distance of only 50 yards. That was followed by a three-second burst and although it was another combat that remained inconclusive, the enemy aircraft was claimed as 'damaged'.

Despite its recent actions, on 24 March 307 Squadron was officially informed by signal number 0/360 that it was to carry out a B-type move (Straight exchange between units) to Colerne in Wiltshire on 26 March. The unit had only been operating out of Squires Gate for six weeks but it had failed to achieve the level of success expected of it by Fighter Command. That in turn had frustrated senior officers at 9 Group HQ and despite the fact that the measures were seen as an act of desperation, Fighter Command was no longer willing to tolerate the situation.

There were several events which led up to the move and the posting of Squadron Leader Tomlinson, to Barton Hall on 18 March can be seen as a one of them. As 307 Squadron's former commanding officer, Tomlinson was almost certainly consulted by the AOC, Air-Vice-Marshal McClaughry, before the decision was finalized.

With such short notice there was little time for 307 Squadron to organize the logistics of the move but two Harrow transport aircraft were called in to carry some 8,000 lb of ground equipment.

Fifteen Defiants, including N1772, N3315, N1769, N1641, N3439 and N3437 were flown to Colerne during the afternoon of the 26th, but only a small number of personnel made the journey by air. Twenty-two officers, thirty-four senior NCOs and 132 other ranks travelled on a special train, routed through Crewe, Stafford, Birmimgham, Gloucester and Bristol. The journey was not without incident. While the train was standing in Gloucester station an enemy aircraft suddenly appeared and began to bomb and strafe it. It dropped a number of bombs and made several low passes over the crowded train before it flew off unchallenged. Although nobody was seriously hurt a number of those in the squadron regarded the attack as the final insult. The unit had been moved because its crews had failed to intercept enemy aircraft and during that very process, the enemy had intercepted them! Fortunately the train was able to continue its journey and it eventually arrived in Colerne station at 1815.

The bitter irony was that on the same night the first 307 Squadron crew was credited with shooting down and destroying an enemy aircraft. Sergeant Janowiak and air gunner, Sergeant Lipinski, from A Flight were flying in N3315 above Bristol. They successfully intercepted an He 111 and after a chase they shot it down near Sherborne in Dorset. The move south had got off to a good start and a piece of the Heinkel was later retrieved and nailed to the door of 'A' Flight's office.

CHAPTER FOURTEEN

96 Squadron: February 1941

The first Defiant delivered to 96 Squadron was N3389, and it arrived at Cranage on 15 January. It was used to start the conversion training because the bulk of the Defiants would not arrive for another month. During the subsequent training period there were a lot of postings in and out, and although many new faces appeared, some disappeared almost as quickly as they had arrived.

The first six Defiants for operational service arrived at Cranage on 15 February; they were N1803, N3327, N3338, N3433, N3434 and N3436. Some of them, such as N1803 and N3433, were cast-offs from 85 Squadron, and they were delivered direct from Debden. On the 28th another three Defiants were flown in: N1766, N1767 and N3374. Each aircraft was painted soot black, a paint scheme known offically as RDM2.

Despite the Defiant's reputation there was great optimism about what lay ahead and the few air gunners who had flown them during daylight operations in 1940 looked forward to a fresh start.

The air gunners entered the turret of the Defiant through side panels which pulled apart like a window. They and the pilots wore bulky Irvin flying suits which protected them from the cold and extreme temperatures. Some pilots had acquired more fanciful flying suits and Sergeant Taylor wore a smart black uniform similar to those worn by members of the *Luftwaffe*. Flying Officer Verity and a few others also wore an Irvin jacket and a customised flying suit but most pilots stayed with the Irvin suit.

Amongst the new arrivals in February were two experienced Czech pilots, Flying Officer Josef Klobucnic and Flying Officer Vlasimic Vesely from 312 Squadron. Vesely already knew some of 96 Squadron's pilots and he had flown Flying Officer Rabone from Speke to Cranage in December 1940. Kloboucnik was posted in on 8 February but he did not stay long; he transferred to 68 Squadron at High Ercall. He was later killed when his Beaufighter crashed during a training flight.

Flight mechanic Leading Aircraftsman Clem Lea was posted from 43 Squadron at Drem in Scotland to RAF Cranage. He was very pleased to be posted to an airfield just down the road from where he lived with his wife at Middlewich in Cheshire. He was posted on a Friday, arrived home on the Saturday and did not have to report for duty until the Monday morning. He claimed living-out allowance and after finishing work he went home to his wife every night, although he still had to do guard duties like everyone else.

One of his friends was a New Zealander, Pilot Officer Harold North, who had also served in 43 Squadron and flown during the Battle of Britain. North had been shot down on 26 August and suffered wounds to his head and shoulders which sometimes caused him a great deal of pain. As a result he did not do a great deal of operational flying with 96 Squadron, Lea remembered him as being one of its characters.

Leading Aircraftsman Clem Lea of 96 Squadron sitting in a Defiant at Cranage. He lived locally at Middlewich and was very lucky to get posted so near to his wife and family. Courtesy of Clem Lea

Sergeant Taylor and Flying Officer Verity were also 'customers' of Lea's and he regularly strapped them in or refuelled their aircraft. At night he would marshall them in by waving two small torches in the air to guide them to their dispersal point. One night while marshalling Sergeant Taylor's Defiant he was walking backwards when he stumbled in the long grass. The whirling propeller was just inches above his body, but fortunately Taylor shut down the engine when he saw him fall, or he might have been cut to pieces.

Having previously worked on Hurricanes Lea was not keen on Defiants but he said everyone worked hard and with great ingenuity. If a spare part was not available a fitter would beg, borrow or steal it, but one way or another the job always got done. Just to add to the amusement on the flight line, Lea's two senior NCOs were Flight Sergeant Salt and Flight Sergeant Pepper. He said they used to take a lot of stick from the 'seasoned' airmen but it was all in good fun and everyone got on well together.

On their nights off or on stand-downs both ground crew and aircrew liked to enjoy themselves and get away from Cranage for a few hours. Unlike some RAF airfields, where officers, senior NCOs and airmen drank in separate establishments, at Cranage everyone drank in the same pub. The Three Feathers, on the outskirts of Winsford, was the most popular place to be and Lea remembered having some very good nights there.

The cold winter weather at the beginning of the year took its toll of airmen of all nationalities; many of them reported sick and were taken off flying duties. Flying Officer Verity recollected that during January and February he felt so ill that he had to visit Flying Officer 'Doc' Blackledge twice a day. The doctor gave him nose inhalations and various tablets so that he could continue his flying duties, but the medication failed to aid a speedy recovery.

Any enthusiasm that crews might have had for the Defiant began to wane when it was discovered that in most aircraft the intercom between the pilot and gunner was more or less useless! Many of the modifications and repairs to the aircraft were carried out by the RAF's own maintenance units, but some work was allocated to private companies such as Reid & Sigrist, which was based at Desford near Leicester, where Boulton & Paul had a second assembly line. Reid & Sigrist was an aircraft manufacturer in its own right and had produced a little known trainer called a Snargasher. A number of 96 Squadron's Defiants were flown to Desford but others were modified in the hangars at Cranage.

Some of the work that was carried out at Cranage was done under the supervision of the CO, Squadron Leader Kellett, who toiled solidly for four days with the engineering officer, Flying Officer Brisket. The technically skilled Brisket had only recently joined the RAF from university, but he played a vital part in rectifying and modifying various electrical circuits. Every Defiant was eventually modified and communications over the intercom between the pilot and gunner were vastly improved.

Flying Officer Verity described the solving of some of the the Defiant's technical problems as Squadron Leader Kellett's 'Finest Hour'. That it may have been, but he received little reward for his work and only a short while later he had a huge row with an air commodore at 9 Group HQ. Kellett told him exactly what he thought of him. For his outburst he was promoted to the rank of wing commander, but posted out from 96 Squadron to North Weald in Essex on 8 March.

The new CO was Squadron Leader Bobby Burns, who had served in the RAF for a number of years and returned from Gibralter at the outbreak of war. Burns, a rugged South African, was posted to Cranage from 54 Night-Fighter OTU and he made no major changes to the running of 96 Squadron except to introduce a safer system of homing the aircraft back to base. This involved positioning aircraft at various heights on QDM to allow them a safe descent through high ground and balloon barrages. Pilots learned to be very wary because there was a large balloon barrage near Crewe, within eight miles of Cranage. There was also what Burns described as a 'veritable wall of them from Liverpool to Manchester'.

Even after the arrival of the Defiants 96 Squadron continued to fly Hurricanes because there were still a number of problems with the serviceability of the two-seaters. Many of the faults involved radio and engine snags but air gunners experienced regular stoppages in the the four .303 guns. Also the Hurricane was to operate at heights above 20,000 ft, where the Defiant could not do so efficiently. On the night of 2 March when there was reasonably good weather, eleven Hurricanes took off on a training flight, but only three Defiants were serviceable enough for their crews to participate in the exercise.

The weather over the following week was very unsettled and on 6 March 96 Squadron managed to get in less than one hour's flying. Within a week morale was boosted when several crews were engaged in combats and one of the pilots was credited with what was effectively 96 Squadron's first confirmed destruction of an enemy aircraft.

Sergeant McNair had accumulated less than fifteen hours of night-flying experience out of his grand total of over 300 flying hours. He had flown all his patrols in Hurricanes and like most other 96 Squadron pilots he had only experienced flying the Defiant on training sorties. On 12 March he flew two sorties in a Defiant, one involving local flying with Sergeant Wirdnam and another on his own practising dusk landings. The practice paid off when, later that night, Sergeant McNair took off on patrol in Hurricane V7752 at 2035. Shortly after commencing his patrol on the Cotton South line near Liverpool, he observed an He 111 heading south. He was flying on a north-easterly course but he managed to do a quick turn, catch up with the enemy bomber and get himself into a position underneath

Squadron Leader Burns (centre), who took over as C.O. of 96 Squadron in March 1941, with flying Officer Veseley (left) and Sergeant Chubb (right) at Cranage. Burns served two terms as the C.O. of the unit and he was regarded as a good leader who was able to inspire others.

the aircraft's tail. He then fired a four-second burst from a range of 75 yards which caused the Heinkel's engine to begin pouring out thick black smoke. Its port undercarriage dropped down as well and as the aircraft began to move unpredictably through the dark sky, McNair ensured its demise with a second burst of fire, approaching the enemy aircraft's port side in a beam attack.

McNair witnessed the Heinkel crashing to the ground in the vicinity of Widnes, but found himself in a precarious position, at only 3,500 ft and in the middle of a balloon barrage. Certainly more by luck than judgement, he managed to avoid the balloons and fly out of the barrage. After clearing the danger area he discovered that the Hurricane's fuel tanks were almost empty. He only just made it back to Cranage, as his Hurricane touched down its Merlin engine spluttered and stopped. It then had to be pushed off the runway – after a sortie lasting two hours and forty minutes, hardly a drop of fuel remained in the tanks.

The destruction of the He 111 was witnessed by the battery commander of an AA gun crew in the Widnes area but he only saw the enemy bomber – McNair's Hurricane remained hidden in the night sky. The army officer had a completely different view of the events which led up to the aircraft's destruction; and he claimed his AA battery had shot the Heinkel down. At 2130 he noted in his log: 'An aircraft was seen surrounded by shell burst and lit up with an orange glow.' Five minutes later the he recorded: 'An aircraft crashed in flames bearing 240 degrees – distance about three miles.' He claimed that the Heinkel only lost height and speed after being hit by a shell from his guns, and that the night fighter attacked it at point blank range, when it was already doomed.

It was later discovered that the German bomber had flown into a barrage balloon cable before crashing to the ground on a sports field near the outskirts of Widnes. Despite the AA's claim, Sergeant McNair was credited with what was 96 Squadron's first confirmed victory.

The enemy aircraft was later identified as He 111, G1 + GP, which belonged to 6 *Staffel* of KG 55. It was piloted by *Oberfeldwebel* Karl Single, but under the command of observer, *Hauptman* Wolfgang Berlin who was the *Staffelkapitan*. They, together with radio operator, *Unteroffizier* Xavier Diem, baled out and survived, while the flight mechanic, *Feldwebel* Leanhard Kuznik and the gunner, *Feldwebel* Heinrich Ludwinski, were killed.

On the same night a number of Defiants were airborne but some air gunners had problems with their guns, including Flying Officer Ritchie. He and his pilot, Flying Officer Rabone, were forced to return early in N1766 from a patrol over Liverpool.

Sergeant Taylor took off at 2355 hours in Defiant T3954, with Sergeant Broughton as his air gunner when they observed a Heinkel and attempted to intercept it. Soon after opening fire, however, the guns jammed and the Heinkel dived steeply to get away. Taylor followed it, down into thick cloud. He then suddenly realized that with the Welsh mountains in such close proximity they were in a dangerous situation and he pulled up into a steep climb. Their efforts might have been worthwhile, as some time later the wreckage of a Heinkel was discovered in the Welsh mountains, but there was no confirmation that it was the same one they had intercepted.

There was a third action that night, when another Defiant crew spotted a Heinkel but again suffered from the guns failing. Flying Officer Veseley and his gunner, Sergeant Haycock, were flying in N1803, but when the guns let them down the pilot persisted and refused to break off the action. Veseley formated on the Heinkel and maintained his station, flying alongside the enemy aircraft at a distance of approximately 100 yards.

Veseley intended to keep in contact until Sergeant Haycock got the guns working again, but the air gunner found it impossible. Without any warning the pilot of the Heinkel put his bomber into a steep dive, but Veseley followed it down. He then manoeuvred his Defiant onto the Heinkel's starboard side, where he then flew in formation with it at a distance of less than 50 yards.

The Defiant crew were taken completely by surprise when the Heinkel's side gunner suddenly opened fire on them and got in two short bursts. The first one hit Veseley and wounded him while the second burst struck the top of the gun turret causing ricochets to fly in all directions. The 28-year-old Czech pilot was wounded in the chest, shoulder and left arm and as a result he temporarily lost consciousness and control of his aircraft.

For a few moments the Defiant went into a spin but then Veseley recovered enough to manipulate the stick and rudder and regained control. It was not easy for him to fly the Defiant but somehow he managed it and he set a course back to Cranage. He was aided in his approach to the airfield by bright moonlight and he was able to see the runway without the goose-neck flares, to make what was almost a perfect landing. He had to be pulled out the cockpit and he was taken to hospital, where he later made a remarkable recovery before returning to flying duties with 68 Squadron.

An enemy aircraft crashed into the River Mersey the same night, although the exact cause of its destruction is not known. The Ju 88, flown by *Feldwebel* Gunther Unger, was probably abandoned after a fire broke out behind the starboard engine and he suspected that it had been hit by AA fire. His assumption may have been correct because the AA battery commander at Widnes, the same one who claimed McNair's Heinkel, reported an aircraft 'blowing up' on a bearing of 290 degrees. That was at 2125, just five minutes before McNair shot down the Heinkel over Widnes. *Feldwebel* Unger and his three crew parachuted to safety, although Unger landed in the river and had to swim ashore. All of them were soon captured and taken prisoners.

Flying Officer Verity did not have much luck to begin with but his fortunes changed during a sortie in Hurricane N6923 on the night of 14/15 March. At 2345 he observed a Ju 88 heading south in a position some 6 miles east of Wrexham. The New Zealander gave chase and eventually overtook the Junkers, before he dropped back to a position 100 yards behind it. Verity then stabilized his Hurricane and made final checks on the range before he lined up and fired an eight-second burst.

The rear of the Ju 88's fuselage was hit and there was a bright red flash from the port engine as the enemy bomber dived away steeply in an attempt to escape. Verity followed it down and managed to get in another four-second burst which struck the top of its fuselage. Searchlights then picked up Verity's Hurricane and the sudden glare blinded him, so that he lost sight of the enemy aircraft. At 0055 he landed at Cranage and during debriefing he heard that there was nothing to confirm his claim that he had destroyed the Junkers. Regardless of the lack of evidence he believed that it did crash; he thought it fell into the sea off the coast of North Wales.

This was Verity's last combat in a Hurricane on 96 Squadron; during future operations he flew with a fellow New Zealander, Sergeant Wake, in a Defiant. Sergeant Frederick William Wake had been posted in from 264 Squadron, which he had joined at Kirton-in-Lindsey in September 1940. The partnership between air gunner and pilot turned out to be one of the most successful in Fighter Command.

The persistent rain created particularly bad conditions on the airfield at Cranage at this time and the water table was recorded as being just 20 inches below the surface. Conversion to the Defiant was, however, going well and the 96 Squadron diary noted in the middle of March. 'Pilots are coming to recognize that the Defiant is the best single-engined night fighter.'

Some pilots still had relatively little experience on the type, especially those who had been detached to Blackpool. On 27 March Flying Officer Rabone flew only his second sortie in a Defiant on a weather test over Manchester at 20,000 ft. Throughout the whole of March he only flew four times and made just one operational sortie.

War Weapons Week began on 23 March and 100 service personnel from Cranage, including elements of 96 Squadron, paraded at Northwich, Middlewich and Winsford. The squadron's Hurricanes put on an aerobatic display and flew alongside eleven Ansons from the School of Navigation, which dropped publicity leaflets. On the 29th, 96 Squadron Hurricanes performed a dramatic 'beat up' of Holmes Chapel to bring the week to a close. For a number of the squadron's pilots it was a last chance to fly the type, as the Defiant was being introduced into operational service and opportunities in the future would be rare.

At the end of March 9 Group was aided by the addition of a new sector which was created when the sector operations room at RAF Rhosneigr (soon to be changed to Valley) opened up. Rather unusaully it was situated in a chapel in the village of Caergeiliog on the main Bangor to Holyhead road. The only other building was a Nissen hut situated adjacent to it because there was not enough room inside the chapel. One of the first staff to arrive was Sergeant Frank Cheesman, who was posted in from Barton Hall. He remembered it being an isolated site. The airmen's mess was 3 miles from the village, with the billets 2 miles beyond that. Airmen were later issued with bicycles but by that time the set-up had changed anyway!

CHAPTER FIFTEEN

Débâcle At Tern Hill:
Incidents Galore

In April Shortshrift and Layers operations were renamed Fighter Nights and their criteria were again redefined by 9 Group HQ. Fighter nights were only to be laid on when there was a full moon, with good visibility and when the enemy was attacking a single objective which could easily be defended. Operations would involve at least nine single-engined night fighters and they could operate as low as 9,000 ft when the AA barrage was shut down. As before, aircraft were to be spaced at 1,000 ft intervals.

The changes came about after Fighter Command had demanded more fighter nights but the operations remained a controversial subject for General Pile and AA Command. To resolve matters an agreement was finally reached about the height at which the night fighters should operate above the gun barrage. There was still disagreement, however about when a gun barrage should be closed down so that night fighters could pursue enemy aircraft alone. Although AA Command shared its HQ at Bentley Priory with Fighter Command its was fiercely independent.

On fighter nights and during routine patrols, communications between pilots and ground control was maintained by VHF radio on a band of frequencies between 100 and 124 megacycles. Every radio set had four pre-set channels, each of which had a specific function. The first channel was used by pilots to contact flying control at the squadron's base airfield. A second was used to communicate with the sector control where the airfield was located. The third allowed pilots to contact controllers in sectors adjacent to their own. The fourth was known as Command Guard, and could be used by pilots to communicate with any sector control in the country. It was the most important channel of all and was regularly tested and checked for interference.

Despite the onset of spring, the weather in April 1941 was very wet and cloudy, but whenever possible training flights went ahead as planned. On the night of 9 April a number of crews were involved in six hours of night flying, practising interceptions and searchlight co-operation. A searchlight intelligence officer had recently visited Cranage and despite some improvements in searchlight techniques, 96 Squadron crews were keen to show him why the searchlights often lagged behind enemy aircraft. There was thick cloud with $^{10}/_{10}$ coverage at 2,000 ft but despite the weather things were going well. Then a training exercise suddenly developed into a full blown combat scenario.

Sergeant Taylor's Defiant was attacked by an unidentified aircraft, but his gunner Sergeant Broughton, spotted it at the last moment and alerted his pilot. Taylor took immediate evasive action but not before the other aircraft had opened fire and badly damaged his aircraft. The starboard wing and fuselage were riddled with cannon fire and the fuel situation became so critical that Taylor considered making an immediate forced landing. Petrol was gushing from the tanks in the starboard wing but he maintained control and was able to return to Cranage, where he made a safe landing.

The incident was the topic of conversation for some time and not everyone was convinced that the 'enemy' aircraft belonged to the *Luftwaffe*. It was generally agreed that the offending pilot had been attracted by the bright lights of Verity's Defiant, which was just ahead of Taylor's. During the exercise Verity was playing the role of the 'bandit' and his navigation lights were switched on for identification purposes. Unfortunately his illuminated aircraft attracted the wrong kind of attention and such incidents highlighted the potential dangers lurking in the circuit of one's own airfield.

Rumours were rife that the other aircraft might have been a night fighter from 29 or 68 Squadron whose crew were 'poaching' on 96 Squadron's patch. Although Broughton had trained his guns on the other aircraft and had managed to get in a short burst, it disappeared as quickly as it had arrived. He caught only a passing glimpse of it and he could not identify it. There was no evidence to support the 'friendly fire' theory and there were a number of similar incidents at around this time.

Just the night before, a 29 Squadron Beaufighter, flown by no less a person than Flight Lieutenant Guy Gibson, was shot up by a Ju 88 while landing at Digby. Gibson's aircraft ploughed through a hedge because the brake pipes were hit, and although he was not injured his radio operator was wounded in the leg. *Luftwaffe* night fighters were regularly penetrating Britain's night defences but most airmen were reluctant to believe it until they experienced their presence for themselves.

The following night, 10/11 April, 96 Squadron was put on standby for a fighter night over Birmingham to work with 256 Squadron, which had just been declared operational. A number of Defiants were flown to Tern Hill in anticipation of a large-scale raid on the Midlands but the operation was plagued by technical problems. A Flight flew down to Tern Hill with five aircraft but two of them became unserviceable, while B Flight's three Defiants were forced to return to Cranage because of extremely bad weather. They only managed to land because of some skilful work by the operator of the primitive Homing Station Bramble and a display of pyrotechnics organized by the signals officer.

In the end 96 Squadron's contribution to the fighter night was to consist of just three aircraft led by Squadron Leader Burns, flying with the gunnery leader, Pilot Officer Smith in T3454. Even that meagre contribution was something of a failure because of further technical problems. Flight Lieutenant Raphael in N3452 suffered a radio failure and returned to Tern Hill without ever reaching his operational height. The newly promoted Flight Lieutenant Rabone in N3438 had his own problems when a hydraulic pump burst and he was forced to return. Only Squadron Leader Burns continued with the operation but he and Smith failed to observe any enemy aircraft. That night was to go down in the annals of 96 Squadron as its darkest hour, and it was some time before the unit was able to make amends for its dismal performance.

Over the next few nights some of 96 Squadron's crews became rather bored because bad weather continually kept them on the ground. On 11 April, conditions were so poor that no aircraft took off after 1535 and the squadron diary declared its crews to be 'earthbound spirits again!' With the boredom came doubts about the usefulness of the moon period in helping crews to see the enemy. Things gradually improved, however, and on 13 April the diary noted: 'Today day flying reached barely eight hours. But even night flying and air test can produce their excitement.'

The excitement was at the expense of Flight Lieutenant Rabone and Flying Officer Ritchie, who were forced to to abandon their aircraft over the Peak District. It was the first of a series of incidents in April involving 96 Squadron's Defiants and it happened on a night cross-country exercise during their return flight from Digby in N1766. At 2120 the Rolls-Royce Merlin III engine started to cough and splutter, so Rabone sent a distress message over the R/T.

Because he failed to get a response to his repeated calls, he assumed that it was unserviceable. The critical situation left him with little choice but to abandon the aircraft above the inhospitable terrain of the Peak District. Both men managed to get out and followed the standard procedure of jumping off the trailing edge of the wing, to avoid being hit by the tailplane. They then parachuted to safety, coming down on different sides of the Derwent Reservoir with Rabone landing on a hill 1 mile to the west of it. The Defiant crashed into the ground 2 miles west of the reservoir on some land known as Rowlees Pastures.

Rabone and Ritchie were very lucky, as they could easily have fallen into the reservoir and drowned or found themselves stranded up on the cold, desolate moors. Others were not so fortunate; on the night of 27/28 April, Sergeant Angell and Flight Sergeant Goldsmith were killed on a night-training exercise. They were flying in N3389, the first Defiant to be delivered to 96 Squadron on 15 January 1941. It crashed near Wellinglore just before midnight. It was thought that the accident was caused because Sergeant Angell became disorientated. The two senior NCOs had previously survived a crash landing at Cranage on the 15th in T3954, but the second time around they had little chance of escaping and the Defiant was a Category 3 write-off.

Flight Sergeant Goldsmith was an experienced airman who had joined the RAF in 1939 and served with 236 Squadron when it was equipped with Blenheims, flying from St Eval in Coastal Command. On 23 September 1940, while with Pilot Officer Russell, he had shot down an He 111 and two days later claimed a Dornier 18 flying boat as destroyed. Goldsmith had met Sergeant Angell at 54 OTU, Church Fenton, in March 1941 when they were going through their flying training.

Flying Officer John Ritchie, 96 Squadron Gunnery Leader. Ritchie was on board the Defiant piloted by Flight Lieutenant Rabone, which had to be abandoned over the Peak District after the aircraft had an electrical failure.

They had become good friends and stayed together as a crew when they were posted to 96 Squadron in early April.

Twenty-four-year-old Sergeant Walter Barrie Angell was buried in Shenfield (St Mary) Churchyard in Essex. The son of Allan Barron and Luisa Giulia, he was laid to rest in Grave 4, Row 14. Flight Sergeant John Ernest Goldsmith was only nineteen years old but his experiences were those of much older and more mature man. Born the son of Percy Charles and Kathleen Elizabeth Goldsmith of Orford, he was buried in Sudbourne (All Saints) Churchyard in Suffolk.

Three days after the Angell and Goldsmith incident, 96 Squadron lost another Defiant when Sergeant Rauls and Sergeant Phillips experienced an engine failure while flying over Gatley in south Manchester. It happened during a night-training interception exercise and both men managed to bale out and land safely. Sergeant Phillips however, had a terrifying experience when his parachute failed to open immediately and he thought it had failed. The Defiant, N3376, crashed in Park Road, Gatley, but fortunately nobody was in the vicinity when it smashed into the ground.

On 2 May Flight Lieutenant Paul Rabone, the flight commander of B Flight, was posted out to 85 Squadron at Hunsdon. He had a total of 662 flying hours and his experience was to be sadly missed by his colleagues on 96 Squadron. He was replaced as flight commander by Flight Lieutenant Raphael, who was also an experienced pilot, but he had a different approach to things and was much stricter.

The same day as Rabone was posted out 96 Squadron lost a Hurricane being flown by a pilot who did not have the correct authority to fly it. Flight Lieutenant Rabone was one of several pilots who might have mourned the loss of the V7621, because it was a former 422 Flight machine in which he had destroyed a Bf 109 on 28 October 1940. The circumstances which led up to the incident began a few days earlier when one of the flight commanders from 2 ANS and a fellow instructor had visited RAF Sealand.

Flight Lieutenant Edwards and his fellow instructor, Flying Officer Wakeford, said that they were both experienced fighter pilots, and were subsequently allowed to 'borrow' a couple of Spitfires. On that occasion they returned them in one piece. A few days later they thought they would try their luck again and see if they could fly a Hurricane. To do so they had to convince someone in 96 Squadron that their story was genuine and persuade them to sign the relevant authorization documents.

They approached Flying Officer Verity, who was acting flight commander of B Flight and told him they were missing the excitement of flying single-engined fighters. Verity was apparently impressed by their stories of how they had flown the Hurricane in combat and yearned to take it into the air once more. Despite a standing order in the Pilots' Order Book which stated that ANS pilots were not to fly 96 Squadron's aircraft, he signed the flight authorization book. V7621 was the only Hurricane fuelled and armed, so Flight Lieutenant Edwards exercised his seniority and went off in it first.

After Edwards had landed Flying Officer Wakeford had his turn, but when he returned to the circuit half an hour later things things began to go wrong. It appeared to observers on the ground that Wakeford was finding it difficult to control the aircraft. As he approached to land, the wheels were still retracted and smoke began bellowing from the aircraft; the first signs of fire appeared just before Wakeford crashed into a nearby wood.

Wakeford was found by those who were first on the scene, staggering around in circles about 50 yards from the wreckage. Despite being badly burned he was not critically injured and after a spell in hospital recovered enough to face a court of inquiry. Its findings resulted in both instructors being censured for their actions. Edwards, who was due for promotion, had it cancelled and he also lost his seniority. It is not known what punishment Flying Officer Verity was given, but he might have claimed mitigating circumstances!

A number of new pilots joined 96 Squadron around this time, including Flying Officer Kenneth Butterworth McGlashan, who had joined the RAF on a short-service commission in January 1939. He had served with 245 Squadron in France and had something in common with Flying Officer Verity. On 31 May 1940 McGlashan's Hurricane had been damaged and he had had to make a forced landing in France. That was the same day as Verity had been shot down in the sea and similarly, McGlashan was forced to return to England by boat.

By the beginning of May and after a bad patch things began to settle down and 96 Squadron had a total of eleven serviceable Defiants on charge. Following the tradition of the RAF, crews adapted their favourite aircraft with various forms of 'nose art'. Caricatures and cartoons began to appear on the Defiants as pilots and gunners began to establish a routine which revolved around training and preparations for operational flying. On the nights when a fighter night operation was not planned, and if the weather permitted, crews flew standing patrols in the hope of catching a glimpse of an enemy aircraft. On most nights nothing of any significance happened but things were building up and expectations were high.

CHAPTER SIXTEEN

256 Squadron: March 1941

On 26 March, the same day as 307 Squadron left Squires Gate 256 Squadron flew in from Colerne in Wiltshire as part of a direct exchange of units between 9 Group and 10 Group. No. 256 Squadron had been commissioned at Catterick in November 1940 and after a brief spell at Pembrey, had moved to Colerne in February. Prior to being posted to Squires Gate its crews had spent a month on night-flying training with other 10 Group units, and because it had performed well, there were great expectations of the results that could be achieved.

Amongst those who had joined 256 Squadron at Catterick was Sergeant John MacDonald. After learning to fly at Brough and Sealand his name had been drawn to transfer to night fighters. Later on most night-fighter pilots were volunteers, but during the summer of 1940 they were sent where they were needed and his expectations of flying Spitfires or Hurricanes were dashed. His experiences of 256 Squadron were typical for the time and even after the move to Squires Gate, he found the organization and administration sadly lacking in many areas.

The CO of 256 Squadron was Squadron Leader W. Gatherall, a medium-term officer who had only recently returned from Singapore. He was judged by most to be a good, efficient officer but he had little experience of modern aircraft or the tactics used by Fighter Command. The squadron adjutant was Flying Officer Ford, a newly commissioned officer who was an extremely resourceful person and a valuable asset to the unit.

There were plenty of rumours going around as to why 307 Squadron had been replaced. The most popular was that the Poles had taken too great a liking to the delights of Blackpool, which were readily available. While a few welcomed the 'wine, women and song' reputation of the seaside resort, many of the newcomers in 256 Squadron ignored such things, or at least were not overwhelmed by the charms on offer. A number were locally recruited from Liverpool and they were more interested in the welfare of their families.

Unlike the muddy grass airfield 256 Squadron had left behind in Wiltshire, Squires Gate, which had been requisitioned by the Air Ministry in 1938, had three concrete runways. They had been laid down in the typical RAF triangular pattern in March 1940, when the Ministry of Aircraft Production chose to build a factory on the airfield to manufacture the Wellington bomber. The main runway, 08/26, was 4,200 ft long and a perimeter track around it connected all three runways with the dispersals. By the spring of 1941 construction of the runways and hard standing areas was still not complete and the runway lighting consisted mainly of goose-neck flares. The paraffin-powered lamps

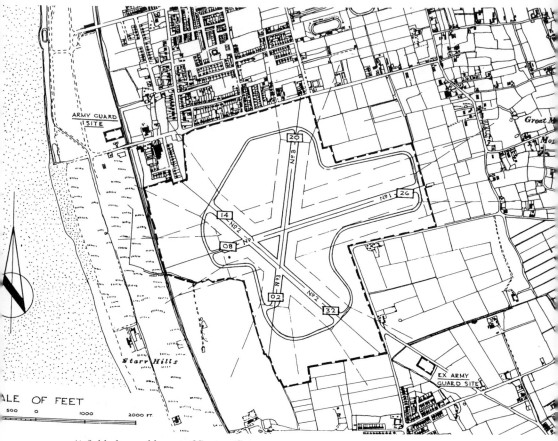

Airfield plan and layout of Squires Gate.

were totally inadequate and failed to illuminate vehicles or aircraft which were widely dispersed all around the airfield.

Accommodation for everyone was basic but for some it was almost primitive, and while some officers were billeted in hotels, most airmen slept in bell tents on a site close to the airfield. Armourer, Corporal Frank Metcalf, had joined 256 Squadron in December 1940 when it was stationed at Catterick. He was quite optimistic to begin with, as he and some others were accommodated in the South Down Hotel. Very soon afterwards, however, that was requisitioned for the officers' mess and he and his mates were billeted in tents on the Pleasure Beach.

While the domestic arrangements were initially worse than those at Colerne, technical and engineering facilities were far better. The unit's Defiants were soon fitted with TR1133 VHF radio and IFF, in most cases without having to be dispersed to maintenance units. No. 256 Squadron was fortunate in that many of the problems associated with the Defiant had already been identified and resolved by 9 Group, through the experience of other units. The problems that remained mainly concerned the interrupter gear on the guns, which was designed to prevent air gunners shooting into the tailplane or propeller.

At Squires Gate all aircraft suffered one additional maintenance problem: sand being blown into the air intakes of the engines. The airfield was situated only a short distance from the shore and strong winds constantly blew sand across the dispersals. This persistent problem was a real hazard and some airmen have claimed that a number of serious accidents were caused by sand getting into engines and vital control systems.

While many of the pilots posted in to 256 Squadron were relatively inexperienced, there were a small number of others who had flown in combat and contributed valuable experience to the night air-war. Most of the New Zealanders generally had more flying experience than the average British pilot and the critics considered that Commonwealth aircrew displayed greater skill and ability. There were those who claimed that they were also more willing to enter into combat with the enemy but that point would have been hotly disputed by those British pilots who had been in action.

One such pilot was Flight Lieutenant Christopher Deanesly, the B Flight Commander in 256 Squadron, who was a former army officer. As a civilian Deanesly had been a salesman but in 1931 he had joined the South Staffordshire Territorial Regiment and served in the army for six years. In 1937 he took a commission in the RAF Auxiliary and gained his RAF wings the same year, before joining 605 Squadron, which was equipped with the ancient Gloster Gladiator biplane. In October 1939 he was posted to 152 Squadron at Acklington, a unit also equipped with Gladiators, but in the summer of 1940 it re-equipped with Spitfires and moved to Warmwell in Dorset.

On 25 July 1940 during the Battle of Britain, he had been credited with a half-share in a Dornier, but was shot down by a Ju 87 during the same combat and ended up in the sea 3 miles off Portland Bill. He was rescued by the SS *Empire Henchman* and taken ashore to Lyme Regis Hospital where he was kept for a month, before returning to service. He had barely recovered from that ordeal when on 26 September, he had a similar experience 10 miles off Swanage.

He baled out of Spitfire K9982 after combat with an He 111 and a Bf 109 but fortunately he was spotted from the air by an Air Sea Rescue Westland Lysander. It kept a watch over him and called in a Royal Navy launch whose crew eventually pulled him from the water. He was wounded in both legs and spent another period in Lyme Regis Hospital before eventually returning to duty as a sector controller. Stationed at St Eval he gained knowledge and experience that would be valuable in his future role as a night-fighter pilot.

At the end of 1940 Flight Lieutenant Deanesly responded to an appeal for flight commanders to join night-fighter units. It was the second time that he had applied to join a night-fighter unit, and in February 1941, he was posted to 256 Squadron. He joined the unit at Colerne shortly after it had moved there from Pembrey and it became partly operational while working up at Middle Wallop. Despite his initial enthusiasm, Deanesly later admitted that he had had plenty of doubts about its future role.

He claimed that after the move to Blackpool the morale of 256 Squadron personnel improved, although the accident rate remained alarmingly high and shadowed that of 307 Squadron. He crewed up with Sergeant Jack Scott as his regular air gunner, a New Zealander who had flown Defiants through the Battle of Britain with 264 Squadron. Scott had a jaded opinion of the way New Zealanders were treated and he claimed they were often shuffled around between training and operational units.

Scott also thought that the tactics used by the Defiant squadrons during the Battle of Britain were very poor; he believed that senior officers did not know what to do with the aircraft. During their training crews had been instructed to fly at a range of 400 yards from and parallel to an enemy bomber, to give the air gunners a clear shot at the aircraft. Scott said he and many others thought it would have been better to have flown in pairs, in loose formation with one aircraft acting as 'shotgun'. He thought that those tactics might have allowed the second Defiant crew to formate on the enemy and get a clear line of fire. His views, and those of many others, were largely ignored and Scott claimed that the lack of a properly thought-out policy contributed to the Defiants being withdrawn from the front-line daylight campaign.

The first of 256 Squadron's many accidents occurred on the day after the unit arrived at Blackpool when two Defiants collided on the ground. On this occasion the incident, which involved N3454 and N3382, caused no casualties and very little damage. Flight Leutenant Deanesly and Sergeant Scott were keen to get on with the job and on the eve of 256 Squadron officially being declared operational they flew what was effectively its first patrol in Defiant N3500 'B'.

On 31 March 256 squadron crews adopted a new rota system and each flight began to operate two nights on followed by two nights off. If necessary the arrangement could be altered at short notice and both flights could be put into action. No. 256 Squadron was declared operational the following day but that did stop some airmen from socialising. Sergeant Reg

Flight Leutenant Deanesly, D.F.C, Flight Commander on 256 Squadron based at Squires Gate. The former army officer used discipline and punitive measure against his airmen that some did not approve of but his tactics were aimed at getting the best out of what was a bad situation. In 1941 he was made the CO of 256 Squadron and by the time he left it in early 1942 the unit was better organised.

Adams noted that he went to a show with Sergeant Trim. Adams also made a note of the fact that Friday the 4th was payday and he received just £4.10 a week. That was not much more than an air-raid (ARP) warden and very soon Adams would be earning every penny!

On the night of 7 April the squadron was involved in its first real action and Sergeant Adams, with his pilot, Flight Lieutenant Don 'Roc' West, destroyed a Ju 88 which crashed into the sea. They had taken off on patrol from Squires Gate just before midnight and West received orders to fly towards the AA barrage that he could see in the distance above Liverpool. He was climbing from 10,000 to 11,000 ft on a heading of 180 degrees when he spotted the enemy bomber at 2359. West decided to use Fighter Command attack A and

Flight Leutenant Deanesly and his air gunner Sergeant Scott, sitting on a Defiant at Squires Gate. Sergeant Scott was another New Zealander who was awarded the DFM for his action while flying with 256 Squadron.

256 Squadron pilot, Flight Leutenant Don West, who with his gunner Sergeant Adams, accounted for the unit's first victory on 8 April 1941. Despite some claims that the airman sitting in the turret is Sergeant Adams, it is thought that the air gunner is someone else who flew with flight Lieutenant West on 141 Squadron. Courtesy of Lancashire County Archives.

Sergeant Reginald Adams (right), Flight Lieutenant West's air gunner who shot down a Ju 88 on the night of 7/8 April 1941. Adams later joined 405 Squadron in Bomber Command and was killed on the night of 30 June 1942. Sergeant Bill Fremlin (left) was killed in a flying accident at Nether Kellet just nine days after this photo was taken 6 May 1941, outside the Rayley Hotel. Courtesy E.M. Marchant & Russell Brown

dropped below and astern of the Ju 88, allowing Sergeant Adams to get in several short bursts of fire.

The sudden attack took *Oberleutnant* Gunther Klemm and his crew from II/KG 54 by surprise, as they were unaware of the presence of the British night-fighter. They were heading for Dumbarton in Scotland and their aircraft had just crossed the Lancashire coast from the Irish Sea when the first few bursts from West's guns found their mark, causing the Ju 88 to catch fire. Klemm was badly wounded; one of his arms was totally shattered during the combat. He quickly assessed the situation as hopeless and ordered that the bombs should be released, but only a single 500 kg bomb dropped from the stricken aircraft.

The incident was witnessed by several observers on the shore, who saw the Ju 88 go into a steep dive before it crashed on Banks Marsh near Lytham. Mr Jameson an ARP warden at Lytham described the aircraft as a 'burning cross' as it fell to earth. Immediately afterwards he claimed he saw Flight Lieutenant West perform a victory roll. It is doubtful, however, if West would have performed such a dangerous stunt in an aircraft like the Defiant, especially at night. He returned safely to Squires Gate and landed at 0012. The ground crew of F for Freddie were jubilant but particularly Corporal Metcalf, who looked after West's Defiant and who had loaded the ammunition belts.

The Lytham lifeboat boarding boat was launched to get out to the wreckage of the Ju 88, which was scattered over an area of a ¼ mile close to the shore. The German wireless operator and flight mechanic were probably killed instantly in the first stages of West's attack, as only *Oberleutnant* Klemm and the observer, *Leutnant* Coster, had managed to bale out. Klemm was captured by Mr Hugh Rimmer, a special constable, while Coster landed on the other side of the estuary in Lytham Street. The bodies of the other two members of the crew were found in the wreckage when RAF investigating officers examined the crash site the following morning. The officer was somewhat surprised to find that two 250 kg bombs remained in what was left of the aircraft. One was partly detonated and the bomb disposal squad were called in immediately.

The enemy aircraft was identified as a Ju 88A-5, coded B3 + 1N and the question of how many bombs it had been carrying caused a certain amount of controversy at the time. A normal bomb load for a Ju 88 attacking Liverpool was two 250 kg bombs, plus a number of smaller weapons. This aircraft had been carrying three bombs and its seems likely that it was also carrying external stores, a capability not fully appreciated in 1941. The search of the wreckage was impeded by the fact that it lay in a tidal gully and investigators were hampered by treacherous conditions. The Ju 88 had disintegrated upon impact with the ground but eventually the bodies of *Feldwebel*s Alfred Hoffman and Herman Ilse were recovered and buried in Southport Cemetery. Their bodies were later exhumed and reburied at Cannock Chase Military Cemetery. *Feldwebel* Hoffman was buried in Block 3, Grave 203, and *Feldwebel* Ilse in Block 3, Grave 204. Because of the

injuries to his shattered arm, *Oberleutnant* Klemm spent a considerable amount of time in Lytham Hospital. In October 1943 he was returned to Germany under an exchange of prisoners scheme and took no further part in the war.

On the same night the squadron lost two aircraft in two separate incidents and which cost the lives of two crew. The first happened at 2330 when Sergeants Stanton and Ross had to abandon their Defiant, N1694, over the sea because of electrical problems and the fact that the aircraft ran out of fuel. Sergeant Stanton made a safe descent by parachute and landed in Maghull, south of Ormskirk. Sergeant Ross, the air gunner, was badly injured after abandoning the aircraft and was taken to Ormskirk Hospital. He was not expected to live his injuries included a fractured skull and a broken leg. His relatives were called for but three days later he was taken off the critical list and squadron personnel were told that he would live.

Sergeant Dennis Cunningham from Ramsgate who was killed on the night of 7/8 April 1941 when the engine of his Defiant failed as he was taking-off from Squires Gate. Courtesy of Sheila Cunningham

The second accident was much more serious and involved Sergeant Cunningham and Sergeant Wood, whose Defiant crashed on take-off from Squires Gate at 0040. It fell into some greenhouses on Marton Moss, off Midgleland Road, Blackpool. The site was almost in a direct line with the extended runway centre line and it was thought that the Defiant's Merlin III engine failed at the most crucial moment as it climbed into the air.

Both airmen were killed outright and the Defiant was listed as damaged to Category 3 status. Sergeant Cunningham's time on 256 Squadron was relatively short; he had only been posted in on 5 March. On 10 April the body of 21-year-old Sergeant John Denis Harold Cunningham was put on a train and returned to his home town of Ramsgate. His funeral took place on Monday, 14 April, in the St Lawrence Plot of Ramsgate Cemetery in Section A, Grave 146. A service was held in St Lawrence Church, under the approach to RAF Manston and it was attended by numerous members of his family, friends and officers and senior NCOs from 256 Squadron.

Known to his family and friends as Denis, the young airman was a keen table-tennis player and footballer and well known in Ramsgate. Before joining up in July 1940 he had worked at Hudson's Mill in a clerical capacity. As might be expected his death had a great impact upon his mother and three sisters, Vera, Mary and Sheila, but previous events had also added to their grief.

Their mother had become a Catholic so that she could marry her husband, who was an Irishman serving in the Royal Enniskillen Fusiliers. After his death she returned to the Church of England but was shunned and ostracized by many of their neighbours. Sergeant Cunningham's younger brother Rory had also died of tuberculosis the year before and the death of the effective head of the family was too much. His mother and sisters felt they had to move out of their home in Southwood Road and they began a new life in Ramsgate in Grange Road.

Sergeant Wood the air gunner, was a 24-year-old New Zealander from Helensville, Auckland. He was buried at St Anne's Cemetery, Lytham, on 12 April. His funeral was attended by Squadron Leader Gatherall and two officers from 256 Squadron as well as ten officers representing the RAF Squires Gate Station Flight. Many of his colleagues, pilots and air gunners also attended the funeral. Sergeant Albert Douglas Wood, the son of Cecil and Voilet May Wood was buried with full military honours and laid to rest in Grave 723.

CHAPTER SEVENTEEN

96 Squadron:
Defiant in the Air

The month of May did not get off to a good start for 96 Squadron. On the night of 1 May its crews made only a small number of visual contacts. Sergeant Taylor, accompanied by Sergeant Waddicar, spotted an enemy bomber while patrolling Cotton South, but it was flying in the opposite direction and too far beneath them to intercept it. Sergeant Hampshire and Sergeant Turner were puzzled when they observed some parachutes illuminated by AA fire but there was no sign of enemy aircraft.

The same night Sergeant Keprt, using the call sign Purley 9, experienced what was by then a common problem: the electrical system failed. The power-operated turret and radio of N1879 would not work and so he and Sergeant Harper were forced to return and eventually made a safe landing at midnight. Flight Lieutenant Raphael completed the only sortie in a Hurricane, patrolling Leek North at 10,000 ft. Although he was vectored onto an enemy aircraft he failed to make any visual contact and he landed at 0040.

During the early hours of 3 May, Flying Officer Verity took off at 0030 to patrol Cotton South and soon got into a good position to make an interception. He and Sergeant Wake then lost sight of the enemy aircraft in hazy conditions, which Verity thought were unsuitable. Flying Officer McGlashan and Sergeant Lazell were vectored onto an enemy aircraft but no visual contact was made. McGlashan then flew a second patrol with Squadron Leader Burns between 0150 and 0215, but both aircraft were recalled because of the lack of enemy action. Despite completing a total of twelve sorties and fourteen hours of night flying, no other contact was made with the enemy that night.

As the moon waxed towards full on the 11th, the airmen became more optimistic about sighting enemy aircraft. On the night of 3 May Flying Officer Verity and Sergeant Wake were airborne at 2300 in N1803, to take part in a fighter night over Liverpool at 18,000 ft. Verity observed that the background behind the fires on the ground was too dark for them to see the silhouettes of enemy aircraft. But he observed that they could be seen quite clearly against the glare from explosions and the subsequent fires. During one particularly bright explosion Verity counted eight enemy aircraft beneath them within the space of less than fifteen seconds.

Not for the first time, the *Luftwaffe* was operating at a lower altitude than that which 9 Group had been advised and there were problems estimating the height of the enemy force. Verity told the sector controller at Speke that he was going to descend to 10,000 ft which proved to be a good move because almost straight away Sergeant Wake spotted an He 111 heading south above Liverpool. Verity tried to intercept it but within a few moments he lost sight of it when his night vision was ruined by the glare from the searchlights.

They climbed back to 16,000 ft and Verity advised Wake that the next enemy aircraft they saw would have to be attacked from above. The reason for this was that Verity thought it would be easier to make an interception that way, especially if the enemy aircraft was converging on their course. While they were making a left-hand turn, Wake suddenly shouted out that there was a 'Hun' visible on the port beam. Pushing the control column forward Verity put the Defiant into a dive, banking steeply as they approached their intended target. Wake opened fire at about 150 yards, with the enemy bomber banking steeply, and he was sure he registered a number of hits along the fuselage and in the area of the cockpit.

After turning to starboard Verity lost sight of the enemy aircraft but three or four minutes after the combat ended, he heard someone shouting over the R/T that an enemy aircraft had crashed. In his combat report Verity stated that both he and Sergeant Wake had clearly identified the aircraft as a Ju 88; an aircraft of that type crashed at Lostock Gralam just before midnight. Verity claimed that his combat took place between 2345 and 2350 and he was convinced that the Ju 88 downed at Lostock was the aircraft Sergeant Wake had fired at. His claim was to become the subject of a bitter dispute with a Defiant crew from another squadron, and it would be nearly two weeks before it was resolved.

The enemy aircraft, serial number B3 + EC, turned out to be a rare Ju 88 A-6, fitted with a balloon fender and cable cutter. This was the first such variant of the Ju 88 to be destroyed over Britain and very soon afterwards the type was withdrawn from operations because it was slow and difficult to control. It was also the first enemy aircraft destroyed

Wreckage of the Ju 88 at Lostock Gralam. It was shot down on 3.5.41 and the claim was disputed by Flying Officer Verity of 96 Squadron and Flight Lieutenant Deanesly of 256 Squadron.

by Flying Officer Verity and Sergeant Wake as a crew, and it was the first enemy aircraft destroyed by 96 Squadron using the Defiant.

On the same night a number of other 96 Squadron crews reported making visual contact with enemy aircraft but that did not always mean that they could intercept them. Sergeant Scott counted at least a dozen beneath him, while his gunner Sergeant Streeter, saw six together. Sergeant Keprt spotted two and his gunner no less than six, inlcuding an enemy aircraft that dropped an HE bomb into the heart of a fire in Liverpool from 7,000 ft. It was again well below the operational height that 96 Squadron crews had been given.

None of the crews could get into a position to make an attack; as Sergeant Hampshire observed, the enemy had taken the defences by surprise. They were again flying a lot lower than the height predicted by the AA barrage and the Defiants were too high to intercept. Rather unusually, Flying Officer Verity spotted nothing during his second sortie of the night between 0155 and 0310. A note in the ORB said that most of the aircrew had now aquired 'cats' eyes and those who were seeing the most enemy aircraft were those with the most night-flying hours!

Because of bad weather, on 4 May only two sorties were flown between 0150 and 0315 by Flying Officer Verity and Squadron Leader Burns. Leading by example, the following night the CO was 96 Squadron's first pilot into the air with Flying Officer Smith at 2355. As they patrolled Leek North beacon in T4052 at 12,000 ft, a sector controller at Tern Hill vectored them towards a suspected enemy aircraft. Burns spotted it 500 ft below them and up-moon, clearly silhouetted against the clouds. Burns closed in on its port side but its crew saw them and it dived away to starboard. Smith managed to get in a two-second burst, in which he fired a total of 116 rounds at the aircraft, which they identified as a Ju 88. Burns followed it down to 5,500 ft but then visual contact was lost and they could only claim it as damaged. This was one of eight sorties completed that night during thirteen hours of operational flying.

On the night of 6/7 May, 96 Squadron flew a further eleven sorties using the Defiants and another two with its Hurricanes. At 0020 Sergeant McNair, with air gunner Sergeant Wirdnam, took off in T4051 to patrol Liverpool at 17,000 ft. At 0105 McNair spotted an enemy aircraft flying below them in a southerly direction and he put his aircraft into a steep dive to catch it. Sergeant Wirdman identified the aircraft as a Dornier and managed to get in one short burst of fire. This combat took place six miles east of Liverpool but there was no confirmation of the outcome.

Verity was in the midst of the action again during his patrol after he and Sergeant Wake had taken off at 0025 to take part in a fighter night over Liverpool. They were scheduled to be on station at 0045. During the first part of their patrol no enemy aircraft were observed but there was extensive AA fire beneath them. At 0115 Verity spotted another Defiant which passed close by and then soon afterwards he saw a twin-engined aircraft, but lost sight of it again as he tried to manoeuvre into a suitable position to intercept it.

During the attempted interception Verity had descended to 13,000 ft and only a short while after losing contact with the first enemy aircraft, he observed an He 111 about 4,000 ft below. He immediately put the Defiant into a dive to the starboard side of it, which gave Sergeant Wake the opportunity to open fire. He got in a one-second burst from a range of 50 yards, which hit the underside of the enemy aircraft's starboard engine. Verity then banked sharply to port to allow Wake a chance to fire another burst into the cockpit and down the fuselage. While Wake was still firing at the Heinkel it exploded so violently that it lit up the night sky and both he and Verity lost their night vision. When they recovered there was no sign at all of the Heinkel. Wake noted the time as being just after 0115 hours.

This was a good night for Verity and Wake, as only a few minutes after finishing the engagement with the Heinkel, the pair observed a Ju 88 flying at 10,000 ft. After Verity had manoeuvred the Defiant into a favourable position below the enemy aircraft, and at a range of approximately 50–70 yards, Sergeant Wake opened fire. The Ju 88 turned to starboard and its flight path crossed theirs giving Wake a further opportunity to rake it with fire. He got in some accurate bursts from the nose to the tail and neither he or Verity saw any return fire. The Ju 88 disappeared from view into the night and it was later credited as a probable. During the course of the two engagements Wake had fired a total of 580 rounds of ammunition.

Sergeant Scott was airborne at the same time as Verity and Wake but in a Hurricane, V6887, operating above Liverpool. He caught sight of a Ju 88 leaving the area and caught up with it in the vicinity of Rhyl at 12,000 ft, and began his attack. He opened fire from 300 yards but closed to 70 yards, noticing that all his shots hit the enemy aircraft but there was no return fire. He then watched the Ju 88 enter a vertical dive through the cloud. He

256 Squadron aircrew outside Windsor Court Hotel, Blackpool, taken in the spring of 1941. Featuring Sergeant MacDonald (in deck chair), with Sergeant Mulligan (on his left). Sergeant Walden is third from the right at the back, with Sergeant Ellmers on his left. The daughters of the hotel owner are centre front. Courtesy of Squadron Leader Macdonald

believed it was out of control, but did not follow it down. The combat took place in cloud above the sea and with no wreckage to confirm its loss it was credited as another probable. There were four other visual sightings on that night, but as the writer of the 96 Squadron records noted, 'Visuals do not shoot down enemy bombers.' Flying Officer McGlashan was one of those pilots who experienced seeing his first enemy aircraft at night, although his attempts at an interception failed.

Despite its success, 96 Squadron was aware that recent changes in the 9 Group structure had prompted an air of competition with its rival at Squires Gate. Feelings were generally running quite high because of the heavy raids on Liverpool, and everyone felt that more had to be done to prevent the *Luftwaffe* bombing at will. What many crews thought was that they needed was a touch of luck, and that given good weather conditions, on the right night things would fall into place. Nobody realized that within a very short space of time this would happen, and all their training and experience would prove worthwhile.

CHAPTER EIGHTEEN

256 Squadron: April 1941

Night-fighter squadrons often had to move at short notice to defend those cities that intelligence sources believed were about to be bombed. In its original role with 10 Group at Colerne, 256 Squadron's primary task had been to provide the air defence for Coventry. As it turned out, the Midlands was where it flew on its first combined operational role during a fighter night above Birmingham. For Flight Lieutenant Deanesly it was familar territory – having been born in Wellington and educated at Birmingham University he had a personal interest in the defence of the Midlands, where his family lived.

On the night of 10 April 1941, 256 Squadron was given less than an hour's notice to move from Squires Gate to a temporary base at Tern Hill in Shropshire, where it was to operate with 96 Squadron over Birmingham. The reason for such short notice was that a number of 96 Squadron's Defiants had failed to reach Tern Hill because of bad weather. Under the control of the 4th AA Division, Birmingham was at the southern end of 9 Group's territory. The detachment was a result of the discovery that German radio beams had been intercepted above the city. The nine Defiants did not even arrive at Tern Hill until 2025 and their crews had little time to prepare and organize themselves.

Flight Lieutenant Deanesly, with his gunner Sergeant Scott, took off from Tern Hill in Defiant N1771 at 2156 and they chose to give top cover at 20,000 ft. At 1,000 ft they flew into industrial haze and the CO, Squadron Leader Gatherall, who had taken off after Deanesly, confirmed that conditions were not suitable for a layers operation but decided to continue anyway. By the time they cleared the Tern Hill area visibility above 5,000 ft was 100 per cent. As they climbed Deanesly and Scott observed a number of fires on the ground. Climbing through 14,000 ft four more were seen to start suddenly, and a number of condensation trails became clearly visible.

This was the moon period, as the full moon was the next night and the brightly lit sky allowed Deanesly to find and follow two trails. He failed to find anything at the end of either, but after climbing to 20,000 ft he followed a third trail and found the enemy aircraft that was its source. On observing it he carefully manoeuvred his Defiant into position so that Sergeant Scott could train his guns on the bomber. Scott fired three short bursts which set his target on fire, and the glow from the blaze clearly identified it as an He 111. The aircraft began to dive towards the ground and Deanesly followed it down but quickly realized the danger that lay ahead in the form of a balloon barrage. He levelled off at 10,000 ft.

It was just as well that he decided not to descend any further because he later discovered that the Heinkel had fouled a cable on one of 915 Squadron's barrage balloons. It crashed in Hales Lane, Smethwick and although two of the crew were killed, three others parachuted to safety. One of them caught his parachute on a chimney and later fell down onto a bay window before dropping into the garden. After the chase Deanesly climbed to 15,000 ft, obtained an accurate homing bearing and landed at Tern Hill at 2315.

Despite their success Deanesly noted that it had been a very unpleasant night because of the dark sky and very bad weather. He wrote in his combat report that as they had taxied out for take-off, Sergeant Scott had said to him, 'Well Sir, I'd rather go with you than anyone else.' That remark boosted his confidence, which was beginning to wane because of the terrible weather.

The following morning Deanesly and Scott visited the crash site and heard that the Heinkel had crashed into the rear of some houses, numbers 281 and 283 Hales Lane. Seven people who had been unable to take to the air-raid shelters because of flooding were killed in their homes. Because of the reception they got the two airmen went away with very mixed feelings.

In light of some detailed research carried out in 2005 by Mark Evans, there is some doubt about the aircraft that Flight Lieutenant Deanesly claimed to have shot down. Evidence from the records of 5 and 6 Barrage Balloon Centres sugggest that the aircraft which crashed at Smethick was shot down by Sergeant Bodien of 151 Squadron, whose air gunner Sergeant Jonas baled out after the Intercom failed and he thought that his pilot had been killed. An unclaimed Heinkel crashed that night in another part of Birmingham and it seems likely that it was Deanesly's victim. This incident and others like it, highlight the confusion that often arose over such night time aerial combats and it is hardly surprising given the circumstances at the time.

When 256 Squadron crews returned to Blackpool they discovered that the airfield had been bombed again in the north-east corner but there had been no casualties and only a small amount of damage. The following night the squadron lost another aircraft after Sergeant Dean experienced severe electrical problems in Defiant N3460. He and his gunner, Sergeant Robinson, were forced to bale out. Fortunately both airmen parachuted to safety, but the Defiant crashed at Cherlyn Hay near Cannock.

On the night of 13 April two enemy aircraft attacked Barrow on separate sorties to bomb the aircraft carrier HMS *Victorious*. Barrow was normally patrolled by 256 Squadron but the second Heinkel to arrive over the shipyard took the defences by surprise and there was no fighter protection. He 111, 1T + EL from KG 28, had taken off from Nantes, flown by *Leutnant* Lothar Horras. It was loaded with armour-piercing bombs but the crew failed to spot the aircraft carrier. With no other comparable targets in sight they dropped their bombs on the quayside in disappointment. Almost as soon as they were released, HMS *Victorious* was spotted on the far side of the bay, where she had been moved after an earlier reconnaissance raid.

As Horras and his crew cursed their luck, the Heinkel was rocked by AA fire which blew out some glass and damaged vital equipment, including the radio and compass. Horras decided to fly back along the Welsh coast but at 0300 the flight engineer shouted a warning that they were over the mountains. Almost immediately the aircraft struck the 2,500 ft Mount Llwtmor and the flight engineer was killed instantly. Horras and two other members of the crew survived. Despite the pilot losing two fingers and being badly injured they were able to walk off the mountain and seek help at a farm at Cydgoed, near Bangor. Where the defences had failed, nature had taken over and the Heinkel was one of several aircraft to be lost in such circumstances.

In the middle of April a number of air gunners were due to go on leave, including Sergeant Reg Adams, who was in A Flight. Because there was a shortage of gunners, however, he and a number of others had their leave cancelled at the last moment. There was some consolation however: a sight worth seeing when a Flying Fortress 1 landed at Squires Gate on 16 April. A number of squadron personnel looked around it and most were impressed by its size and design. The identity of this aircraft is not certain but it was most probably destined for 90 Squadron at Watton, the first of two RAF units equipped with the type.

American aircraft were becoming regular vistitors to Squires Gate, particularly Liberators. After the arrival of the first aircraft in March, two more Liberators, AM260 and AM910, passed through on 6 and 7 April, direct from Gander, while others flew in from Prestwick, which was the main transatlantic staging post.

British Summer Time began at 0200 on Sunday 20 April but the new season started badly for 256 Squadron. In the early hours of Monday morning there was a tragic incident, which arose out of the mishandling of the guns on a Defiant that had just returned from a night-flying test. There is no clear account of exactly what happened but it is understood that an air gunner was trying to recock the guns safe when they accidentally went off. Aircraftsman 1st Class George Skevington, who was standing on the wing of the Defiant was killed, while another airman, Leading Aircraftsman Bob Noble, was fortunately only wounded.

Unlike their colleagues in Bomber Command, air gunners on night-fighter squadrons did not maintain their own guns and that fact might have contributed to the accident. The air gunner was convinced that he had made the guns safe before they began to fire but investigators proved that this was impossible. With the guns in the forward position he had somehow overlooked the failsafe mechanism and activated the guns. A court of inquiry was convened and it is understood that the air gunner was let off with a severe reprimand. Twenty-four-year-old Aircraftsman George Roy Skevington, the son of James and Lizzie Ann Skevington of Selston, was buried in Selston Churchyard, Nottinghamshire, in Section B, Grave 360.

Despite the events of the previous day and the shortage of crews, 256 Squadron performed a flypast of Fleetwood with nine Defiants on Tuesday, 22 April to promote War Weapons Week. There were only five pilots and four gunners available in A flight and no less than six airmen were sick, two of them seriously. Nevertheless there was an air of expectation in the squadron as the new moon was due on Friday the 25th and it seems everyone knew what was about to happen.

Despite the dismal weather at the beginning of May the squadron began to fly more regularly and on the night of 1/2 May two crews were scrambled after an enemy aircraft circled overhead at 2200 hours. It dropped four HE bombs, one of which exploded only 50 yards away from a Liberator parked on the apron. Flight Lieutenant West and Sergeant Adams had a lucky escape when the mainplane of their Defiant, N3445, began to move during a dive from 9,000 ft. Sergeant Adams estimated that they had nearly reached a speed of 400 mph when they realized what was happening. On the ground they found that the mainplane had moved 3 inches from the centre section. Sergeant Adams described it as a 'shaky do' and thought that they were lucky to be alive.

The next night, 2/3 May, was typical of many for 256 Squadron. Its crews completed nine patrols between 2200 and 0125, but failed to make a single visual contact. The evening of Saturday, 3/4 May however, marked the watershed and 256 Squadron crews flew twelve patrols into the early hours of the morning on a fighter night over Liverpool, when approximately 200 enemy aircraft were active over the region.

After taking off from Squires Gate in N3450 at 2230, accompanied by the aircraft of Sergeants Frogatt and McDonald, Deanesly climbed to 12,000 ft and was ordered to patrol to the west of Liverpool. Visibility was fair in a quarter moon and it was bright enough for Deanesly to spot an enemy aircraft by the glow from its exhaust stubs. He identified it as a Ju 88 less than 150 yards away at about the same altitude. Owing to the changing relative positions of the two aircraft, the enemy was suddenly less than 50 yards away and turning sharply to starboard.

Manoeuvring his aircraft to starboard and beneath it, Deanesly put his aircraft into a position from which Sergeant Scott could get in several short bursts which were seen to hit their target. For a few moments Deanesly and Scott were convinced that the bomber was on fire but then they realised that it might have been the glow from the exhaust stubs as the pilot applied power. The Defiant then overshot the Ju 88 and Deanesly was unable to turn quickly enough to attack it again. However, they observed it entering a steep dive, before it finally disappeared from view. There was at least one burst of return fire which struck the superstructure of Deanesly's Defiant, although the damage was not noticed straight away. After the combat, Sergeant Scott experienced some problems with the turret; he had great difficulty in getting it to rotate properly.

Despite this problem, the two airmen estimated that they had enough fuel to remain on patrol until midnight. Another enemy aircraft was soon observed but then lost in haze and cloud. At 2355, when they were immediately above Liverpool, they suddenly spotted another enemy bomber, which they identified as a Dornier. It was 250 yards to port at the same height of 14,000 ft, and it flew right over the top of them travelling in the opposite direction, But its crew failed to notice them. Deanesly turned, dropped beneath it and got into position astern of the bomber.

The first burst from Scott's guns hit the belly of the bomber and it dived away very steeply. Its crew failed to return fire as Deanesly swung the Defiant from side to side in pursuit. Scott got in another accurate burst of fire but Deanesly realized that they were already down to 2,000 ft. He did not want to go any lower for fear of hitting the balloon barrage or high ground. There was a hazy industrial sky but they managed to maintain visual contact and soon witnessed a terrific flash, typically made by an aircraft crashing on the ground.

Sergeant Scott had used a total of 415 rounds of ammunition during the two combats but two of his four guns had stopped during the second interception because of snags in the belt links. Deanesly made a safe landing at 0030 on 4 May. When the ground crew dipped the Defiant's fuel tanks they discovered that they contained less than 20 gal. Deanesly was surprised to find some bullet holes very close to the glycol header tank and a number of others on the port aileron hinge, the main spar, the port self-sealing fuel tank and at the rear of the fuselage.

There is a problem with the identification of both the aircraft engaged by Deanesly and Scott on this night, especially the claimed Dornier. No Dorniers were shot down on that particular night in the north of England – or anywhere else in Britain. It is possible that the aircraft fell into the sea but the fact that they witnessed an explosion suggests that it almost certainly crashed on land. The only other possibility seems to be that they wrongly identified the aircraft and it was a Ju 88.

The total enemy aircraft that were shot down over England on that night included five Heinkels and two Ju 88s. The most likely candidate for one of Deanesly's claims was a Ju 88 from KG 54 based at Bretigny. It crashed at Lostock Gralham near Northwich at around midnight, which fits into the timescale quite well. The only problem with that is that it was also claimed by Flying Officer Verity of 96 Squadron. Despite that it remains distinctly possible that it was the same enemy aircraft.

Flying Officer Verity was certain that his gunner, Sergeant Wake, had scored a number of hits on the enemy aircraft, which they identified as a Ju 88, and that it then dived away out of their sight. If it was already damaged it could explain why Deanesly and Scott did not experience any return fire. Another interesting point is that after landing, Deanesly found some marks on a propeller blade to suggest that it might have made contact with a balloon cable. The Ju 88A-6 which crashed at Lostock Gralham, B3 + EC, was fitted with a balloon-cutting fender. If it was the same aircraft that flew above Deanesly's Defiant just before they attacked it, that might explain how its propellers were slightly damaged.

Of the four men on board the ill-fated enemy bomber, two were killed in the crash; the pilot, *Leutnant* Hans Glanzier, and the wireless operator, *Unteroffizier* Gerhard Baumgard, were the unfortunate victims. Glanzier's parachute failed to open, while the wireless operator had failed to properly secure his parachute harness properly and paid the ultimate price.

To add to the confusion, the two survivors, *Unteroffizier* Hans Stettweiser, the observer, and *Feldwebel* Hans Richter, the flight mechanic, failed to agree on what had caused their aircraft to crash. They had dropped their bombs on Liverpool and had just turned on a course for home when there was severe jolting and the port engine suddenly stopped. Glanzier could no longer control the aircraft and ordered his crew to bale out, but the two survivors failed to agree whether they had been attacked by a night fighter or hit by AA fire. Although anti-aircraft fire was heavy that night the flight mechanic thought that either a high-calibre shell had hit them or there was a mechanical failure. Not for the first time amongst downed *Luftwaffe* aircrew, he seemed to be reluctant to accept the truth, that they had been caught unawares by a night fighter.

Investigating air intelligence officers inspected the burned-out remains and their conclusions were that it had been shot down by a night fighter and not AA fire. Amongst the wreckage they also found two manufacturers' plates which indicated that the Ju 88 had originally been built as an A-5 model, but later converted to an A-6 when it was fitted with a balloon fender. It was later established that it was the first of the Ju 88 A-6 type to be shot down in this country.

Flight Lieutenant Deanesly and Sergeant Scott later visited 75 MU at Wilmslow to examine the wreckage for themselves. They found a number of bullet holes around the area of the top turret, where Sergeant Scott claimed to have scored a number of hits. They left the unit convinced that it was their actions which had caused the aeroplane to crash but Flying Officer Verity and Sergeant Wake of 96 Squadron also went to sift through the wreckage. Verity later recalled that he only went to investigate the wreckage of an enemy aircraft on one other occasion and that was after hearing that an AA gun crew had claimed to have destroyed the aircraft. He did not question Deanesly's claim but said that he just wanted to check whether the wreckage had .303 bullet holes in it. It was ten days before investigators credited the pilot they thought had shot down the aeroplane – and even then there were a few more twist and turns.

Of the other eleven 256 Squadron Defiants which operated on the night of 3/4 May, only three crews made visual contact with enemy aircraft. Sergeant Frogatt, with Sergeant

Deane as his gunner, attempted to make three interceptions but all of them failed to produce any results. Pilot Officer Hughes and his gunner, Sergeant Smith, made two visual contacts, but also failed to make any interceptions. The final patrol of the night was flown by Flight Sergeant Stenton and Sergeant Low who took off at at 0130 and returned at 0310, reporting making just a single visual contact made.

After each sortie combat pilots and air gunners were debriefed by the squadron intelligence officer, Flight Lieutenant Bragg, who compiled the intelligence combat reports. Pilots often wrote up their own accounts of sorties, known as personal combat reports, which then formed the basis of the intelligence officer's report. In his personal combat report dated 5 May, for the action on the 3/4 May Flight Lieutenant Deanesly strongly criticized the AA GL on that particular night. The combat report was in the form of a letter, rather than being filed on the official Fighter Command Form 1151 F, and a copy was sent to Fighter Command HQ at Bentley Priory.

Deanesly claimed that what was lacking, as it had been on previous occasions, was knowledge of the height at which the enemy bombers were operating. The flight commander suggested that the AA ground defences should fire a tracer shell or devise some other method of notifying pilots of the enemy's height by R/T. He also commented that accurate information about heights should be passed on to pilots from the AA's Gun Laying Elevation Finding. Deanesly knew that in the south a network of GL was established in those areas where no other radar cover existed. The fact that he mentioned GL 1 E/F at all suggests that it was still the only type of radar in the region capable of detecting the height of enemy aircraft.

Not all crews were successful in intercepting enemy aircraft and Deanesly said he understood the difficulties that his crews encountered while trying to find enemy aircraft at night. He admitted that there were many problems, one of the main ones being that crews had very little live-firing practice in the air. Secondly, the recommended Number 1 method of attack from astern at night, which crews were ordered to use, was normally ineffective. That type of attack often caused little damage, except to the tailplane and it involved a high risk of being hit by return fire.

There was also the fact that to begin with, the type of ammunition that 256 Squadron air gunners were issued with was inferior to that being issued to other night-fighter units. Deanesly was aware that Sergeant Scott had often fired many rounds of ammunition at a target but caused very little damage, despite the accuracy of his aim. Then he discovered that other night-fighter squadrons were being issued with a more powerful type of ammunition called brittle bullets.

The patent for the De Wilde incendiary bullet had been purchased from Belguim in 1939 and its supply was reserved exclusively for squadrons in 9 Group. As 256 Squadron had originally been part of 10 Group its issue had been overlooked, but eventually the unit did receive it and subsequently crews achieved better results. Deanesly thought at the time that such ammunition might have been in breach of the Geneva Convention, but despite his concerns it was widely used and often mixed with armour-piercing rounds when they were available.

The Flight Commander and Sergeant Scott were elated on 6 May when they received news that they had been credited with destroying the Ju 88 three days earlier. It was a bitter blow for Flying Officer Verity and Sergeant Wake of 96 Squadron, who were convinced that they had shot it down. That took 256 Squadron's total of enemy aircraft destroyed to three, and it was just the boost that the crews needed. Things were to get even better and on the night of 7/8 May, many factors all worked together to give them their best night yet.

CHAPTER NINETEEN

Fighter Night: 7/8 May 1941

On 5 May 1941 the rules and regulations which governed how the night fighters operated were amended under Standing Operational Instructions 45 (A). The reason for the changes were that while it was accepted that the night fighters had inflicted heavier losses on the enemy than the AA guns, there were occasions when conditions were bad and they did not make contact with any enemy aircraft. On the nights when there was low visibility and when the moon was below the horizon it was decided to give priority to the AA guns, which the authorities thought had a better chance of destroying enemy aircraft.

Future night operations and fighter nights would only be ordered when the moon was going to be above the horizon and when visibility and light would be good enough to give crews a chance to spot enemy aircraft. There were other factors: fighter nights operations were only to take place if the enemy's attack was concentrated on a clearly defined target in a specific area. Night-fighter crews were to patrol within a 10 mile radius of the centre of the town over which the fighter night was ordered but that could only be authorized by the 9 Group controller with the express consent of the AOC 9 Group.

In effect the night fighters were changing their tactics to patrol within a 10 mile area of the town under attack, rather than patrolling the lines of approach. The tactic of patrolling the enemy's lines of approach had been strongly criticized by a number of officers, including Flight Lieutenant Deanesly in his combat report of 3 May. One of the most significant parts of Standing Operational Instructions 45 (A) stated that under normal circumstances only single-engined night fighters would be used in fighter night operations. As many Defiants as possible were to fly at 500 ft intervals, while other single-engined types such as Hurricanes had to maintain 1,000 ft separation.

For 96 Squadron personnel 7 May was a busy day, with an official visit by the Inspector General of the RAF, Air Chief Marshal Sir Edgar Ludlow-Hewitt, DSO, MC. Ludlow-Hewitt was later described by Air Chief Marshal Arthur Harris as one of the most capable commanders in the service. When the former Commander-in-Chief of Bomber Command was appointed as Inspector General the move was seen by many senior officers as an attempt to 'sideline' him. The post was traditionally given to a senior officer as a form of retirement but Ludlow-Hewitt continued to influence events and improve morale.

After the formal business of the inspection was over Ludlow-Hewitt invited a number of pilots to take tea with him in the officers' mess. The invitation was mainly aimed at the officers but it was extended to included a small number of the more experienced senior NCO pilots. To the surprise of everyone, he began an open discussion and encouraged those present to speak their minds and voice their opinions. He had pushed through the idea of OTUs and he was particularly interested in suggestions as to how things could be improved. A long debate took place which was concluded by Ludlow-Hewitt telling everyone that most of their opinions were similar to those of the Air Staff.

The air chief marshal went on to say that he and Lord Trenchard were the only members of the Air Staff that Churchill could not sack. He claimed that they were using their authority to modify some of the Prime Minister's extreme ideas about how the RAF should be used, while at the same time seeking the backing of others for a change of tactics. The meeting almost certainly boosted the confidence of a number of pilots but Flying Officer Verity was so inspired by it that a few hours later he openly challenged the authority of a senior officer.

That evening it became clear that for the eighth consecutive night, another major air raid was about to take place on Liverpool. The conditions for the authorization of a fighter night were ideal, with bright moonlight and generally good visibility. The 9 Group diary noted that the weather conditions were very favourable with $^7/_{10}$ cloud at 2,500 ft but visibility moderate to good. The group controller made arrangements with the duty air commodore at Fighter Command and arranged the 'zero' hour for the start of the operation. Details about searchlight exposure and the height the of the Liverpool gun barrage were passed on to the gun operations room at Barton Hall. The 9 Group operational strength available on that night was forty-two Hurricanes and eleven Spitfires, with twenty Defiants for night-time defence.

For some reason a decision was made not to include 96 Squadron in the fighter night and defensive operation and it was ordered only to operate standing patrols. No. 256 Squadron was to take part, along with a number of AI equipped Beaufighters from lodger units in the south. The decision was probably made at group level, and it effectively left 96 Squadron out of the plans for operations on that night, much to the dissatisfaction of its crews.

At Squires Gate, Sergeant Leonard, with his air gunner, Sergeant Harris, was the first 256 Squadron pilot into the air, taking off in T3981 at 0010. Wing Commander Oliver, who never missed an opportunity to take part in an operation, took off at 0012 in a Hurricane. They were followed by Sergeants Olney and Simmonds at 0017 in T3983 and Pilot Officer Toone and Flying Officer Lamb at 0021, with Pilot Officer Caldwell and Sergeant Trim at 0031.

Deanesly and Scott took off in Defiant N3450 at 0028 hours and climbed to their assigned height, which had been pulled out of a hat earlier that evening. Deanesly had drawn 14,000 ft, which he considered to be very promising given the conditions. They were on station above Liverpool by 0045 and Deanesly noted that there was good visibility aided by the light from a three-quarters moon, which would illuminate the night sky until 0430.

With 96 Squadron not assigned a role in the fighter night, everyone at Cranage became increasingly frustrated by the fact that enemy bombers were flying directly over them. Verity said that some seemed to be so low that he and others felt like throwing rocks at them. Three of the squadron's Defiants had taken off on standing patrols, led by the CO, Squadron Leader Burns, they were airborne between 2340 and 0145.

Flying Officer Verity was so upset about being able to do nothing about the *Luftwaffe*'s presence that he decided to act. At about 0030 he phoned 9 Group HQ at Barton Hall and demanded that the group controller allow 96 Squadron to get airborne and participate in the fighter night. He was put through to the duty staff officer, who who was reluctant to

24. Jan. 1941

GB 50 82 b
Nur für den Dienstgebrauch

Bild Nr. 1060 R 36

Aufnahme vom 4. 9. 40

Liverpool-Waterloo
Hauptkraftwerk am Clarence-Hafen
Länge (westl. Greenw.): 3° 00' 00" Breite: 53° 25' 00"
Mißweisung: − 12° 19' (Mitte 1940) Zielhöhe über NN 5 m

Maßstab etwa 1:19 200

Genst. 5. Abt. November 1940
Karte 1 : 100 000
GB / E 12

Ⓐ GB 5082 krafiwerk am Clarence-Hafen
Ⓑ GB 5282 Gaswerk ostw. Nelson-Hafen
Ⓒ GB 5041 Krafiwerk Wallasey mit Gaswerk
Ⓓ GB 5683 Großmühle und Getreidespeicher am West Float
Ⓔ GB 5681 " " , " " East Float
Ⓕ GB 5687 Viehställe, Schlachl· u. Kühlhäuser am Viehumschlaghafen

Luftwaffe aerial photograph of Liverpool–Waterloo, dated January 1941.

listen to Verity's argument. This was almost certainly Air Commodore George Maxwell Lawson, who served at 9 Group from February to July 1941. He said that all the controllers were busy and there were not enough staff on duty to deal with any more aircraft.

Verity persisted with his demands. At some point during their conversation the air commodore became frustrated and angry, declaring the matter would have to be referred to the AOC. Air Vice-Marshal McClaughry was aroused from his sleep and Verity said that at first he sounded very cold and distant. However the New Zealander was not put off by the 'silent treatment' and he incited the AOC to respond. McClaughry told Verity that he was being a bloody fool, but after a heated argument he gave way and told him to get on with it! McClaughry however, demanded that Verity report to his office first thing the following morning.

The AOC imposed a couple of conditions, the main one being that he would be held personally responsible for the lives of every airman. Verity agreed terms and his spirit and determination allowed 96 Squadron to have its finest hour of the war. The first Defiant was airborne in minutes, after the crews were briefed to pass on any information about the location and height of the enemy force to each other over the radio.

CHAPTER TWENTY

Verity Gets His Way:
State of Confusion

Sergeants Taylor and McNair took off at 0050, followed by Flying Officer McGlashan with Sergeant Scott at 0100 hours and Sergeant Black at 0120. Verity was amongst the last to get airborne because he was forced to sign the flight authorization book for all those crews taking off. Fed up with the delay he scribbled his initials on some blank pages and then left a new flight commander behind to fill in the details.

Ironically the first 96 Squadron success went to Sergeant Hibbert and his gunner Sergeant Haycock, who were one of the three crews assigned to carry out the standing patrol. They had taken off in T3997 at 2355 and were patrolling beacon Cotton South at 15,000 ft when Hibbert observed an He 111K south of Chester at 0055 hours. He quickly turned his Defiant around and positioned himself beneath the enemy aircraft's starboard wing while Sergeant Haycock fired a short burst from 150 yards. The Heinkel dived first to starboard and then to port, almost vertically towards the ground, but then disappeared from view in the clouds.

Their victim was probably flown by *Leutnant* Dunkerback, who crashed on the River Dee marshes near Buckley, with the loss of three of the five-man crew; it was G1 + LL from 3/KG 55. Dunkerback gave the order to bale out when the bomber was at 14,000 ft but he and the observer, *Feldwebel* Fritz Kitzing, were the only two who managed to escape. *Unteroffizier* Joachiam Salm, *Feldwebel* Alfred Gentzsch and *Feldwebel* Mildenburger were still aboard the Heinkel when it hit the ground with a full bomb load and exploded. This aircraft was also claimed by Pilot Officer Toone of 256 Squadron, but credited to him and Hibbert as a probable.

As Flight Lieutenant Deanesly and Sergeant Scott of 256 Squadron reached their allocated height they observed a number of large fires in the area of the River Mersey. What really drew their attention, though, was a large, eerie orange glow on the distant horizon. Although they must have had their suspicions, only later did they learn that it was the skyline of Manchester.

Keeping a sharp look-out, Scott soon observed an enemy aircraft about 2,000 ft below them and attempted to direct his pilot, but Deanesly could not see it. A short while later at 0115 hours both he and Deanesly spotted another enemy aircraft at the same height as them, flying out of the GDA above Liverpool. The aircraft was on the Defiant's port side astern of their position, so Deanesly was forced to pull around quickly. He estimated that the enemy aircraft was over 500 yards away, but they soon caught up with it.

When the aircraft's glowing exhaust stubs came into sight Deanesly dropped beneath it on the starboard beam and immediately identified it as an He 111, with its large black crosses beneath the wings clearly visible in the moonlight. Although it was not the ideal position from which to launch their attack, Sergeant Scott opened fire from 100 yards into the underside of the bomber. The results were not immediately noticeable, but there was no return fire from the Heinkel before it fell into a steep dive. Deanesly followed it down and overtook it, guided by Sergeant Scott, who had a better view from his turret. While they were descending the range had closed to within 50 yards and Scott continued to fire his guns. His action had an almost immediate effect, as both engines of the Heinkel were set on fire and it went burning furiously towards the ground. Deanesly followed it down to 3,000 ft but, seeing the ominous shape of some barrage balloons silhouetted against the ground, he decided to pull up.

As he climbed to a safe height he called over the radio to get a bearing and confirm their position. He was quite surprised to hear that they were 8 miles south of Manchester. The combat had lasted barely five minutes and in that time they had launched two attacks during which Sergeant Scott had used a total of 796 rounds of ammunition on the four guns. That was broken down into 323 De Wilde, 414 armour-piercing and 59 incendiary rounds. Scott had previously never used more than 500 rounds to destroy an enemy aircraft and Deanesly blamed the ineffectiveness of their first attack on its underside.

On board the ill-fated Heinkel, *Oberleutnant* Adolph Knorringer was struggling with the controls after experiencing a number of loud explosions. He was not a man to be

Crash site and remains of the Heinkel 111 shot down by Flight Leutenant Deanesly 08.05.41., on the golf course in Stockport. The photograph was taken in the morning after the crash, with the Gas Officer Ted Price and an air raid warden looking on.

unduly concerned about such things but when his aircraft began to shudder and vibrate, he realized that it had been badly damaged. Smoke began to fill the cockpit and when the first signs of a major fire manifested themselves, he ordered his crew to abandon the aircraft. The four German airmen took to their parachutes and jumped out into a black abyss above Stockport, which was illuminated only by the glow from exploding bombs and incendiaries being dropped by their colleagues.

Meanwhile their blazing Heinkel was observed by people many miles away; fire watchers on the roof of the forge at Chinley in the Peak District were amongst those who reported the sighting. During its final moments it flashed past a Home Guard unit based in a field close to Fairey Aviation, where barrage balloons were flying for the factory's protection. The Heinkel narrowly missed the Heaton Chapel works which had produced some of the first Beaufighter 1fs and had just begun manufacturing a batch of 1cs for Coastal Command. Home Guard volunteer John Walker recalled that his sergeant ordered the men to load their weapons and be prepared to take prisoners, by force if necessary. Within seconds the Heinkel crashed to the ground on the sixth green of Torkington Golf Course and the subsequent explosion lit up the night sky.

The following morning all that remained was a smouldering pile of burning metal in a deep crater on the golf course. News of the incident spread fast and by early morning hundreds of local people had arrived at the crash site looking for souvenirs. Ironically the spectacle was to be repeated twenty-six years later when a British Midland Argonaut crashed in Stockport. Security measures had to be taken to protect the crash site and the Heinkel, which had taken off from Melum-Villarche, was later identified by RAF intelligence officers as G1 + LH from KG 55.

Of the 96 Squadron Defiants that had taken off from Cranage to join the fighter night, Sergeant Scott and Sergeant Streeter were amongst the first into action. They were patrolling the Leek North line on a vector of 280 degrees at 12,500 ft when they saw an enemy aircraft approaching from the opposite direction at 0120. Scott quickly banked his Defiant around and spotted the aircraft's exhaust stubs before he manoeuvred into a position which allowed Sergeant Streeter to get in a burst from 25 yards' range.

The fire power raked the starboard engine and after breaking to port, Scott side-slipped beneath the port wing and Streeter put another burst into the port engine. A total of three attacks were carried out and Scott and Streeter observed the enemy aircraft crashing at 0120. The aircraft crashed into a small wood at Cefn Park near Wrexham, and none of the crew managed to escape from the doomed bomber. The remarkable thing was that the CO, and gunnery leader, Squadron Leader Burns and Flying Officer Smith were just 2,000 ft below Scott and Streeter when the action took place. They were slightly bemused when they saw the burning Heinkel flash past their starboard wing tip and crash to earth. The secretive conditions of night flying had hidden the fact that a combat had taken place immediately above them and they had not even been aware of it.

At 0120, about the time that Scott and Streeter were starting their combat with the Heinkel, Flying Officer Verity was taking off from Cranage, using the call-sign Purley 6. He claimed that the language over the radio was blue as the excitement built up. He was attracted to the western end of the patrol line, where he and Sergeant Wake immediately observed three enemy aircraft being attacked by night fighters. After climbing to 17,000 ft Verity sighted a Ju 88 below them but he noticed that its crew were being extremely cautious and carrying out evasive manoeuvres. Not to be put off he managed to get his Defiant in a position to port and below the aircraft at a range of 75–100 yards.

Remains of the Ju 88 on Goldsitch Moss shot down by Flying Officer Verity of 96 Squadron 08.05.41. Photograph taken in 1974.

Sergeant Wake fired a four-second burst into the Ju 88's port engine and almost immediately Verity put on power and they overshot it before he throttled back. The Defiant fell back into almost the same position as before, which allowed Wake to fire another four-second burst into the port engine and cockpit. At that point the Defiant crew observed the first flames as oil began to gush out of the damaged engine, then the Ju 88 began a banking turn to starboard, before entering a steep turn and rolling onto its back. At 9,000 ft it was still diving, emitting black smoke and flames from its port engine, but as Verity gave chase he observed that the whole structure was engulfed in flames as it dived towards the earth.

Leutnant Dither Lukesch, a pilot from the same *Luftwaffe* unit, was flying another Ju 88, F1 + FR, over Liverpool when he heard a familiar voice over the R/T. *Hauptman* Von Zeihlberg's radio operator, *Oberfeldwebel* Rudolf Schwalbe, was sending out a last desperate message. Lukesch had taken off from Leuwarden just before Von Zeihlberg and his final memory of the charismatic commander of KG 76, was watching him playing cards with his crews, typically dressed in a long leather coat. The short message transmitted by Von Zeihlberg's wireless operator just said that the aircraft had been hit but there was no mention of their situation or position. Von Zeihlberg did not approve of long or unnecessary broadcast, and his wireless operator obeyed his orders to the last moment.

The wreckage was discovered some time later by two local policemen on the moor at Goldsmith Moss at Gradback, near Stafford. Investigators found that the heat from the fire had been so intense that it had almost completely melted the wings and cockpit. Two badly charred bodies lay close by, with a third alongside the wreckage of the fuselage, but they could not find a fourth body and it seemed that at least one of the crew had escaped by parachute. Then a more detailed inspection was made and eventually the remains of a fourth body was found in what was left of the cockpit. It was later confirmed that the enemy aircraft was the Ju 88, F1 + AD flown by *Hauptman* Von Zeihlberg from III/KG 76. The bodies were initially taken to Leek Memorial Hospital and later buried in Leek Cemetery, before finally being exhumed and laid to rest in Cannock Chase Cemetery.

When Verity broke off the combat with Von Zeihlberg's aircraft he immediately spotted another Ju 88 closing in, with its crew apparently showing a great deal of interest in the proceedings. This second Ju 88 had appeared in between Verity's Defiant and Von Zeihlberg's aircraft and the New Zealander made an immediate decision to intercept it. But before he realized what was happening the second Ju 88 turned around and attacked his Defiant head on. Only by performing a steep banking turn and side slipping across the nose of the Ju 88 did Verity avoid being hit. The sudden unexpected manoeuvre kept the Defiant away from the enemy aircraft's deadly fire power and Verity managed to get inside its turning circle and position himself slightly below it. After milling around for what seemed like an eternity, Sergeant Wake got in a long burst from a range of approximately 100 yards.

The Ju 88 disappeared from view, but then Sergeant Wake suddenly spotted it again on their tail and shouted a warning to Verity over the intercom. The New Zealander pulled up into a sharp climb and performed a banking turn, while the Ju 88 passed under their tailplane and then appeared in front of them. It was only 10–15 feet above the Defiant and Sergeant Wake took the opportunity to get in another burst of fire. There was some return fire from the enemy aircraft but after another three-second burst from Sergeant Wake at point-blank range it suddenly stopped as it went into a steep dive.

Verity followed it down and from a range of 75 yards Sergeant Wake fired a final four-second burst into the its fuselage and port engine. They then followed it down through the clouds to below 6,000 ft, when it finally disappeared from sight. In the final moments both Verity and Wake thought that it had turned over onto its back, but they could not be certain it had crashed. Verity got a fix from Tern Hill at 0205 and after resuming their patrol he returned to Cranage and landed safely at 0235, having been airborne for one hour and fifteen minutes. It was an experience that he would never forget because he said it was the first time that the crew of an enemy aircraft had challenged him in such a way.

Early on Verity had suspected that the enemy aircraft might be a deadly Ju 88 C-4 night fighter with two cannon fitted into its nose. He later admitted that he had made a big mistake and may have needlessly put his own life and that of Sergeant Wake at risk. The engagement had lasted between eight and ten minutes and Sergeant Wake fired a total of 1,034 of his 2,400 rounds of ammunition. Although Verity and Wake were certain that the aircraft had crashed into the sea there was no confirmation, and it was credited only as a probable.

Sergeant McNair and Sergeant Wirdnam of 96 Squadron were patrolling the Leek North Patrol Line to the south of Liverpool at 14,000 ft when they spotted a Ju 88 flying east. McNair turned and Wirdnam got in a short burst but as they turned around the pilot observed another Ju 88, above his first target and to starboard. The two enemy aircraft then flew towards each other and continued in loose formation but Wirdnam got in another long burst from 75 yards. He aimed at the aircraft on their starboard side and claimed to have hit one of its engines and damaged the fuselage. However, his actions seemed to have little effect and the pilots of both Junkers opened up the throttles and left the Defiant behind. At 0140 an He 111 was spotted flying north but it was also lost because of the bad visibility.

CHAPTER TWENTY-ONE

Clearing Up:
The Best Night Yet

It was 0140 when Flight Lieutenant Deanesly landed and in his subsequent combat report (RAF Form 1151) he complained that the AA barrage had crept above the permitted height of 12,000 ft. Deansely was also unhappy about equipment failures and the fact that his gunner Sergeant Scott had suffered stoppages in two of his four guns. Moreover because of continous chatter over the radio on frequency stud D while they were over the target area, he had to switch to channel C.

As Deansely and Scott were landing, Sergeant Taylor and Sergeant McCormack of 96 Squadron were just beginning their patrol and at 0140 they observed an He 111 less than 250 yards away. Taylor ordered guns starboard and a two-second burst from McCormack at a range of 70 yards damaged both engines and caused flames to pour from the port engine. The starboard wing dropped and the machine flipped over onto its back and crashed to the ground at Egerton Hall Farm at Malpass in Cheshire. It is understood that it was coded 6N + FL, an elite pathfinder from 3/KG 100 and only the pilot, *Unteroffizier* Karl Schmidt, survived.

After completing their first combat Taylor and McCormack climbed to 10,000 ft and continued their patrol. Within minutes the air gunner spotted another enemy aircraft. It was in a shallow dive flying across the tail of their Defiant and he told Taylor to hold his course. He fired a three-second burst at the unidentified twin-engined machine and scored hits on the port engine and cockpit roof. When last seen the aircraft was diving into the clouds, going through the vertical and almost certainly about to crash. In the two combats McCormack had fired a total of 687 rounds of ammunition.

No. 256 Squadron's Flight Lieutenant West, together with his air gunner, Sergeant Adams, had been the first crew to achieve success on 7 April. On this night they also intercepted and shot down an He 111 belonging to 6/KG 55 after a combat above the Southport marshes. The Heinkel, coded G1 + HP, exploded in the air and the wreckage fell on Llwnyn Knottia Farm, near Wrexham, at 0200. Their action was all the more remarkable because, like Sergeant Scott, Adams had suffered stoppages with his Browning machine-guns and only a single gun remained in working order. He was so determined to destroy the Heinkel that in his combat report, he claimed that he would have done it even if it had meant 'throwing the control column at it'. All four airmen aboard the Heinkel were killed and *Oberfeldwebel* Hottenrott and his crew became what was effectively 256 squadron's second victim of the night. The other three airmen were *Unteroffizier* Gotze, *Oberfeldwebel* Gerstle, and *Oberfeldwebel* Reese.

Pilot Officer Don Toone and his air gunner, Flying Officer Bob Lamb, from 256 Squadron took off from Squires Gate at 0021 and soon afterwards they shot down an He 111, which turned out to be the unit's third victim of the night. They had observed the enemy aircraft over Liverpool Docks and Lamb opened fire at a range of 150 yards, then watched as it turned over onto its back and dived into the ground on the Liverpool waterfront.

Several other enemy aircraft were claimed as damaged by 256 Squadron crews. Pilot Officer Caldwell and Sergeant Trim attacked an He 111 over Manchester. Trim claimed to have scored a number of hits behind the wings of the enemy aircraft but it disappeared into cloud. Sergeant MacDonald, whose call sign was Purley 5, and his air gunner, Sergeant Walden, were on their way back to Squires Gate when they spotted an He 111. Walden opened fire and he claimed it went into a stall turn and then completely disappeared. Sergeants Olney and Simmonds also claimed to have hit and damaged a Ju 88 over Liverpool but no result was confirmed.

No. 256 Squadron did not get away completely unscathed. Squadron Leader Gatherall and the gunnery leader, Flying Officer D.S. Wallen, were forced to abandon Defiant N3500. They were engaged in combat with a Ju 88 over Liverpool and Walden claimed to have scored a number of hits around the enemy aircraft's wing roots. However they were hit by return fire which damaged their Defiant's Glycol tank and that caused the cockpit to fill with smoke. The two airmen baled out at 0140 and made safe landings in Widnes, while the Defiant crashed near St Helens.

There is some evidence to suggest that Squadron Leader Gatherall's Defiant was shot down by one of his own crews. A 256 Squadron air gunner, flying on the next allocated flight level below him reported opening fire on an unidentified aircraft at about the same time. It is thought that Gatherall's aircraft lost height and in the heat of the battle was identified as an enemy bomber. Intelligence sources might have been aware of what had happened but kept quiet to save the repuations of those who were involved in the incident.

A total of twenty sorties were flown by 256 Squadron crews on this night, including the single sortie flown from Squires Gate by Wing Commander Oliver in a Hurricane. The squadron's final tally was three aircraft confirmed destroyed and another three probables. Despite the loss of one of its Defiants, it was the squadron's finest hour and telegrams arrived at Squires Gate from Sir Charles Portal, Sir Archibald Sinclair and Fighter Command.

It was also 96 Squadron's finest hour. It completed eighteen sorties, totalling twenty-six hours of operational flying, which resulted in four enemy aircraft confirmed destroyed and three probables. All but one were flown in Defiants and Flying Officer McGlashan carried out the only sortie in a Hurricane when he patrolled Leek North between 0100 and 0240. Most pilots completed two sorties and by the time that Sergeant Black returned from his second, the moon was already setting. With his air gunner, Sergeant Cadman, Black landed at 0425, just two hours before sunrise, noting in his combat report: 'The bombers had long since turned for home.'

Flying Officer Verity said that he could not recall whether the AA barrage was shut down when 96 Squadron took off from Cranage, but he thought it had remained quite active throughout the fighter night. One thing that stuck in his memory about the following day was the silence, followed by loud giggling from a group of WAAFs when he walked into the 9 Group Sector Operations room at Tern Hill. He was told later that they had been on duty the night before when the radio channel used by 96 Squadron had been connected to the tannoy.

The colourful language used by many of the squadron's pilots had amused the girls, but not all those present found it so funny! Wing Commander Aitken, the CO of 68 Squadron, had also been in the operations room and he was not happy to hear 96 Squadron crews celebrating their victories over the air. Some of the jibes may have been aimed at the Beaufighter crews, who according to Verity had everything that technology had to offer. However they had failed to intercept a single aircraft and the gamble to use aircraft equipped with AI had on this occasion not paid off. The technology was within weeks of being perfected and within a short while it would turn around the situation in the night air war.

Amongst the various messages of congratulation received by 96 Squadron one was from Sir Edgar Ludlow-Hewitt and it probably saved Verity from a 'carpeting' by the AOC. Ludlow-Hewitt almost certainly sorted out any disciplinary measures that Verity might have faced, because he had known McClaughry since 1918, when he had commanded 10 Brigade. At that time McClaughry's 4 Squadron of the Australain Flying Corps had been directly under the command of Ludlow-Hewitt. His influence was probably enough to sway McClaughry, and as far as we know no action was taken against the New Zealander.

The success of 96 and 256 Squadrons and that of other RAF night fighter units during this period, curbed the *Luftwaffe*'s ambitions for domination of the night sky over England. It was a bitter blow to the Germans, but particularly for Hermann Goring. Former Ju 88 pilot *Feldwebel* Peter Stahl recalled in his book *The Diving Eagle* that a message was read to all the crews that night as part of their briefing, in which Goring claimed that High Command had information to prove that it was only a matter of weeks before the 'island people' gave in. Many *Luftwaffe* airmen knew this was not true and made very rude comments under their breath as the message was read out.

On the night of 7/8 May Fighter Command flew a total of 339 sorties and claimed a record number of twenty-one enemy aircraft destroyed. Another five were credited as probables and thirteen more as damaged. There were sceptics who claimed that, in terms of the overall number of enemy aircraft deployed by the *Luftwaffe*, the percentage of those destroyed was quite small. Nevertheless it was a great night for Fighter Command and effectively the watershed in the night air-war in the North-west.

CHAPTER TWENTY-TWO

Mixed Fortunes:
Introduction of GCI

After their achievements on the night of 7/8 May, subsequent events proved to be something of an anticlimax for the Defiant crews. The following evening 256 Squadron crews completed only six operational sorties but not a single one of them made contact with the enemy. Despite the squadron's efforts four bombs fell on the airfield at Squires Gate.

No. 96 Squadron did not do any better, its crews completed just nine sorties totalling fourteen and a half hours, but only one visual contact was reported. That was made by Flying Officer McGlashan, who was on patrol between 0135 and 0335 with Sergeant Lazell. They spotted an enemy aircraft heading south but lost sight of it in the murk and haze caused by the fires of the previous night.

Because of poor weather conditions, which persisted over the next few days, very little operational flying was done by either unit. No. 256 Squadron completed six operational sorties, but no interceptions were made. There was some movement of personnel at this time. Flight Lieutenant Hamilton and Sergeant House were both posted to 256 Squadron and joined A Flight. Sergeant House was an air gunner who reported for duty from 54 OTU at Church Fenton.

Two days later Pilot Officer Peter Caldwell, who had recently damaged an enemy aircraft over Liverpool, was posted to 54 OTU as an instructor. Caldwell was a popular officer amongst all sections of 256 Squadron and many were sad to see him go. He avoided a lengthy train journey by being personally flown to Church Fenton by Squadron Leader Gatherall.

At Squires Gate 256 Squadron's accident rate remained alarmingly high. On 15 May Sergeant Taylor and Sergeant Fremlin (RNZAF) were killed. At 0145, Defiant T3955, was seen to dive as if it was out of control. It hit the ground and exploded on impact at Nether Kellet, 2¹/₂ miles south of Carnforth. At the subsequent inquiry several factors were found to have contributed to the accident. The training system was criticized and in particular the practice of posting inexperienced pilots directly to night-flying squadrons from OTUs.

It was also suspected that Sergeant Taylor had only lost control of the aircraft because of a technical malfunction of the flight instruments. The artificial horizon and gyro compass were linked by a flexible rubber tube to a vacuum pump which controlled the instruments. An instrument failure was likely if the tube became kinked or bent and it was suspected that Sergeant Taylor was the victim of such a breakdown. At night or in bad weather even the most experienced pilots would probably have found it difficult to maintain control.

Sergeant Peter Taylor came from Nottinghamshire and after attending Worksop College had joined his father's fruit and vegetable business in Mansfield. He was an aviation enthusiast even before joining the RAF, and one of his hobbies was making models of the types of aircraft that he later hoped he would fly. He also liked fast cars and owned an MG which he loved to drive and show off to his friends whenever the opportunity arose. Only the week before the tragic incident, he went home on leave and took Sergeant Fremlin with him. The New Zealander received a warm welcome from the the Taylor family and he struck up a good relationship with his pilot's father, John.

As a result, Mr Jack Taylor requested that his son and Sergeant Fremlin should both be buried in Mansfield Cemetery. Squadron Leader Gatherall agreed and after official permission was granted, the CO played his part in making the arrangements. A Roman Catholic priest officiated at the burial and a firing party from 256 Squadron accompanied the coffins which, as tradition demanded, were covered in Union Jacks. Pilot Officer McKinnon and Sergeant Mulligan of the RNZAF represented Sergeant Fremlin and they were accompanied by the Taylor family and many other members of 256 Squadron. As the bodies were being lowered into the grave the Last Post was sounded and a flight of the squadron's Defiants flew overhead as the final tribute. Twenty-year-old Sergeant Peter John Taylor is buried in Mansfield (Nottingham Road) Cemetery, Grave 2402, while 19-year-old Sergeant Erle Rutherford Fremlin, the son of Charles Clement and Mabel Norah of Kawau Island, Auckland, is buried in Grave 2603.

The following day, on 16 May, 256 Squadron received its first honours when Flight Lieutenant Deanesly heard he was to be awarded the DFC and his air gunner, Sergeant Scott, the DFM. The celebrations might have been muted by the fact that three days earlier, Deanesly and Scott had received some unwelcome news. The Ju 88 which they had been credited with destroying on 3/4 May was given to Flying Officer Verity of 96 Squadron, reversing the earlier decision. It was a bitter blow that was felt by everyone on the squadron, but particularly Sergeant Scott. For him it was a double blow because on the same day he received the news about his DFM, he was admitted into hospital with a bad case of measles.

During the afternoon of the 16th there was a bit of excitment when the wheel fell off Sergeant MacDonald's aircraft as he was taking-off. The Defiant was inspected by the pilot of another aircraft in the air and consideration was given to diverting to High Ercall. However, MacDonald did not have the right maps and the fuel state was quite low. He eventually made a forced landing by the side of the main runway with both wheels retracted and he and his gunner, Sergeant Walden, escaped injury.

Within twenty-four hours of receiving news of his DFC award, Flight Lieutenant Deanesly's fortunes took a downward turn when he was involved in an unfortunate accident. It was the first of two similar incidents involving the flight commander which happened while taxiing around the airfield at night. Deanesly had landed from a fruitless patrol and was returning to his dispersal when he ran into the NAAFI tea van. Although the Defiant was only slightly damaged, the vehicle was completely wrecked. More seriously a number of its occupants were badly injured and the flight commander was lucky to escape lightly from the subsequent court of inquiry.

Over at Cranage 96 Squadron was having a far better time of things. Its crews were only too pleased to show off when the unit finally achieved a 100 per cent serviceability status. During the evening of 16 May it was put on immediate standby and detached to

High Ercall in anticipation of a bombing raid on the Midlands. Crews flew four patrols in thick layers of cloud, which were unsuitable for visual conditions, and no contact was made with the enemy. When the squadron left High Ercall the next day its twelve Defiants and two Hurricanes climbed overhead and joined up, to fly back to Cranage in perfect formation.

The display was not put on just to impress 68 Squadron, but also finally to avenge the débâcle of the night in April when so many of its aircraft had been unserviceable. Every aircraft which had flown to High Ercall returned fully serviceable and they made a perfect spectacle over Cranage. The aircraft broke off one by one to land and their return was met by an appreciative audience from 96 Squadron and the ANS.

The first Ground-Controlled Interception (GCI) radar station in 9 Group was located at Hack Green in Cheshire, to the south of Nantwich and approximately 15 miles south of the RAF airfield at Cranage, covering the approach to the Ternhill Sector. GCI radar had an all round view scanning the approach routes of enemy aircraft, so that its controllers were able to vector crews onto them. It did have its limitations, however, and to start with controllers could only handle one aircraft at a time.

Trewan Sands, the second GCI station, was set up at Rhosneigr Golf Course on Anglesey, to cover the approaches through St George's Channel. Many of its staff were transferred from the 9 Group operations room at Caergeiliog and it worked closely with it and other units based at nearby RAF Valley. It became operational on 9 May 1941, under its CO, Flight Lieutenant John Kemp. He was an excellent controller and responsible for a number of successful interceptions.

As GCI radar was introduced new operational policies were put into place. Standing Operational Order 45 (A), dated 5 May, was one of many new orders written at this time. Under these instructions fighter nights were only to be ordered when:

(i)   The moon is over the horizon
(ii) Visibility and light are such that that fighter aircraft are likely to sight enemy aircraft
(iii) The enemy attack is obviously concentrated on a clearly defined target which covers only a limited area.

The Liverpool guns were restricted to firing up to 14,000 ft and night-fighter pilots were ordered to give them 2,000 ft clearance. Controllers could use their discretion and the height of the barrage could be changed. Sector commanders were also to use their discretion in exposing searchlights and marker beacons to help pilots maintain their position during patrols or returning to base.

As a result of the introduction of GCI radar and the beginning of operations with the Beaufighter, the existing system of patrol lines was largely replaced in May by fighter boxes. These were not boxes as such, but two large clusters of flares situated approximately 30 miles apart and connected by a hypothetical line. Box A ran across the Lleyn Peninsula. Box B was situated to the south of Chester down the Welsh Borders and ran from Ruabon to Welshpool, Box C was to the east of that between the Liverpool and Crewe GDAs. Some marker beacons, consisting of clusters of Tilley Lamps or electric flares were retained and those in the Speke Sector were coded with the letter 'S' and were numbered 1–10.

On 19 May there were further changes to the orders and policy controlling night fighter operations in 9 Group because it was claimed that the operation of single-engined night fighters on geographical patrol lines was ineffective. The main points were as outlined below:

(i)   During suitable conditions of the moon single-engined fighters will be employed on layers patrols concentrating over the target area of the enemy's attack.

(ii) During dull moon periods single-engined fighters will be ordered to orbit over focal points marked by clusters of flares from which positions they will be vectored by the sector controller to intercept raids.

(iii) Should the GCI controller be able to accept more aircraft than the number of twin-engined aircraft available, single-engined fighters may be operated under GCI control provided that this does not prejudice their availability for the roles outlined in paragraphs i and ii above and is not likely to bring them into contact with friendly twin-engined fighters.

While they were not meant to establish a precise and rigid procedure, orders laid down the different operational roles of single-engined and twin-engined night fighters. The principle was that twin-engined fighters were to protect the lines of approaches, while single-engined aircraft were mainly to concentrate on the objectives of the attack and fly above it at staggered heights.

When twin-engined and single-engined fighters were airborne on operations at the same time, each 9 Group sector was to use code words to warn them of each other's presence, one to warn pilots and the other to inform them that the danger had passed. When they received the warning, pilots of single-engined aircraft were ordered to cease all offensive operations, while pilots of twin-engined fighters were warned to take great care not to engage single-engined fighters.

On the 19 May some airmen got their first night off duty since the end of April – probably not as a result of the policy changes, more because of a lack of enemy action. Sergeant Adams of 256 Squadron finally got his leave on the 23rd, some twenty-seven days late, but after receiving some good news. Flight Lieutenant West had told him in confidence that he, West, had been recommended for the DFC, while Sergeant Adams had been recommended for the DFM. It was something to ponder over during the thirteen hour train journey, via Preston and London, to his home at Marten in Wiltshire. Adams arrived just in time to participate in War Weapons Week, which was taking place in the neighbouring village of East Grafton and he thoroughly enjoyed his seven days' leave in the countryside.

Despite the operational restrictions and the fact that many airmen went on leave which was long overdue, 96 and 256 Squadrons continued to operate normally on those nights when the weather and the moon permitted. On 27/28 May 96 Squadron carried out nine sorties with the same number of aircraft but only a single crew made visual contact. The enemy aircraft was subsequently lost in thickening cloud conditions which provided sufficient cover for enemy bombers to hide.

No. 256 Squadron flew a total of eleven sorties but failed to intercept any of the attacking force, which comprised forty aircraft that targeted various objectives over Lancashire and North Wales. To add insult to injury four 50 kg bombs were dropped on the airfield at Squires Gate by a single enemy aircraft, although no 9 Group aircraft were hit, a number of Blackburn Bothas belonging to 3 School of General Reconaissance (SGR), a Coastal Command training unit based there, were damaged.

Sergeant Stanley Walker was posted to 256 Squadron in June, fresh from training at 56 OTU, Sutton Bridge, after completing his elementary flying training in Canada. He had trained at 11 Elementary Flying Training School, which was run by Quebec Airways under the British Commonwealth Training Plan. Amongst the twenty-eight members of his course was Sergeant Percy Belgrave Lucas, later known as Wing Commander 'Laddie' Lucas, CBE, DSO and Bar, DFC. The luck of the draw meant that while Lucas was posted to 52 OTU on his return to the UK and flew Spitfires, Sergeant Walker was posted to a night-fighter OTU and flew Defiants.

Sergeant Walker's reception at Squires Gate was not promising. Flight Lieutenant Deanesly told him to go and have a look around a Defiant. Sergeant Walker was helped into the cockpit of an aircraft by a flight mechanic, who was explaining the layout when Deanesly appeared and began to ask the Walker some questions about the aircraft's performance. Walker told him that he had not got a clue, because he had trained on Hurricanes and never been in a Defiant before! Deansley openly expressed his displeasure and walked away.

Just after he arrived Sergeant Walker had to attend a civic luncheon in Liverpool to honour the night-fighter pilots who had flown through the May Blitz. The occasion was a duty but as he had only just arrived on the squadron he felt guilty about taking credit for something that he had not been involved in. He never felt completely at ease at Squires Gate, and a few weeks later he was glad to receive the news that he had been posted to 456 Squadron at Valley.

CHAPTER TWENTY-THREE

Enter the Beaufighter: June 1941

By the end of May the operational strength of 9 Group available for night fighting was five Blenheims, six Beaufighters and twenty-eight Defiants. The Beaufighters belonged to 68 Squadron which had only just begun to re-equip with them; its crews had yet to experience their first successful action.

On the night of 31 May/1 June there was a considerable amount of activity with some eighty enemy aircraft above Merseyside and Barrow. This was the first occasion that 219 Squadron operated in the region. Equipped with Beaufighters fitted with AI radar Mk IV, 219 Squadron was based at Tangmere but a detachment from A Flight moved north to operate out of Valley. Its presence in the region suggests that the authorities were aware that a large-scale raid was imminent.

On that night Squadron Leader Colbech-Welch of 219 Squadron engaged an enemy aircraft over Anglesey, and after a short combat destroyed it. The aircraft was seen to crash into the sea off the coast near Aberystwyth and although Colbech-Welch failed to make a positive identification, it is believed to have been a Ju 88.

No. 96 Squadron was also active that night and flew a total of thirteen patrols, with crews making a total of four visual contacts, but not a single interception. In each case the enemy was lost almost immediately because of hazy conditions, which were hardly suitable for cat's eyes operations. A comment in the 96 Squadron diary claimed that the reason enemy bombers got away was because the Defiant was too slow to chase them. The speed factor frustrated the Defiants' pilots, because once the enemy knew of their presence they were normally outrun. It seems that the crews were coming to terms with the fact that the Defiant was being outclassed, and not just in speed.

The aircraft was capable of speeds in excess of 300 mph but on patrol it was normally flown at around 260–280 mph to conserve fuel. By comparison the Beaufighter could cruise quite comfortable at speeds well in excess of 300 mph, with a maximum of 330 mph, and it had the further advantage of a far greater range. The other important factor was firepower: the Defiant's four Browning .303 machine-guns were no match for the Beaufighter's four 20 mm cannon and later up to six .303 machine-guns.

The *Luftwaffe* mounted what the 9 Group operational diary called a medium-scale raid on Manchester during the night of 1/2 June with a force of at least sixty aircraft. Enemy aircraft flew towards Manchester from the east coast but because others flew up Cardigan Bay on a mine-laying operation the night-fighter defences were split. Beaufighters of 219 Squadron were operating out of Valley for a second night running, under GCI control with 68 Squadron from High Ercall.

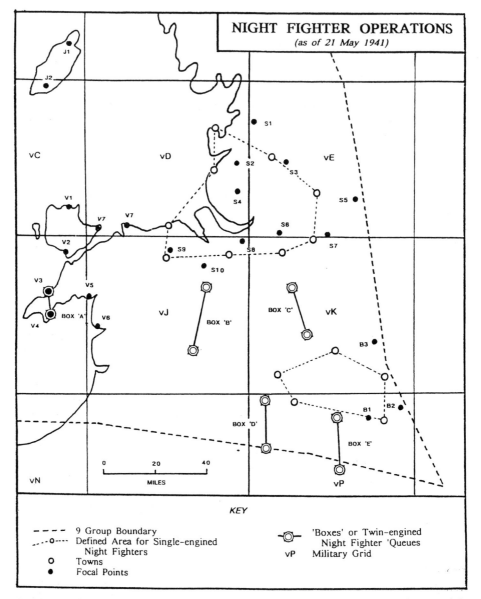

Diagram of Fighter Boxes and Patrol Lines as from May 1941 after the introduction of the Beaufighter. Courtesy of Derek Pratt and Michael Grant

It was on that night that Salford Royal Hospital was bombed and the devastation resulted in the death of fourteen nurses. Locally this was regarded as a totally unnecessary and deliberate act of inhumanity. In fact there is some evidence to suggest that by 1942 the *Luftwaffe* was deliberately targeting hospitals. It comes from a map found on Gatow airfield in July 1945 by Leading Aircraftsman R.F. Jones of 2848 Squadron, RAF Regiment. The 1:10,000 scale map of Stockport's Bredbury area was dated 15 March 1942, and on it were marked a number of legitimate targets such as steel works, rolling mills and a gas works on Great Portwood Street. Also clearly highlighted, however, with a thick black cross, was Steeping Hill Hospital, which leaves little doubt as to its intended purpose.

No radar-equipped night fighter made any interception that night; 96 Squadron was the only unit to engage an enemy aircraft in combat. Squadron Leader Burns intercepted a Ju 88 above the Wirral, and although the combat was inconclusive, he claimed to have damaged it. A Ju 88 which crashed near Brighton might have been his victim, the only other enemy aircraft lost was a similar type from KGr 606 which crash landed at Caen in France.

On the night of 17 June 68 Squadron claimed its first enemy aircraft destroyed, but the action did not take place in the north-west. Beaufighter X7554, flown by Flight Lieutenant Pain, DFC, and Flying Officer Davis of A Flight intercepted an He 111 with the aid of Comberton GCI station near Malvern. Hack Green GCI station was off the air because of technical difficulties which had plagued the radar unit since it had been declared operational.

The interception, at 17,000 ft, was controlled by Radar Technical Officer David Davies who although he was not a properly qualified navigator, flew on a number of operations. Davies said that the aircraft had almost certainly dropped its bombs and was flying very fast, so they had to go flat out to catch it. Flight Lieutenant Pain opened fire at a range of 250 yds with a burst lasting just one second. It was enough to make the Heinkel catch fire and within a short while it exploded, with only the pilot having time to escape. The main part of the aircraft crashed at Timsbury, 6 miles south-west of Bath and the bodies of the other four crew were found in the wreckage. The authorities were soon on the scene and a number of documents concerning radio beams were found amongst the debris and sent directly to the Air Ministry.

Just over a week later, on 28 June, the Beaufighter crews consolidated their dominance of the night sky, when an He 111 was shot down over North Wales by the crew of a 604 Squadron Beaufighter operating out of Middle Wallop. It was tracked by Sopley GCI station and its details passed to Wing Commander Appleton and his observer, Pilot Officer Jackson, at 0020. It was flying very fast at 15,000 ft and Jackson made contact three times, but there was interference with the signal from the ground. Appleton experienced problems with searchlights illuminating his aircraft and he was reluctant to fly too close in case the enemy crew spotted them.

Finally at 0113 hours the controller at Sopley gave Appleton some updated information. He was told to orbit to starboard and then 'flash' on a heading of 010 degrees. Appleton approached from dead astern and closed in from 3,000 yds to 1,200 yds, At a range of 200 yds he opened fire. When the first shells exploded underneath the Heinkel, the pilot, *Leutnant* Helmut Einecke, thought that it was AA fire. There was a second blast underneath the starboard wing and a third immediately in front which rocked and badly damaged the aircraft. Most of the instruments and dials in the cockpit were destroyed and Einecke began to experience problems controlling the aircraft. He ordered his crew to bale out. It was a wise decision; only moments after the last man jumped out the aircraft blew up.

The radio operator, *Unteroffizier* Hans Muhlhan, was in a state of shock as he floated to earth in a long, cold descent from nearly 12,000 ft. As he approached the ground he took his pistol from its holster and fired off several shots to attract attention in a naive attempt to raise the alarm. The shots were heard by a number of people in the vicinity of Hendre on the Nercwys – Mold road and Muhlhan was extremely lucky not to attract return fire from an over enthusiastic member of the Home Guard.

Just after landing he was approached by Mr Llewelyn Roberts, a mature member of the ranks and he surrendered to him, handing over his gun. He was well treated and given a cup of tea while his injured head was dressed by the district nurse, Mrs Thomas. Intelligence sources later discovered that Einicke's crew were from the 7th *Staffel* III/KG 27 and had taken off earlier in the day from Orleans in He 111, 1G + CG to provide air cover for the *Bismarck*. After becoming airborne at 2308 their orders had been changed over the radio to bomb Liverpool.

While in custody in Mold police station Muhlhan received the good news that all his crew, including the navigator, *Unteroffizier* George Hartig and the flight mechanic, *Gefreiter* Konrad Baron, were safe. As a parting gesture to Mr Roberts, Muhlhan happily handed over his signals lamp and holster. Within a short while he was reunited with his crew and they were later sent to Canada and interned in Prisoner of War (PoW) Camp No. 23.

By the summer encounters with the *Luftwaffe* were rare. Because of further changes in the 9 Group order of battle, the cat's eyes units were almost non-operational. One of the few combats to take place during this period occurred on 7 July when Sergeants Mulligan and Parks of 256 Squadron, in Defiant N3480, sighted an He 111. They closed to within a range of 500 yards but despite the close proximity and their finest efforts to intercept it the Heinkel got away. No. 96 Squadron also took part in operations over Birmingham that night on what was becoming an increasingly rare fighter night. No. 256 Squadron continued to see the occasional action and on the 9th visual contact was made with a Heinkel from a range of 800 yards but the aircraft managed to get away.

CHAPTER TWENTY-FOUR

456 Squadron: July 1941

RAF Valley opened in February 1941 although it was at first known as 'RAF Rhosneigr', but that name caused a lot of confusion. No. 9 Group wanted to change the name but Fighter Command resisted any such move. The Air Ministry finally made its mind up and supported 9 Group, so that the station officially became RAF Valley from 3 April 1941. The airfield had three concrete runways laid down in the typical RAF pattern, the longest being 4,200 ft. RAF Valley was Commanded by former 9 Group Staff Officer, Wing Commander Oliver, which must have been quite confusing as the Commanding Officer of 456 Squadron was Wing Commander Olive.

Despite the fact that the Beaufighter had largely superseded the Defiant, at the end of June 1941 there was still one squadron in 9 Group being equipped with the single-engined aircraft. 456 Squadron was formed at Valley on the Isle of Anglesey and Sergeant Brian Wild was one of the first pilots to arrive, on 7 July. He had only just completed his flying training at 56 OTU, Sutton Bridge, and it was an exciting time for him when he arrived at his first operational squadron.

Sergeant Wild was a Lancashire lad from Bolton, who had been weaned on aviation at Barton Airport, Manchester, before the war. When he attended an air pageant at Barton in 1931, huge fabric sheets were hung on metal poles to prevent non-paying guests from seeing the aircraft. At the end of the day Brian and his friend were paid a few pence to carry the poles away to a lorry. As his friend

Individual photo of Sergeant Brian Wild of 256 Squadron. Born in Bolton the senior N.C.O. pilot was first posted to 456 Squadron at Valley, where he survived a collision with a mobile cooker. He was later posted to 256 Squadron and in 1942 he was commissioned before being posted overseas.

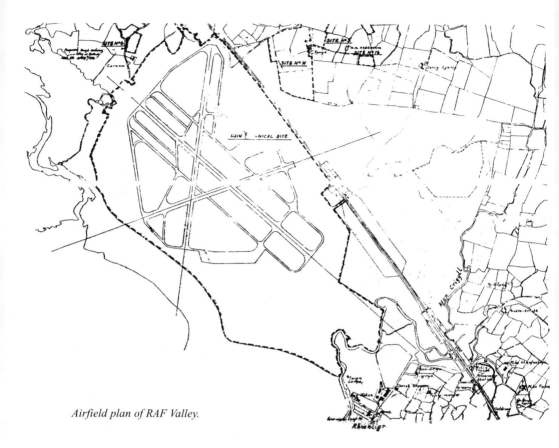

Airfield plan of RAF Valley.

turned around with a pole over his shoulder, Brian was hit on the nose and injured quite badly. He lost his sense of smell, so the air pageant was a day that he would never forget!

At Sutton Bridge he had mixed in illustrious company. His flight commander was Flight Lieutenant Derek Dowding, the son of Air Chief Marshal Hugh Dowding, the former Commander-in-Chief of Fighter Command. He was also posted to Valley at about the same time and on 1486 Fighter Gunnery Flight, which towed drogues and targets. Flight Lieutenant Dowding was known to be a bit of a 'joker' and on one occasion he ordered airmen to parade in their Grey coats on a hot summers day. The inspection went ahead but most realised it was only a joke when he told them that it was just in case they were posted to Siberia!

Towards the end of their course at 56 OTU, pilots were asked if they would volunteer to join a night-fighter squadron but only three of them did so. Sergeant Wild was posted to 456 Squadron at Valley, along with his colleagues Sergeants Ward and Wills. No. 456 Squadron was sponsored by the Australian Government and for the first few weeks after he arrived at Valley Sergeant Wild was forced to fly alone as the Australians had not yet arrived. Eventually Sergeant Wild was temporarily crewed up with a Sergeant Walker, one of a number of RAF air gunners who were filling in for the Australians.

On 26 July they had a lucky escape when Wild was forced to make a crash landing on the airfield. The accident happened as they were about to land in Defiant N1569, when to Wild's horror, something suddenly appeared out of the gloom straight ahead. There was nothing he could do to avoid hitting the obstruction, which turned out to be the tall chimney of a mobile field kitchen being towed under the approach to the runway without permission from flying control. Fortunately he managed to maintain control, but he was forced to overshoot, go around again and make a crash landing on one wheel. He and Walker were very lucky to get away unscathed, but their Defiant was badly damaged. It was sent to Reid & Sigrist to be repaired, but was later involved in a fatal accident in June 1942, while in the service of 289 Squadron. The mobile kitchen that had been delivering meals to the airmen working on the dispersals, was a write-off. Many airmen at Valley went hungry that night and there was a lot of grumbling from empty stomachs and raised voices about careless fighter pilots.

For Sergeant Wild it was just one of a number of dangerous moments in his flying career which could have killed him. On one occasion his radio became unserviceable while he was flying over Snowdon and he was left not knowing his exact position. He flew in the direction of the Irish Sea until he found a clear patch of sky and then managed to find his way back to Valley. On another night, the lever to lower the undercarriage snapped off while he was approaching to land. In the end he had to take his flying boot off, hit the selector stud by the side of the lever and then shake the wheels down by violent manoeuvres.

When the Australians arrived in August Wing Commander Olive the CO, began the process of forming his pilots and air gunners into crews. For some reason pilots and gunners were reluctant to mix so the CO was forced to organize a meeting in the mess. He told the airmen that pilots had to choose a gunner, or gunners a pilot; he was not bothered which way they did it, but it had to be done. The bar was then opened and as the beer began to flow the airmen mingled in a more relaxed way, overcoming their inhibitions.

Sergeant Wild said that after he had spoken to several air gunners a small stocky figure approached him, poked him in the chest and asked, 'Have you got a gunner?' Wild replied that nobody had yet offered their services and he was still looking around. The Australian poked him in the chest again and said, 'I'm your gunner.' He introduced himself as Sergeant 'Ack' Greenwood. At twenty-nine the pushy Australian was considerably older than his pilot, but despite that the two men got on well from the start.

A little while later the CO took Sergeant Wild to one side and congratulated him on his choice of air gunner. He told him that he was a lucky man. In Australia Sergeant Greenwood was well known because he was the bantam-weight boxing champion of Victoria. He said Greenwood was very strong and jokingly warned Sergeant Wild not to shake his hand for fear of damaging his fingers! The other thing the CO told him was that Sergeant Greenwood had passed out of gunnery school classed as 'exceptional'; he was certainly the best air gunner on the squadron and probably the best in 9 Group. Wild felt reassured about the future!

Sergeant Stanley Walker also arrived at Valley on 7 July, having been posted in from 256 Squadron at Squires Gate. One of his most interesting experiences involved an Irish air gunner who against all the odds, damaged his own aircraft. At the time of the incident they were flying to the west of the Isle of Man close to the Irish coast. Without any warning the air gunner suddenly opened fire. The burst passed perilously close to Sergeant Walker's shoulder and vital instruments and controls. Bullets passed through the arc of the propeller, hitting and damaging the blades and causing the engine to vibrate. The aircraft made an awful noise but Sergeant Walker managed to get back to Valley and make a safe landing. The air gunner claimed that he had fired accidentally, but Sergeant Walker suspected that his real motive was to force a landing in Northern Ireland. The Irishman had regularly complained that he never got to see his family, but it was never proved that he had deliberately endangered the aircraft.

Sergeant Walker was on 456 Squadron when it was declared operational on 5 September, but by the time it scored its first victory in January 1942, he had moved on to another unit in 9 Group.

One of the ground crew who missed his supper the night Sergeant Wild wrote off the mobile kitchen was Leading Aircraftsman Clem Lea, who was posted to Valley from Cranage in July. He lost the comforts of living in his own home in the process, but still managed to return to Winsford quite often. His old friend from 96 Squadron, Sergeant Taylor, regularly dropped in at Valley and flew him back to Cranage. The first time it happened Clem's wife got the surprise of her life to see him walking down the garden path when he should have been many miles away in Wales. After that it became a common practice and he managed to get home most weekends. He maintained contact with many of his friends at Cranage and kept in touch with what was going on there.

Back at Cranage, 96 Squadron was having a bad time. On 22 July the gremlins returned when another aircraft was lost after taking off from Squires Gate. Defiant T4071 was on an air test after undergoing maintenance and crashed into Eddisbury Hill in Cheshire killing Pilot Officer Smithson and the air gunner, Sergeant Robinson of the RNZAF. The 20-year-old pilot had been commissioned just five days before his untimely death, on 17 July.

Sergeant Ivan Norton Robinson, the son of William and Anneta Voilet of Mount Albert, Auckland, was buried locally in Byley churchyard, in Section B, Grave 11. Twenty-five year old Pilot Officer Richard Smithson, the son of Johnson and Susan Marion, was buried in his home town of South Hetton, in the Holy Trinity churchyard, Grave Number 815.

Despite the accidents, the airmen and officers of 96 Squadron had reasons to celebrate in August when 96 Squadron received its first honours; Flying Officer Verity was awarded the DFC and Sergeant Wake the DFM. August though, was generally a bad month for 96 Squadron and it lost two aircraft and one crew in just four days during training flights. The first incident happened on 2 August when Pilot Officer Keprt, with Sergeant Harder on board, undershot the runway at Cranage and hit a tree. Although Defiant T3924 was badly damaged, neither Keprt or the air gunner were badly hurt.

On 4 August Pilot Officer Duncan and Flight Sergeant Allcroft were killed on a night-training exercise when N3447 crashed and burned out. Flight Sergeant Frederick Augustus Allcroft is commemorated on Panel 1 of the Memorial in Brighton's Woodvale Cemetery. Pilot Officer John Rodger Duncan, the son of John Rodger and Mary, also the husband of Gwndylyn Jean of Blackpool, is commemorated on Panel 10 of Manchester Crematorium.

The month also ended badly when Pilot Officer Jacobs suffered an engine failure on 31 August and crash landed Defiant N3383 in some fields near Sandbach Grammar School. Fortunately neither Jacobs or his air gunner, Sergeant Arnold, were seriously injured.

CHAPTER TWENTY-FIVE

A Black August for 256 Squadron

At Squires Gate 256 Squadron was not faring much better. On 14 August Flight Lieutenant Deanesly had his second accident on the ground. It happened while he was carrying out a taxiing manoeuvre and his Defiant collided with a bus which had been left on the airfield. There were no casualties but the bus was badly damaged, as were the Defiant's propeller blades and the leading edge of the wing.

Pilot Officers Eric Raybould and Jack Sharpe arrived at 256 Squadron in July after completing their flying training at 56 OTU, Sutton Bridge. Pilot Officer Raybould had 165 hours' flying time and the story of his arrival is similar to that of Sergeant Wild. At Sutton Bridge pilots were requested to volunteer for night-fighting duties, but Raybould recalled that very few seemed interested. Only he and Pilot Officer Sharpe put their names down, so they were posted to Squires Gate together.

The two men became good friends but on 18 August Pilot Officer Sharpe was killed on a training flight while carrying out a homing exercise. The explosion of the impact was heard by a Home Guard unit, who instigated the search for the aircraft. The Defiant had crashed on Lee Fell, bleak open moorland between the hamlets of Marshaw and Quernmore to the south-east of Lancaster, and the wreckage was not discovered until the following day.

Pilot Officer Jack Sharpe of 256 Squadron who was killed on 18 August 1941 in the Trough of Bowland. Courtesy of Eric Raybould

When rescuers eventually arrived at the scene they could not find the body of the pilot and so another search began. Pilot Officer Sharpe had been flying on his own and because he did not have time to bale out he had remained with the aircraft. The young pilot was very badly injured and had suffered terribly after dragging himself from the wreckage and struggling for over a mile across rough countryside to try and get help. When the rescue party found him he was in a state of severe shock but still alive when he arrived at Lancaster Royal Infirmary.

As the news broke at Squires Gate that Sharpe's aircraft had been found, Pilot Officer Raybould, together with Squadron Leader Gatherall and the engineering officer, drove over to the crash site. They inspected the aircraft and were amazed to discover that it was partially intact. They also found some blood on the armour-plated seat. That suggested to them that Sharpe's head had been pushed very hard against the head-rest of the seat during the initial impact. It was a bleak and desolate location and Raybould recollected that the thought of his friend spending all night out there on his own made him shiver.

Pilot Officer Eric Raybould, colleague and good friend of fellow pilot Jack Sharpe. They were on the same course at O.T.U. and posted to 256 Squadron together. After the incident when Sharpe was killed he became unsettled and was soon transferred to 68 Squadron. Courtesy of Eric Raybould

The three officers drove to Lancaster, but when they arrived in the late afternoon they were told that Pilot Officer Sharpe had just died. His injuries were far worse than anyone had first thought, and his death was caused by severe head wounds, including a fractured skull. The body of 20-year-old Pilot Officer Sharpe was transported to Golders Green Cemetery in London on the 22nd and Pilot Officer Raybould accompanied the coffin. He also attended the funeral in Golders Green Crematorium with the Sharpe family. Pilot Officer Norman Jack Sharpe, the son of Cecil and Madeleine Sharpe from Southampton, is commemorated on Panel 3 at Golders Green Crematorium.

On 27 August 1941, just nine days after the death of Pilot Officer Sharpe, Blackpool was the scene of one of the worst crashes in the region during the war. The incident began on a warm sunny afternoon as rigger Dick Longson was about to take advantage of the weather and go on a test flight in a twin-engined Botha.

He and his friend, Norman Midgeley, were both engineers who worked for Brooklands Aviation, which was contracted to the Air Ministry. In between jobs they regularly had the opportunity to fly in the aircraft that they serviced and on that fateful afternoon, Dick shouted to Norman that he had a couple of parachutes and would he go up with him.

Norman wiped his hands and put on a parachute as the Botha's engines were started up by its pilots, Pilot Officer Horne and Pilot Officer Sale. Both the officers and the aircraft were from 3 SGR.

Dick boarded the Botha but as Norman was about to climb in, he heard his foreman shouting to him above the roar of the engines. He was complaining that there was work to be done on another aircraft, so Norman reluctantly told Dick he could not go and jumped out. He was given the job of fixing some petrol tanks into another Botha but he kept looking up at the sky to see where the aircraft was.

He spotted it high above the Central Promenade, and as he worked he continued to look up to monitor its progress. He saw a formation of Defiants suddenly appear above it and they began to break off. He stopped work to see what they were doing. One by one they dived towards the Botha making mock attacks, then suddenly one of them appeared to fly perilously close to it. The next instant the two aircraft collided and a huge pall of black smoke filled the sky as debris began to fall to earth.

There were a large number of eyewitnesses, one of which was 13-thirteen-year-old Albert Smith, who watched the tragedy unfold with his older brother from the Central Pier. They were from Coventry and having survived the November blitz and more recent bombing raids on that city, they were enjoying a holiday at the seaside with their father, who had been given a few days off work. They saw the twin-engined 'bomber' approach the pier from the sea. As it came nearer it came under attack in what he realized was a mock combat involving a number of fighters.

The scene as one of the fighters hit the bomber's tail and crashed to earth stuck in Albert's memory, but it was something else that really affected him. As he looked up he saw something falling to earth amongst the debris which looked just like a spinning propeller. The following day he heard that one of the crew had fallen into the sea and the body had been recovered. It was then that the awful reality struck, that what he had seen was one of the airmen falling to his death with his arms and legs outstretched.

The tail of the Botha broke off and it crashed into the sea but the bodies of Pilot Officer Horne and Pilot Officer Sale fell from the fuselage. The main section, including its engines, landed on Blackpool's Central railway station which was packed with servicemen and civilians. The impact and subsequent fire caused absolute chaos and killed fourteen people, with many more seriously injured.

Eight-year-old Percy Featherstone from Barnsley was at the station with his family and was one of those badly hurt. On a week's holiday to Blackpool, his father was visiting the ticket office to get their tickets regulated and ensure seats on their return journey. They had just left the ticket office when a sudden commotion began and someone shouted that there were some planes overhead. His father, who was a miner and a part-time fireman in the AFS (Auxiliary Fire Service), told Percy and his mother to take cover and he went outside to see what was happening. At that point there was a terrific crash and the horrific sound of tearing metal as the Botha hit the ground less than 15 yards away!

Percy and his mother were showered in aviation fuel and he was convinced that they were going to die, as they were engulfed in flames. Fortunately, his mother was wearing a long thick coat, so she was able to hold him close and shelter him from the worst of the fire. They shuffled towards an area where they thought the exit was and along the way Percy saw the horrific sight of a woman in a flimsy dress running away covered in flames. As he and his mother escaped through the station entrance they bumped into his father, who had heard the explosion and was on his way in to find them. On their way out of the station his father saw a small baby abandoned in a pram, so he picked the child up and they ran to safety.

Percy and his mother were taken to a nearby chemist who applied first aid until the ambulances arrived and then they were taken to Blackpool's Victoria Hospital. On examining Percy, the doctors found that the blast from the explosion had blown the skin off the back of his hands and because he was wearing short trousers, his legs were also badly burned down to his ankles. His mother was also burnt but she was more concerned that her handbag had blown open and that its contents were scattered about, including money, ID card and ration books!

Amongst those who witnessed the carnage were a number of servicemen who were waiting for trains. Corporal Thomas Hill who was standing at the barrier of No. 3 platform also missed death by just a few feet when the bulk of the Botha crashed through the station roof. He was blown off his feet by the explosion and overwhelmed by the intense heat, but saw others with their clothes on fire. He tried to beat out the flames with his jacket and dragged three people out from under the wreckage of the rubble and tangled metal.

The scene at the crash site of the Defiant was less dramatic because there were far fewer people involved and the destruction was on a smaller scale. The aircraft crashed down on a house at 97 Reads Avenue. Although the property was totally devastated, the occupants of the house, Mr and Mrs Francis, miraculously escaped without injury but they were deeply shocked. Sergeant Ellmers was still in the aircraft at the time of its impact with the ground and his body was entangled in the wreckage. What remained of the Defiant was completely covered with debris from the house and it was 2100 before rescue workers recovered the pilot's body.

The Defiant's air gunner, Sergeant Clifford, managed to escape and attempted to deploy his parachute, but probably because the aircraft was too low it failed to open and his body was found in Regent Road. Some local people ran around to the police station in Albert Road but they said that it was not their responsibility and the RAF had been informed. They covered his body in a sheet borrowed from one of the residents and some time later a van arrived and Sergeant Clifford's body was finally removed.

Although a separate inquest investigated the deaths of the eighteen people killed, it was the Court of Inquiry set up by the RAF that examined the cause of the accident. It

Head and shoulders shot of Sergeant Ellmers, the pilot of the ill-fated Defiant that collided with a Botha over Blackpool on 27 August 1941.
Courtesy of Russell Brown

looked at all the circumstances and the records of the pilots in detail, especially that of the Defiant's pilot, Sergeant Lincoln John Ellmers. It convened at 1000 on 31 August at RAF Squires Gate. It was a sombre occasion and evidence was taken from a large number of civilians and service personnel. There was no shortage of eyewitnesses.

Constable John Williams gave a graphic account at the subsequent inquest of how the two planes collided. He said that the Botha was flying near the tower at about 2,000 ft when the first of three Defiants dived from west to east. One dived down upon the Botha, then a second and finally the third, but then the slow, lumbering twin-engined aircraft began to bank to the right. The left wing of the third aircraft to dive, hit the Botha and cut it in two, with the tail breaking up into fragments.

The Inquiry's findings have only now been revealed and much of what was apparently witnessed by the public and thought to be the cause of the collision proved to be something of an illusion. It was established that four 256 Squadron Defiants had taken off from Squires Gate on an authorized flight to practise formation flying. Shortly after take-off the flight commander was recalled to the airfield to take an urgent message and handed over command to his deputy.

Just a few minutes later the deputy flight commander ordered the Defiants to break away and it was that order that was responsible for the collision.

The Court of Inquiry found that the accident was primarily due to the fact that the deputy flight commander failed to observe the Botha aircraft in the vicinity of his formation when he gave the order to break away and Sergeant Clifford was killed while attempting to use his parachute at a low altitude.

No blame was attributed to either pilot.

The findings went against the popular belief that Sergeant Ellmers had deliberately dived on the Botha and caused the accident. In fact there was evidence to suggest that the Botha only flew underneath him as he broke away and he would not have seen it until the last moment. After being ordered to break he put the Defiant into a steep dive and was unable to recover in time to avoid colliding with the Botha. It is not known at what height the aircraft were flying but the fact that Sergeant Clifford's parachute failed to open, suggests that it was not much more than 3,000 ft.

Pilot Officer Jack Horne, staff pilot at 3 School of General Reconniassance, one of the two pilots of the Botha who was also killed 27.08.41.
Courtesy of Russell Brown

256 Squadron aircrew standing by a Defiant, with the C.O Squadron Leader Gatherall (standing third from right). Next to him on the right are Sergeants Mulligan and Parks. Flight Lieutenant West is on the wing nearest to the aircraft, sitting next to Sergeant Ellmers, Flying Officer Bragg and Sergeant Gordon Walden is at the end. Sergeant John Macdonald is standing on the left at the end.

Sergeant MacDonald probably knew Sergeant Ellmers better than anyone else because he had shared a room with him at The Corona Hotel. He recalled that during get togethers in the evenings, which were sadly only too rare, they sat around and sang the bawdy New Zealand song, 'Ring Bang Du' together. MacDonald described Sergeant Ellmers as being an excellent pilot who just loved flying. However, he said he was sometimes a little over-exuberant and should have been cautioned about his actions by someone in authority. The fact that he was never

Pilot Officer Jack Sale, second pilot of Botha who was killed in the seaside tragedy. Photo taken when he was a senior NCO.
Courtesy of Russell Brown

Another photo of Pilot Officer Jack Sale shortly after had been commissioned and wearing his officer's uniform. Courtesy of Russell Brown

Civilian mechanic, Dick Longson, employee of Brooklands Aviation who was on board the Botha and was killed. Courtesy Russell Brown

given a warning might have contributed to his death and that of four others. To remind him of their friendship, Sergeant MacDonald kept Ellmers' safety razor.

The two New Zealanders were buried in Lytham Park Cemetery where Sergeant Lincoln John Ellmers, a Nonconformist and the son of Frederick and Mabel Ellmers of Auckland, was buried in Grave 725, Section D. He was awarded the 1939–45 Star, the Aircrew Europe Star, The 1945–45 War Medal and the New Zealand War Medal. The medals were eventually forwarded to his sister in May 1950. Sergeant Noel Anthony John Clifford, a Roman Catholic and the son of Denis and Margaret Clifford of Wellington, was buried in Grave 514 Section D (RC) some distance away from his pilot. Sergeant Clifford was awarded the same medals and his mother also received them in May 1950.

As late as 1948 inquiries were being made by the Air Department in New Zealand on behalf of the families of Sergeants Ellmers and Clifford. The accident had a deep impact on those who were involved and Percy Featherstone and Albert Smith are just two people who have struggled to come to terms with what happened many years ago. However, they bore no grudge against any of the aircrew involved nor did they wish to deny them the honours they received.

Because of the secrecy and confidentiality of RAF records little is known about the service history or backgrounds of the two British pilots, except for the fact that Pilot Officer Aubrey Abraham Horne was Jewish and came from Willesden in Middlesex. He was buried in Willesden Jewish Cemetery in Grave 172, Section HX, Row 4. His co-pilot,

A view of Blackpool's Central Station where the main parts of the Botha landed after the mid-air collision. Photo taken from the air Circa 1950. Courtesy of Russell Brown

Pilot Officer Kenneth Jack Sale was from Impington in Cambridgeshire and he was buried in St Andrew's Churchyard in that village, in Grave number 50. Both officers were members of the RAF Volunteer Reserve.

The home of Mr Lionel Francis, MBE, JP, after it was hit by the stricken Defiant.

Ten year old Percy Feathstone from Yorkshire who was badly burned at Central Station, when the Botha fell upon it.

Mrs Featherstone – Percy's mother who saved him by covering him with her coat.

CHAPTER TWENTY-SIX

96 Squadron Moves to Wrexham: Autumn 1941

On the day that the court of inquiry opened into the tragedy at Blackpool, 256 Squadron lost another aircraft after Pilot Officer Reynolds experienced engine trouble while flying along the coast of North Wales near the town of Rhyl. He struggled to get it working properly but ordered his gunner, Sergeant Smith, to bale out. He parachuted to safety from 6,000 ft and landed 1/2 mile inland. Reynolds then made a forced landing on the beach close to the shoreline but was concussed by the impact. Fortunately help arrived very quickly and rescuers dragged him from the cockpit and took him to Rhyl Memorial Hospital, where he made a full recovery. Within fifteen minutes N1770 had been completely covered by the incoming tide and Reynolds was lucky to escape a watery grave.

Squadron Leader Gatherall, who had been the CO of 256 Squadron since December 1940, was posted to 54 OTU (Night-Fighter) at Church Fenton on 1 September, to train on Beaufighters. Flight Lieutenant Deanesly was promoted to Squadron Leader and given

The Squadron Petrol Bowser which served the unit at a number of airfields, probably photographed by LAC Tom Wilkinson at Ford.

his first command when he replaced Gatherall, but he was not a popular choice. A number of officers felt that the A Flight commander, Flight Lieutenant Coleman, would have made a better leader. He had a lot of charm and charisma and there was great disappointment when he was not selected.

The 9 Group AOC, Air Vice-Marshal McClaughry, made one of his regular airfield inspections on 11 September when he visited Squires Gate to interview a number of senior NCOs from 256 Squadron who had applied for commissions. Those on the list included the pilots, Sergeants Olney, Leonard and Froggart, who had flown through the period of the May blitz. Not all were succesful but those who were selected to become officers were promoted in the New Year.

On the same day Sergeant John MacDonald was posted out to become an instructor at the Beam Approach Training School, Watchfield. He had been sent on a blind landing course there between 3 and 16 August and achieved such high marks that Training Command had requested that he be posted back. He was sorry to leave 256 Squadron behind and particularly Sergeant Walden who had become a good partner and friend.

New air gunners and pilots were still arriving at 96 Squadron and amongst those who were posted in September were Pilot Officers John Birbeck, Tom Smith, Dan Maskell and George Dyke. They had all trained on Number 5 Course at 60 OTU East Fortune and were part of a group of pilots who had been together since they had learned to fly on the Tiger Moth at Hatfield. Afterwards they were posted to Canada and underwent advanced training on Harvards before returning to the UK.

The pilots and air gunners had already been formed into crews at East Fortune and Pilot Officer Birbeck flew with gunner Sergeant Stanley Sim. Pilot Officer Smith, who had a total of 135 hours flying experience, was crewed up with fellow Glaswegian Sergeant

Group shot of members passing out from 60 O.T.U. at East Fortune, including Pilot Officer Tom Smith (front row 5th from left), Sergeant Stanley Sim (back row end left), Pilot Officers John Birbeck (front row 4th from left), Maskell (front row 6th from left) of 96 Squadron. It also features Pilot Officer Eaton (middle row end right) of 256 Squadron, who having been detached to 3 Delivery Flight, was killed in 7 December 1941 in an accident involving a Dominie near Ellesmere Port.
Courtesy of Tom Smith

Andy Allen. Whereas Smith was the son of a ship's captain, Sergeant Allen came from a mining background and he claimed to be a communist. Pilot Officer Smith had his doubts because the air gunner was always playing cards for money and Solo was his favourite game. He repeatedly tried to convert Smith and other aircrew into the ways of communism but he did not have a lot of luck.

One of Pilot Officer Smith's first duties on 96 Squadron was to fly to Hucknall to collect some baffles for exhaust stubs which had been manufactured by Rolls-Royce. They had been ordered by Wing Commander Kellett some five months earlier and they were to stop soot and exhaust fumes from restricting the visibility of the crew. Smith had quite a good opinion of the Defiant but not the airfield at Cranage with its steel planking runway. He nearly came to grief several times when the steel mesh rucked up in front of him and he thought it was quite dangerous.

Not long after Pilot Officer Smith and the others arrived at Cranage, 96 Squadron had a distinguished visitor in the form of Air Marshal Sholto Douglas. The Commander-in-Chief of Fighter Command wanted to know how a fighter night worked and so a special fighter night was laid on during the day. Squadron Leader Burns and Sholto Douglas took-off in a pair of Hurricanes and the idea was that he could observe the various layers of aircraft and what went on.

After they landed Smith recalled that Burns and Sholto Douglas walked through the mess, informally dressed, with scarfs around their necks and maps stuck down their flying boots. Officers from the School of Air Navigation probably recognised Burns but not Sholto Douglas, and they looked on in horror as the two officers slunk past with their hats on the back of their heads. Someone from the ANS later complained that 96 Squadron's officers were setting a bad example to younger airmen and in future they should dress as per regulations. Smith often mused if anyone at the ANS ever realised that it was the Commander-in-Chief of Fighter Command they had complained about!

Because of the lack of enemy action in 9 Group's sectors, some pilots on 256 Squadron were posted out to Beaufighter units. At the end of September Pilot Officer Eric Raybould was approached by Squadron Leader Deanesly. He asked Raybould if he would volunteer to train on twin-engined aircraft – an offer he could not refuse.

Because Raybould had only joined the squadron in July, he was still something of a 'new boy' and he never had a regular gunner to crew up with. With the exception of Flying Officer Oakes and Sergeant Walden, he did not fly more than four sorties with anyone. As a result he missed the friendship that naturally came from the pilot/air gunner partnership and he did not have many close acquaintances on the unit. One of his few friends was Flying Officer Bob Lamb who was that much older and wiser in the ways of the world than others. He also had an 'eye' for the ladies and Pilot Officer Raybould was one of several young officers who he took under his 'wing'. Raybould learned a lot from Lamb and not all of it was about flying.

Altogether Raybould completed fifty-one sorties with 256 Squadron from Squires Gate but most involved searchlight or Army co-operation exercises. With 262 hours' flying experience he was posted to 68 Squadron at High Ercall. He never regretted his decision to move out and he had a far better time in his subsequent years in the RAF.

Night flying was a very dangerous business and every pilot knew that whatever the circumstances of an accident, luck played a great part in determining whether an airmen lived or died. An accident involving a 96 Squadron crew highlighted this phenomena when on 13 October, Pilot Officer Hilton and Sergeant Brankhurst flew into the top of Shining Tor, just 400 yards from the Cat & Fiddle Inn. The site had been the scene of several air accidents in the past and many of the people involved in them were not so fortunate. Although Hilton and his gunner were in a state of shock they walked away completely unharmed except for a few scratches. Some twelve hours after the accident they were found strolling along the Buxton – Macclesfield road, still in a state of shock but very happy to be alive.

The following day Sergeant Stanley Walker was posted to 96 Squadron from 456 Squadron at Valley, to join his third unit in 9 Group in four months. He crewed up with air gunner Sergeant Arnold who had already survived a crash landing with Pilot Officer Jacob on 31 August. Sergeant Walker's first flight was a sector reconnaissance sortie on 14 October and he completed his first operational patrol on the 20th.

There were changes ahead for both 96 and 256 Squadron personnel in October. At Squires Gate airmen who were still living in tented accommodation finally moved out into the relative comfort of requisitioned hotels. The move was only made possible because a number of personnel in 256 Squadron's A Flight were leaving to form the core of the newly commissioned 153 Squadron, which moved to Northern Ireland. The main reason for this squadron's formation and move was that the *Luftwaffe* had begun to attack the Short's aircraft factory and other industrial targets in Northern Ireland. At 1030 on 15 October its nine Defiants departed for Ballyhalbert, County Down, followed by two Harrow transports carrying personnel and ground equipment.

No. 96 Squadron was struggling to keep its pilots occupied. While they were engaged in routine training flights, many of the old hands yearned for further action. On 17 October its crews completed just five hours of day flying and eight at night; the following day they flew for only three hours. Both pilots and air gunners became quite bored and no one was looking forward to another wet cold winter at Cranage. On the 20th, however, there was an air of jubilation. After flying what turned out to be its last three sorties from Cranage, 96 Squadron received a movement order from 9 Group HQ, to be carried out with immediate effect.

An advance party was dispatched to the base at Wrexham and the next day 96 Squadron's twenty-one officers and 261 airmen began the move. Some time later its fourteen Defiants and two Hurricanes took off from Cranage for Wrexham, which was a purpose built night-fighter station with three concrete runways. It had excellent dispersals and many other facilities which Cranage lacked, but according to the wag who compiled the Squadron Diary, its main attraction was Wrexham lager, which was consumed in large quantities at the Sun Inn, one of the most popular amenities.

The airfield at Borras was a flying ground which had been endorsed by Alan Cobham in 1932 and in 1940 it was used by 5 FTS as a relief landing ground. Towards the end of that year the RAF chose it as the site of a night-fighter station and the contractors, McAlpine, began work on it in December that year. The first unit to move in was the 9 Group AACF flight and in October 1941 it was still the only permanent unit on the site, although both 229 and 315 Squadrons had used it. The facilities were a vast improvement on those at Cranage; modern living accommodation was arranged on six separate sites for WAAF and RAF personnel.

Wrexham had three concrete runways. The main one (10/28) was 4,600 ft long and 158 ft wide and it was built on foundations of shale to prevent it from flooding. Following

Sergeant Les Seales (left), a 96 Squadron air gunner who was then posted to, 275 Squadron, an Air Sea Rescue unit equipped with the Defiant at Hawkinge. Late in life he went on to become the oldest wing walker in the world. Sadly Les died in May 2004 aged 89. Courtesy of Les Seales.

the fall of Crete and the airfield at Maleme, many changes were made to the defence of the Wrexham airfield, and it incorporated many new features. In case of an assault by airborne troops the runway was mined and explosives were packed into tubes and built into foundations. The airfield was defended by three self-contained mutually supportive dispersal areas to the north, south and east which had direct communication with the control tower and a battle HQ bunker.

Some 55 acres of the airfield site was requisitioned from Wrexham Golf Club but the planners left nine holes intact. They were situated behind B Flight's dispersals and when they were off duty aircrew used to sit and watch the local dignitaries play. Most of them were well-to-do people and some were rather unpopular in the community because they openly displayed their wealth and power. When one of them was arrested for the misappropriation of petrol it caused quite a bit of amusement both amongst the locals and RAF contingency.

The move to Wrexham raised the morale of 96 Squadron crews but did not improve flight safety; only four days after arriving there the unit suffered its first accident, when Pilot Officer Pat Phoenix struck a goose-neck flare on take-off, which damaged the elevators and rudder of T3999. Phoenix found it difficult to control the Defiant and he was told by flying control to climb as high as he could, then abandon the aircraft. He managed to climb to 3,000 ft, but his air gunner, Sergeant Les Seales, had a feeling that something was wrong with him.

The Defiant was vibrating badly and when he got no response from his pilot over the intercom, Sergeant Seales decided to find out what was happening. He climbed out of the turret and walked along the wing to the cockpit, where he found that his pilot was struggling to release himself from his safety harness. He helped him to get out before walking back along the wing and jumping off. As a result of this deed Sergeant Seales was given the nickname 'Dizzy'; little did he realise that his exploit was to lead to his taking up wing walking as a pastime many years later.

Leading Aircraftsman Tom Wilkinson, an engine fitter, was posted to 96 Squadron at Wrexham from 19 Squadron, where he had worked on Spitfires. The Glaswegian was assigned to work on B Flight. He took no nonsense from anyone and told people exactly what he thought of them. That sometimes made him very unpopular and he fell out of favour with a number of senior NCOs who tried to catch him out. One gave him some technical notes and insisted that he memorize every section and then sign it to confirm that he had done so.

The Glaswegian had a feeling that he was being set up, so he refused and complained to the engineering

LAC Tom Wilkinson at Wrexham 1942. Working as an airframe fitter he joined 96 Squadron at Wrexham and served with the unit right through the war.

officer, who supported him. That angered one particular senior NCO, and he decided to put LAC Wilkinson in his place. One night a plot was hatched to catch him. The NCOs knew that he was rostered to be the duty cook for the supper. It was standard practice to heat the suppers with oxygen from the aircraft. The oxygen was used to fire up the grill plate, although it was strictly against orders.

That particular night, however, Wilkinson had a lot of work to do on an aircraft, and so he swapped cooking duties with another airman. The change was unofficial and so Wilkinson's name remained on the duty board in the crew room. Just after the other airman had begun heating the grill plate, the NCO, accompanied by a number of service police, appeared from nowhere. There was a lot of confusion but the other poor airman was taken away and eventually received a stiff sentence. Wilkinson knew that he had had a lucky escape, but despite the experience he enjoyed his time on 96 Squadron and remained with 'B' Flight for the rest of the war.

CHAPTER TWENTY-SEVEN

Business as Usual:
Conversion to Defiant Mk II

October was a good month for 68 Squadron and after a slow start the combination of the Beaufighter's power and improvements in GCI and AI radar began to take effect. On the 12th Pilot Officer Mansfield and Sergeant Janocek were scrambled from Valley when a number of enemy aircraft were seen approaching from the south. The fighter controller on duty that night was Flight Lieutenant Kemp, and as Mansfield reported over the R/T he instructed him to steer 180 degrees

Both Mansfield and Janocek were Czech and had only a limited understanding of the English language which sometimes made communications difficult. After being given the initial vector Mansfield was directed into a position astern of an enemy aircraft. As Flight Lieutenant Kemp watched the two contacts merge on his screen, Mansfield called, 'New vector, please,' and the controller directed him onto a second contact.

Flight Lieutenant Kemp observed the blips merging together and then Mansfield called again, 'New vector, please,' and he was directed onto a third enemy aircraft. Within minutes the call came again for 'New vector, please,' By now Mansfield's Beaufighter was almost half way to the Isle of Man. Kemp gave him a fourth vector and watched the contacts merge but suddenly he heard a call over the R/T, 'Engine on fire, vector for base.' Thinking that Mansfield's aircraft had been hit by enemy fire, Kemp gave him a course for Valley. He was extremely worried about the situation, and put the fire section there on alert. He was relieved when he heard that Mansfield's Beaufighter had landed safely.

The controller later learned from an intelligence officer that it was not Mansfield's Beaufighter which had been on fire but the engines of the last enemy aircraft that he had attacked. Mansfield said he had observed all four of the enemy aircraft and fired at three of them. He and Janocek were credited with two enemy aircraft destroyed and another damaged. The next day Mansfield was given the immediate award of the Czech DFC, while Sergeant Janocek received the Czech DFM.

By late 1941, with priority being given to the twin-engined night fighters, engagements with the enemy by the Defiant squadrons were rare. However, on 22 October Flight Lieutenant B.S. Coleman and Flight Sergeant Smith destroyed a Ju 88 near Woore in Shropshire, in what turned out to be 256 Squadron's last combat of the year. They had taken off from Squires Gate in Defiant T3995 and engaged and shot down Ju 88 7T + CH from KGr 606 at 2135. *Gefreiter* Hennemann and *Unteroffizier* Kolar escaped by parachute and were taken prisoner. *Oberfeldwebel* Datzert, aged twenty-six and *Feldwebel* Neukirchen were killed in the crash. The German airmen were buried with full military honours the following day at Stoke-on-Trent Cemetery. The burial party was from 5 FTS at Tern Hill, and the Station Commander was also in attendance.

The same night that Coleman and Smith won their victory Flying Officer Winward and Sergeant Wood of 68 Squadron were credited with destroying a Ju 88. On the 25th Warrant Officer Welch and Pilot Officer Bennett claimed another Ju 88 as damaged; the tide was beginning to turn in favour of twin-engined operations. Pilot Officer Shepherd and Sergeant Oxby of 68 Squadron were credited with destroying an He 111 over North Wales. Another of its crews was credited with the destruction of an He 111 on 1 November. There was not much action for the Defiant crews and some airmen thought they would probably sit out the rest of the war.

In October 256 Squadron began to equip with a number of Defiant Mk IIs, which were fitted with the more powerful Merlin XX engines rated at 1,260 hp. The new model had a pressurized fuel system and larger fuel tanks that gave it a longer range. Improvements also had been made to the design of the engine cowling and radiators, and it was supposedly capable of 313 mph at 19,000 ft. It had, however, arrived too late to influence the night air-war and was rarely flown on operations.

Sergeant Walker of 96 Squadron gained his first experience of flying a Hurricane IIc on 1 November but the sortie was only a ten-minute trip around the local area. Sergeant Haycock was one of Sergeant Walker's regular gunners on the Defiant, but he also flew with a number of others including Sergeants Scales and Lazell. He also made a number of flights with Flight Lieutenant Verity's former air gunner, Sergeant Freddy Wake. Wake's partnership with Verity had probably split up because the latter was spending more time on his duties as a flight commander.

256 Squadron's 'A' Flight gathering at Christmas Party at Jenkinson's Cafe in Blackpool late 1941.
Courtesy of Russell Brown

Aircrew from Squires Gate in a formal photo taken in late 1941, with the Mayor of Lytham, featuring an unidentified air commodore and a wing commander from the Medical Branch. Also featuring flight Lieutenant Pat Gibson (pushed up from the middle row fourth from the right), *a New Zealander who was on a course at 3 S.G.R. In the late 60s he was to become the Commanding Officer of R.A.F. Preston at Barton Hall. Two of the air gunners in the photo are Sergeant Jack Scott D.F.M.* (third from right back row) *and Sergeant Gordon Walden* (third from right middle row).
Courtesy of Russell Brown

The night of 2/3 November proved to be an eventful one for both 96 and 256 Squadrons but for all the wrong reasons. At 0140 on the 3rd, Squadron Leader Burns of 96 Squadron, with Flying Officer Smith, in Defiant T4008, was practising some radar interceptions with Hack Green GCI station when his aircraft had a complete instrument and R/T failure. They were flying over mid-Wales and running short of fuel at the time, but because the area was blacked out, searchlight homing was not available. They had little choice but to abandon the Defiant near Llanidloes; although Burns made a safe descent Smith broke an ankle on landing at Newtown.

The situation then became almost farcical when 96 Squadron sent up another two Defiants, flown by newly promoted Flight Lieutenant Verity and Sergeant Scott, to search for Burns and Smith. While they were flying over Newtown the engine of Verity's N1575 caught fire and he and Sergeant Wake had to abandon their aircraft. Sergeant Scott had taken a corporal from the ground crew to act as his observer, and when they became lost in bad weather the pilot had to stay with his aircraft. The corporal had not been given any training or instruction in parachute drill so Scott had to make a forced landing in a Shropshire field, which badly damaged N3327. It was a bleak night for 96 Squadron with two aircraft lost and another badly damaged; the only consolation was that nobody was killed.

Informal line up of airmen from 256 Squadron early in 1942, with Sergeant Greenwood (at the back), *Sergeant Joe Berry* (third from right) *and Sergeant Ray Jeffs* (second from right). *Dressed in their tunics, with shorts, football boots and sock on they appear to be impersonating the Seven Dwarfs.* Courtesy of Brian Wild

On 4 November 256 Squadron crews were taking part in a practice fighter night when, at 2240, Sergeant Berry got into difficulties: the oil pressure in the engine of Sergeant Berry's T4053 suddenly dropped. Berry ordered his air gunner, Flight Sergeant Williams, to bale out while the aircraft was still over land in the vicinity of Cleveleys at 4,700 ft. After failing to resolve the problem, Berry followed him over the side from a height of 2,700 ft and made a safe landing. The Defiant crashed a few minutes later at Shard Bridge, one mile south of Hambleton. Flight Sergeant Williams was not so lucky – his parachute was blown out to sea by strong winds and he came down in the water.

A local newspaper wrote an account of the incident but it failed to get past the Ministry of Information censor in Manchester. The report simply stated:

In the early hours of Wednesday two airmen baled out of an aeroplane, which crashed near Shard Bridge and caught fire. One of the airmen fell into the sea off Cleveleys. He was heard to shout several times. The Fleetwood lifeboat put out but a two-hour search was in vain. The body was washed up at Fleetwood later in the day.

Nevertheless it was considered too sensitive.

Sergeant Edward Vivian Williams, the son of John and Mary Williams of Southend, was buried at Lytham Park Cemetery on 8 November in Section D, Grave 227. Sergeant Berry was commissioned in September 1942 and he was destined to become one of the RAF's top wartime pilots.

Sergeant Brian Wild was posted to 256 Squadron on 7 November, the day before Sergeant Williams's funeral. He had left 456 Squadron after being sent on a twin-engined conversion course at South Cerney in October. There he had completed approximately twenty hours on Airspeed Oxfords which would give him an advantage over other pilots when the unit converted to Beaufighters. His air gunner Sergeant 'Ack' Greenwood accompanied him and they both soon made plenty of new friends.

On 13 November Pilot Officer Best, who had been posted from 256 to 153 Squadron at Ballyhalbert, was paying an unofficial visit to see a friend in Blackpool when his Defiant, V1175, crashed and he was killed instantly. Despite being ordered to return to Ballyhalbert if the weather conditions were unfavourable, Best continued and tried to land. The young pilot made his turn onto final approach too late and as the speed dropped off the aircraft went into a spin. His passenger, Sergeant John Bentley, the son of a senior officer, survived but was very badly injured. Squadron Leader Deanesly later said that he had a great deal of respect for Pilot Officer Best but he could not dismiss the possibility that the accident might have been caused by him being a little over confident. The tragedy was made worse by the fact that Best was married and had two young children who were just one and two years old. Pilot Officer Brian Bertram Horace Best was buried in Lytham St Anne's Park Cemetery in Section D, Grave 728.

No. 96 Squadron began to re-equip with Defiant Mk IIs in November. Four of them were delivered on the 18th, although the first aircraft, AA290, was delivered to the unit at Cranage on 13 October. The delivery of airframes, AA312, AA317, AA318 and AA320 was followed by another batch, including AA297, AA295, AA313, AA315, AA350, AA351 and AA352, in December. The squadron completed 295 training sorties in November but flew on only a single operational patrol.

At about this time Pilot Officer Smith and Pilot Officer Maskell drove to Sheffield, in an old Morris 8. Maskell, who lived in Handsworth Road, owned the car but as he was going on leave he lent it to Smith, who after a short stay in Sheffield, had to return to return to duty at Wrexham. Smith drove through the Peak District but as he travelled along the Buxton to Macclesfield Road, it started snowing heavily and he only just managed to reach the safety of the Cat & Fiddle Inn before the worst of the weather set in.

For seven days all the roads in the area were blocked with drifting snow and Smith had to stay put and reluctantly enjoy the hospitality of the house. When he eventually returned to Cranage Squadron Leader Burns read the Riot Act to him. He said that there was no excuse because his friend Maskell had made it back to Cranage on time by rail. He pointed out that the trains were running normally and said he should have caught one. Smith knew that would not have been possible but as the CO was going to take no further action he did not argue, but thought himself quite lucky to get away with it!

During the remainder of 1941 there was little going on as far as operations were concerned. At Wrexham 96 Squadron crews had time to reflect upon the changing fortunes of war over the past year. Of the original contingent from 422 Flight only Flight Lieutenant Verity and Sergeant Scott and Flight Sergeant Hampshire remained. Flight Lieutenant Taylor and Pilot Officer Black were the only ones left of those who had joined 96 Squadron at Cranage. Taylor, who was a former sergeant pilot and member of B Flight in January 1941, had risen through the ranks to become a flight commander.

There was a change of command in December when Squadron Leader Burns was posted to 9 Group HQ at Barton Hall and Squadron Leader R.C. Haine took over 96 Squadron. Burns had done a lot of work on 96 Squadron and he had a special relationship with its officers and airmen. He did not like the desk job at HQ and the following spring he returned to flying with his old unit.

The year ended badly for 256 Squadron. On 7 December it lost one of its most proficient pilots in an incident which was not directly connected with operational flying. Pilot Officer Eaton was considered by Squadron Leader Deanesly to be one of the squadron's finest pilots. He had trained at East Fortune and had been on the same course as a number of pilots who had been posted to 96 Squadron pilots in September, including Pilots Officers Smith and Birbeck. To improve his experience and local knowledge of the area with daylight cross-country flights, he was temporarily attached to 3 Delivery Flight at Hawarden.

On the day of the accident a howling snow storm swept in from the sea during the afternoon and flying conditions deteriorated rapidly. A number of other aircraft were also caught up in severe icing conditions and there was an electrical storm which wiped out radio communications, causing four Spitfires from 57 OTU (formerly 7 OTU) to crash. Pilot Officer Eaton was on board a de Havilland Dominie, serial number Z7354, being flown by Pilot Officer J. E. Moodie, ferrying four pilots from Lichfield back to Hawarden, when it flew into the atrocious weather.

After the Dominie was struck by lightning Moodie ordered his passengers to abandon the aircraft and three of them successfully baled out. For some unknown reason Moodie and Eaton failed to escape and both pilots were killed when the Dominie crashed at Hordley in Shropshire at 1720. The body of 20-year-old Pilot Officer George Kingston Eaton was returned to Squires Gate and then sent by rail to his home town of Norwich, where he was buried on the 12th. Pilot Officer George Kingston Eaton, The son of Frederick Ray and Ruth Evangeline, was laid to rest in St Andrew's old churchyard, near Norwich.

The year did not end well for Squadron Leader Deanesly. Apart from losing one of his best pilots, he was involved in a landing accident at Walsall. He overshot the runway on 23 December at the start of a seasonal visit to his family in the Midlands. He was not the first pilot to come to grief on Walsall's short grass runway. The pilot of a Handley Page Harrow had recently done the same thing and ended up on the main road. He claimed that engine failure had forced him to land but it was later discovered that, like Squadron Leader Deanesly, he was really visiting family and a girlfriend in the area.

The senior NCOs who remained at Squires Gate for the festive season were entertained in the officers' Mess on Christmas day. At 1400 the officers served a traditional Christmas dinner to the airmen and NCOs, before taking their own meal at 1800. For senior NCOs and officers alike it had been a turbulent year and the squadron had suffered a number of casualties. There was however, an air of optimism amongst those present, and everyone hoped for better things in the New Year.

CHAPTER TWENTY-EIGHT

Bleak Times: January 1942

In late 1941 there were a number of changes to the structure of 9 Group and the layout of its sector control system. The Valley and Andreas Sectors remained the same but the Speke Sector was absorbed into the newly created Woodvale Sector. The changes were largely the result of the opening of the airfield at RAF Woodvale and the operation of its sector control room. This was originally set up as a temporary facility in Aughton Springs School, 5 miles east of Woodvale, but it was later moved to a permanent building in Brood Lane.

In the North Midlands the Tern Hill Sector became the Atcham Sector, named after the airfield just a short distance to the south. Atcham had Wrexham under its control and it

Changes to 9 Group's Sectors made in December 1941. Courtesy of Derek Pratt and Michael Grant

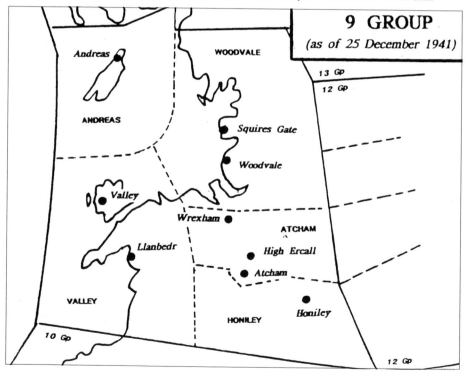

256 Squadron Defiant JT – J in the air being flown by Sergeant Ray Jeffs and Sergeant Derek Hollindrake. Taken by Sergeant Greenwood, from another aircraft, flown by Sergeant Wild. Sergeant Greenwood was killed in February 1942 while flying with Pilot Officer Olney. Courtesy of Brian Wild

was selected because activity at Tern Hill was restricted by the construction of concrete runways. The Baginton Sector, based around Coventry, was renamed the Honiley Sector.

In January 1942 there very little enemy activity, and 256 Squadron was assigned to operating convoy patrols over Liverpool Bay. It took over the responsibility for the dusk patrols from 308 Squadron which had moved into the new purpose-built airfield at Woodvale in December 1941. The first 256 Squadron sortie was flown on 9 January by Pilot Officer Johnson and Sergeant Hughes who patrolled the Mersey Estuary between 1729 and 1813. Sergeant Jefferson and Sergeant Hollindrake took over from 1727 to 1827 but like most other patrols it proved to be uneventful.

The following night 456 Squadron, based at Valley, scored its first victory after re-equipping with the Beaufighter II in September 1941, Squadron Leader Hamilton and his navigator, Pilot Officer Norris-Smith, were scrambled at 2200. A number of enemy aircraft were laying mines in the approaches in Liverpool Bay but their attempt to intercept them was plagued by technical problems at Trewan Sands GCI station. Hack Green took over the interception but it was nearly midnight before Hamilton and Norris-Smith made contact with a Do 17 at 12,000 ft. They pursued it for several minutes before they came into range and fired a burst of cannon which caused the Dornier to crash. The victory opened the book for 456 Squadron, but its crews saw very little action in the next few months.

The beginning of 1942 was very wet and for much of the time bad weather kept the aircraft on the ground. As a result there were fewer accidents and none at all involving

256 Squadron in January. Sergeant Wild was temporarily detached to 3 Delivery Flight at High Ercall from 7 to 14 February and during that short time he flew three marks of Spitfire. While he was delivering a Mk II to Llanbedr he was involved in a freakish incident that might easily have killed him.

It happened as he flew over the airfield and opened the canopy to look down through the cloud. Suddenly the canopy shot back and the catch at the top of the cupola caught his goggles on the bridge of his nose. His head was jerked back violently, causing him to lose control of the Spitfire, which plunged towards the ground. Fortunately he was flying at 3,000 ft and his height gave him the opportunity to recover, but he came very close to crashing into the ground.

On the very day that Sergeant Wild flew to High Ercall, his air gunner and good friend, Sergeant 'Ack' Greenwood was killed in a tragic accident when his aircraft crashed into the sea off the coast of Lytham. He was flying with Pilot Officer Olney, who was carrying out mock attacks on an ROC post in Defiant V1116. The aircraft failed to recover from a steep dive and although Sergeant Greenwood's body was later recovered that of Pilot Officer Olney was never found, despite an extensive search of the area.

Although Sergeant Greenwood held Australian nationality he had been born in England, at Hessle, near Hull, in September 1912. At the request of family and relatives living in England, his body was sent to Hull, where he was buried on the 11th. Sergeant Stanley Wheatley Greenwood, the son of George Albert and Harriet, was buried in Haltemprice Cemetery, Hessle, in Plot 13, Grave 1. Pilot Officer William John Paterson Olney is commemorated on Panel 71 of the Runnymede Memorial.

Sergeant Wild heard nothing about the death of his friend until he arrived back at Blackpool. As he walked into the sergeants' mess at the Fairhaven Hotel it suddenly went very quiet. A fellow sergeant pilot he knew looked around, then walked over and broke the bad news. For a while Sergeant Wild was reluctant to crew up with another air gunner but he later flew regularly with Sergeant Fred House and Sergeant 'Red' Squires.

The court of inquiry into the accident convened on 10 February and on the very same day there was another serious but unusual incident. Pilot Officer John Tweedale had just landed at Squires Gate and was in the process of taxiing to his dispersal when his Defiant collided with an open-topped Morris Standard car. Sergeant Carr, who was in the car, was killed instantly, while another senior NCO, Sergeant Dane, lost some fingers and part of his hand, which he had held up to defend himself from the aircraft's propeller.

The car was being driven by a civilian and the accident further highlighted the dangers of unauthorized vehicle movements on an operational airfield. The body of 24-year-old air gunner Sergeant Thomas Edward Carr was transported to his home city of Glasgow for burial. The son of William Adams and Mary and husband of Margaret, he was buried in Glasgow (Eastwood) Cemetery, in Section H. Grave 363.

In early 1942 96 Squadron began to operate in a different way when experimental AI radar was fitted into a number of aircraft, which were categorized as Defiant 1a. The workload of the pilots was increased, as they had not only to set up the equipment but to read off the distance and range, as well as fly the aircraft. If a contact was made it appeared as a dot in the middle of a small cathode-ray tube and as the Defiant closed in it appeared to grow wings. At a range of 250 yards the signal merged into the side of the screen and at that point the pilot should have been in a position to make an attack.

The range of the Mk VI AI radar was limited but it was approximately equal to the height at which a Defiant operated, so it was never more than 3 miles. Nicknamed 'the christmas tree' because of the shape of the aerial on the wing, the radar also had a number of other restrictions, including limiting the speed of the Defiant to approximately 180 mph. The air gunners had no control over an interception, except for acting as look-outs, and many were unhappy with their diminished role. The Defiant Mk 1a invoked very little enthusiasm amongst the aircrew in 96 Squadron. Everyone knew that the unit's future would be with twin-engined aircraft.

Newly promoted Flying Officer Smith was one of the few who thought that the pilot operated radar was operationally acceptable. He had flown a number of the Defiants to Silloth where the sets were fitted and he had talked to the 'Boffins' about it. When it was decided not to continue with the radar he flew some of the aircraft back to Silloth to have it removed. He said that the Boffins were quite dismayed about the situation and the fact that all their good work and development had been done for nothing!

Throughout January and February updated Defiant Mk II continued to arrive at Wrexham to replace 96 Squadron's Mk 1s. Many of the Mk IIs had originally been built as Mk 1s and only modified during production. Because of previous modifications that had been carried out, not all Mk IIs could take the larger fuel tanks which were normally fitted to this type. One such aircraft was AA297, which was consequently handed over to 256 Squadron to replace another Defiant which had recently been lost.

During February there was a lot of movement backwards and forwards between maintenance units to complete the modifications. As the Defiant Mk IIs arrived, some of the Mk Is, such as T3936 which left on 24 February for 60 OTU, were flown away and delivered to training units in 81 Group. Rather remarkably, all of six Defiants delivered to 96 Squadron on 15 February 1941 survived to the end and went on to serve with other units.

In February, for the second month running, 96 Squadron did not fly any operational patrols and its crews completed only one-hundred-and-five sorties in total. There were a number of minor accidents and one very serious one involving a Defiant Ia which crashed at Sealand on 17 February. Pilot Officer Potter-Smith was on an AI acceptance flight in AA319 when it stalled and crashed on the approach. The aircraft, which had only 45 hours on the airframe, burst into flames and Potter-Smith was killed instantly, while his passenger leading Aircraftsman Steed, died later that night in Chester Hospital.

Both airmen came from Wales. Pilot Officer Potter-Smith was buried in LLanshan Cemetery, Grave 135, in his home town of Cardiff. Leading Aircraftsman Steed was from Cwmbran and he was buried at Cwmbran Cemetery, Section F, Grave 7.

On 26 February 256 Squadron lost its second aircraft and crew in three weeks when a Defiant dived into the ground on a training flight. Sergeant Joyce and his gunner, Flight Sergeant Walden, were flying in T3995, a former 255 Squadron Defiant which had been damaged in July 1941 when its crew had intercepted an He 111 near Hull. The chain of events which led up to the accident began when Squadron Leader Deanesly ordered Sergeant Joyce to take off and practise circuits and landings. The weather was appalling and Corporal Metcalf, an armourer, could not believe that anyone was flying that night. Visibility was down to the absolute minimum, with the cloud almost on the ground.

As Sergeant Joyce was getting ready to go he was approached by his gunner Flight Sergeant Walden, who offered to accompany him. Walden had only recently returned from an instructors' course at East Fortune, where had met Sergeant Joyce who was then just finishing his flying training at 60 OTU. The two men were almost certainly old friends because they both came from the same area around Wanganui and had worked for New Zealand railways before the war. On his return to Squires Gate, Flight Sergeant Walden asked Squadron Leader Deanesly if he could arrange for Joyce to be posted to 256 Squadron. Somewhat reluctantly the squadron leader agreed to Walden's request and Joyce was posted in.

Sergeant Joyce had only completed his flying training twelve days before the accident and he was not familiar with either the local area or the airfield circuit. After taking off he managed to complete just a single circuit before the Defiant stalled and crashed halfway down runway 08 at 2005. Corporal Metcalf recalled that the aircraft crashed at supper time, when most accidents and incidents tended to happen.

Metcalf and several other airmen from the flight hut were the first to arrive on the scene and a sergeant took control. He shouted for everyone to lift the tail and get the gunner out before it exploded. They eventually managed to get Flight Sergeant Walden out of the wreckage but he was already dead. There was no chance of recovering Sergeant Joyce for some time because his body was buried deep in the ground beneath the wreckage. Corporal Metcalf described it as the most emotive incident that he experienced at Squires Gate because Sergeant Joyce should never have been ordered to fly in such conditions.

The official accident report said that Sergeant Joyce had made a faulty approach and crashed in bad visibility while trying to land in difficult weather conditions. The Form 1180 also stated that the Station Commander had made an 'error of judgement' when he authorized the flight. Squadron Leader Deanesly later admitted that he was partly responsible and said he had failed to realize just how extreme the weather conditions were, in relation to Sergeant Joyce's experience.

Sergeant Joyce had passed out of Number 2 EFTS, New Plymouth, in March 1941 and completed a total of just 196 flying hours. Flight Sergeant Walden had recorded 222 hours as an air gunner and was credited with flying on sixteen operational sorties. Walden, who was married, had embarked for England on 6 October 1940. His ship was the *Mataroa*, and he was in the same batch of airmen as Sergeants Ellmers and Clifford, who had been killed in the previous August. Like them and several other of their countrymen, Sergeant Joyce and Flight Sergeant Walden were buried with full military honours in Lytham Park Cemetery. Walden has been described by his former pilot on 256 Squadron, Sergeant John MacDonald, as fearless and cheerful and he was very sad to hear of his death.

Twenty-two-year-old Sergeant Francis William Joyce, the son of Frank and Annie Maud of Wanganui, was laid to rest in Section D , Grave 729. Twenty-six-year-old Flight Sergeant Gordon Fitzgerald Walden, from Palmerston North, the son of Richard and Ada Evelyn and husband of Mrs Vera Olive Walden, was laid to rest in Section D, Grave 730, next to his friend.

At Wrexham a number of 96 Squadron's longest-serving pilots were being posted out during this period, amongst them Flight Sergeant Hampshire and Sergeant Scott. Hampshire, one of the original pilots from 422 Flight, was promoted to warrant officer in February 1942. He was then posted to 60 OTU at East Fortune as a flying instructor, before being commissioned in July. After being posted to 286 Squadron at Zeal, he was involved in a flying accident at Locking and he spent a year in hospital. He later recovered and was given a post with the 2nd TAF as an administrator, before being finally discharged in 1946.

Sergeant Scott, also one of the first pilots to join 96 Squadron from 422 Flight, was posted to 245 Squadron which was operating Hurricanes from Middle Wallop. He was commissioned soon afterwards but was killed in action on 19 August 1942. The body of Sergeant Alfred Scott was never recovered and he is commemorated on the Runnymede Memorial on Panel 71.

Of the original 96 Squadron pilots from December 1940, only the former senior NCO pilot, Flight Lieutenant Taylor remained. Flight Lieutenant Victor Verity was posted out to the Middle East in March, and he was very bored and very seasick during a long voyage which lasted thirteen weeks. Before he left 96 Squadron Verity managed to get involved in a controversial incident concerning Flying Officer Smith, who was involved in a forced landing on 17 March.

On that night Smith had taken-off in a Defiant Mk. II, AA317, on a sortie to practise GCI interceptions. His passenger was Flight Sergeant Motley who had recently been involved in an accident and was being given flying experience to renew his confidence. However his nerves were tested to the limit again when a hydraulic pipe burst on take-off and Smith was forced to return immediately because the engine overheated. The undercarriage failed to lower but Flying Officer Smith managed to pump it down using the emergency handle.

There was hardly any hydraulic pressure left and with the engine about to seize up and without the aid of the flaps, Smith got the Defiant on the ground. It was a heavy, bumpy landing but at least both he and his passenger walked away from it, despite the fact that Smith banged his head on the instrument panel as they touched down. There was some damage to the Defiant but it was more or less intact and Smith was therefore surprised when he was called to the Station Commander's Officer for a 'Ticking Off'.

Wing Commander Tomlinson told Smith that because of his negligence the Defiant had been badly damaged. Tomlinson said he had been informed by 9 Group that Flying Officer Smith should receive a severe reprimand and have his log book endorsed. Smith protested but the wing commander claimed he was also not happy about it, but it had to be done. He then told Smith that he had been reprimanded and so he should leave his office at once. Flying Officer Smith was puzzled by the whole business and he did not discover the truth and Flight Lieutenant Verity's part in the affair for several months.

The last of 96 Squadron's remaining Hurricanes left Wrexham at around this time and one of the final aircraft to depart was V7732 on 28 March. It had been on the strength of 96 Squadron since February 1941 and after being passed on to 59 OTU it went on to serve with 263, 137 Squadrons. The Hurricane which had first been delivered to 48 MU in December 1940, was not struck-off charge until January 1945. Such was the strength of the Hurricane's robust design and many pilots and ground crew on 96 Squadron were sorry to see the type leave Wrexham.

Over at Squires Gate, 256 Squadron pilot Sergeant Joe Berry was commissioned on 14 March and he used the occasion to keep a long standing promise to his fiancée, Joyce. The couple had first met when they had worked at a branch of the Inland Revenue in Nottingham. They had been engaged since August 1940 when he had joined the R.A.F. Volunteer Reserve and Pilot Officer Berry and Joyce were finally married on 19 March.

The happy occasion was held in their home town in the Midlands and so few of his colleagues from 256 Squadron were able to attend the ceremony.

The following month there were major changes in 256 Squadron. Squadron Leader Deanesly was posted out and replaced by Wing Commander Adams. The squadron leader noted his departure by making an entry in the Operational Record Book on 8 March, which also recorded the arrival of some Wellingtons from Cranwell. He wrote that he was 'extremely sorry to be making this my last entry for the squadron' and he wished everyone 'Good Luck!' He was promoted to wing commander and posted to Castle Camps in Cambridgeshire as the CO.

Sergeant Cornwall with Flight Sergeant Haycock over Crew during an air defence exercise on 26 February 1942. A rare shot of Defiant MkIa equipped with A.I. radar MkVI. Note 'Christmas Tree' aerial on the starboard wing, leading edge. Aircraft coded ZJ-T.

CHAPTER TWENTY-NINE

Re-equiping With Beaufighters: April 1942

On 1 April Air-Vice Marshal McClaughry visited Woodvale on what was probably his final tour of inspection before taking up a new post in the Middle East as AOC Egypt. He welcomed the Polish pilots of 315 Squadron and said goodbye to those of 308 Squadron, whom they were replacing. A few weeks later he handed over the command of 9 Group to Air Commodore William Dickson. He took over during an interesting period, as 96 and 256 Squadrons prepared to convert to the Beaufighter.

On 13 April an Airspeed Oxford arrived at Wrexham for 96 Squadron pilots to train on and practise flying a multi-engined aircraft. The Defiant was rapidly approaching the end of its front-line service as a night fighter, but it had served well in a role for which it had not originally been designed. There remained a few technical problems, but when serviceability allowed it could still be flown in large numbers and put on a show.

During the afternoon of the 22nd, a formation flight from 256 Squadron was made up of nineteen Defiants, which must have been an impressive sight for those who witnessed the fly past from the ground. It was a busy day, especially as the Chief Constable of Lancashire turned up at Squires Gate, accompanied by thirty policemen. He announced that they were expecting to see a demonstration of how to rescue aircrew from a crashed aircraft, but nobody was expecting them. As might be expected, there was a bit of confusion before the practice rescue could be laid on and the police were satisfied.

For the moon period from 28 April, a minimum of two aircraft were kept on a state of immediate readiness and four others on thirty minutes' standby. That evening Woodvale Sector Operations informed 256 Squires Gate that there was enemy activity in the area and all training flights were cancelled. The following night training was back on, but Pilot Officer Jones was taken over by a 12 Group sector controller for operations while he was flying near Dishforth.

This was during the period of the so called 'Baedeker' raids, named after Carl Baedeker's tourist guide of Britain. The attacks were mainly against cathedral cities such as Canterbury, Exeter and York. Pilot Officer Jones was given a vector towards an enemy aircraft which had bombed York and although his Defiant passed very close to it, neither he or his gunner saw it. Seconds later, there was a burst of fire and Jones had the frightening experience of seeing tracer heading towards them. Fortunately it missed and they were able to return safely to Squires Gate.

There was a practice fighter night on 30 April involving both 96 and 256 Squadrons, during another night of increased activity by the *Luftwaffe*. No. 96 Squadron started the night with an exercise over Wrexham but later its pilots were ordered to patrol the Liverpool area. Twelve of its Defiants were involved in the operation but none made contact with the enemy. No. 256 Squadron also carried out patrols that night with twelve Defiants but none of its crews saw any action either.

The fact that 96 Squadron aircraft were already airborne suggests that it was pursuing a new policy which was aimed at getting aircraft into the air before being given the order by 9 Group HQ. As former Valley sector controller Sergeant Frank Cheesman has pointed out, only the group controller could authorize a night fighter squadron to take part in operations and there were often lengthy delays before orders were issued for them to take off. The squadrons were however allowed to organize training flights and exercises without the permission of anyone at 9 Group HQ. To the get around the problem it became standard practise for them to take-off on the pretence of an exercise. With the night-fighters already airborne, their crews were in a better position to catch the enemy over the target.

At Squires Gate 256 Squadron had experienced an unprecedented two months without a serious accident but that happy run was broken on 1 May when a Fairey Battle crashed on take-off. The engine cut out on Sergeant Cotterill just as he became airborne, and he crashed on to a hangar near A Flight's dispersals. He escaped without injury but the Battle was badly damaged, with its undercarriage ripped off and engine shock loaded. An investigation revealed that the accident was the result of a Glycol leak, which had caused the engine to overheat.

96 Squadron 'B' Flight personnel at Wrexham in June 1942. Sergeant Stan Walker is 3rd from left with his Radar Observer, Sergeant Bishop, 7th from left.

96 Squadron Beaufighter at Wrexham in May 1942. Note that the aircraft in the background is still in 307 Squadron markings 'EW – L'. Courtesy Group Captain R.C. Haine, D.F.C.

Personal aircraft of then Squadron Leader Haine, D.F.C., C.O. of 96 Squadron, Beaufighter 'ZJ – M'. Courtesy of Group Captain R.C. Haine, D.F.C.

Despite the fact that it was about to re-equip with twin-engined aircraft, 96 Squadron continued to receive deliveries of Defiant Mk IIs. Most of them remained at Wrexham for only a short time. At least three of them were handed over to 256 Squadron, and others were sent back to maintenance units and eventually assigned to other units for special duties, Air Sea Rescue and telecommunications duties.

On 2 May 96 Squadron received its first Beaufighter Mk II. It began to convert to the type seven days later. Most of the aircraft had been in service with 307 Squadron at Exeter; the Polish unit was exchanging them for the Mk VI. The Mk II had a violent swing to port on take-off and the pilot had no control over the tail-wheel. Some pilots have claimed that they could wear out a tail-wheel tyre in just a couple of landings. A new type of ribbed tyre was later introduced which corrected the problem of drag, and in later models the tail-wheel was controlled through the rudder.

Squadron Leader Haine, the CO, flew in a Beaufighter on the 4th and was pleasantly surprised by its performance. He thought that the Mk II, with its 1,280 hp Rolls-Royce Merlin XX engines, compared favourably with the Mk I and it might not be the killer that its reputation had suggested. He did not remain at Wrexham long enough to experience 96 Squadron becoming operational with the aircraft, however. Within the month Wing Commander Bobby Burns returned to 96 Squadron and resumed his command.

Between 4–14th May a number of 96 Squadron's pilots were sent on a Beam Approach Training Course at Collyweston near Stamford. Amongst those who attended the course were Flying Officers Smith, Maskell, Dyke and Birbeck. All the 96 Squadron pilots were graded 'Above Average' but Flying Officer George Dyke was judged to be 'Exceptional'. His ability was such that it was decided that he should be retained as an instructor and subsequently 96 Squadron lost a good pilot.

The first Beaufighter was delivered to 256 Squadron at Squires Gate on 8 May and two more aircraft followed within a week. It was to be equipped with the much more favourable Beaufighter Mk. 1 fitted with Bristol Hercules engines. During the conversion all the flights were completely reorganized and there was a huge turnover of personnel in the coming weeks as the squadron also prepared to move out of Squires Gate.

To get their hands on the controls of a Beaufighter, pilots had to complete ten hours on the Airspeed Oxford, followed by eight hours on the Blenheim. Although the first Oxford had arrived at Wrexham in April, the first Blenheim, K7117, was not allocated to 96 Squadron until 6 May. Sergeant Walker had his first flight in an Oxford on 23 May with Squadron Leader Haine but it was another two weeks before he got to fly in a Beaufighter. Most of the pilots were looking forward to flying the Beaufighter but not all of them would make it and 96 Squadron's last accident involving the Defiant denied one of them at the last moment.

On 27 May Pilot Officer Bowran was carrying out an army co-operation exercise on a bombing range near Stafford. While he was 'beating up' a gun post his aircraft went into a half-role and flew into a hillside. Bowran was killed instantly but his air gunner, Pilot Officer Cadman, was saved because the turret detached from the aircraft and rolled away. Those first on the scene opened the turret expecting to find a mangled body inside and were quite astonished to find Cadman alive.

Flying Officer Tom Smith was a good friend of Flying Officer Bob Bowran and he led the burial party and laid the wreath at Cannock Chase War Cemetery. Many men from 96 Squadron attended the funeral but the parade was carried out by airmen from a local RAF unit. Flying Officer Robert Bernard Bowran, the son of Thomas and Nellie Eliza and husband of Margaret, was buried in Plot 2, Row A, Grave 2.

Such was the condition of Pilot Officer Cadman that he was not expected to live and a collection was made for a wreath. When he began to recover it was hung inside a telephone kiosk near the officers' mess, in the hope that it would not be needed. After extensive surgery to his face and jaw Cadman made a full recovery and he was sent to a holding unit at Brighton. When he arrived at the hotel he walked straight into some antics taking place between rival groups of officers and was immediately thrown out.

Probably feeling vulnerable and a little confused after his ordeal, Cadman did not know what to do, so he caught a train and ended up back at Wrexham. It was a good move because only minutes after he left, the hotel was hit by a bomb and a number of airmen were killed. Two days later a signal arrived at Wrexham informing 96 Squadron that Pilot Officer Cadman was dead. The news was quite appropriate because the wreath intended for his funeral remained hanging in the telephone kiosk and Pilot Officer Cadman was able to see it before it was finally thrown out.

No. 96 Squadron flew its final sortie with the Defiant on 30 May. Sixteen months after the unit had first been equipped with the type, its operational service came to an end. Its phasing out meant that air gunners were surplus to requirements and decisions had to be made about their future. When AI had first been introduced in 1940, air gunners had been simply retrained to operate it, but by 1942 there was a selection procedure. The main choice for air gunners was to remain in that aircrew category and transfer to another command or to face a selection board and train for another role in Fighter Command.

The category which air gunners could normally apply to join was radio operator (air). Several changes were made to this category by Air Ministry orders and it is not our aim to detail them all. Suffice it to say that up to July 1941 the senior NCO or officer who operated the AI radar were classed in the category radio operator (air). After that they were classed as observer (radio).

Ironically, had things worked out differently many air gunners might never have had to choose. They might have remained in that role, because during this period two Beaufighters, which were designated as the Mk V, were fitted with a four-gun Boulton & Paul power-operated turret. One of the experimental Beaufighters served on 29 Squadron, but although extensive trials were carried out, the type never entered operational service.

For those air gunners in 96 Squadron who wanted to retrain as observers, an Anson arrived at Wrexham on 15 May, fitted out with equipment to test their aptitude. One of the ten air gunners who passed the selection board was Sergeant Stanley Sim, who had regularly flown with Pilot Officer Birbeck. He flew with 96 Squadron for the last time on 6 May and was then sent on a six-week navigation course, which was followed by intensive training on AI radar at an OTU. He did not return to operational flying until 30 June 1943 when he joined 153 Squadron.

Sergeant Willie Streeter, who had performed so well with Sergeant Scott on the night of 7/8 May, was also selected for training. He was posted out but he was destined to be reunited with a former 96 Squadron pilot, Sergeant Stanley Walker the following year. Some air gunners were lucky enough to remain on Defiants and Sergeant Les 'Dizzy' Seales was posted to 277 Squadron. It was an Air Sea Rescue unit based at Shoreham but Sergeant Seales joined a detachment at Hawkinge. He remained as a gunner/observer in the specialist Air Sea Rescue role for the rest of the war.

At Squires Gate 256 Squadron air gunners went through a similar procedure. Sergeant Derek Hollindrake was one of those selected for training as an observer. After completing his training he was also reunited and crewed up with his old friend Pilot Officer Brian Wild from 256 Squadron.

Many of the remaining air gunners in 96 and 256 Squadrons were sent to 1484 Flight at Driffield for further gunnery training. After completing a refresher course the majority were then posted to OTUs, before joining squadrons in Bomber Command. Within two months a number of them had been killed on operations, and amongst the first was Flight Sergeant Fred House.

After leaving 256 Squadron he had been posted to 10 OTU at Abingdon and he was killed on the night of 25/26 June 1942 in Whitley P4944, which was lost over Hamburg. His crew had not even finished their training programme but were taking part in the last '1,000 bomber' raid on Bremen. Like many others from OTUs they were there to make up the numbers, and Bomber Command lost fifty aircraft that night. The body of Flight Sergeant Frederick Clifford House, the son of George Henry and Emily, was never found and he is commemorated on the Runnymede Memorial, Panel 74. He was from Southend on Sea and he was married to Lottie Beatrice House.

Just a short while later another former 256 Squadron air gunner, Flight Sergeant Reg Adams, was killed when his Halifax bomber

Sergeant Derek Hollindrake, air gunner on 256 Squadron. He later became a Radar Observer and flew Mosquitos with fellow northerner Brian Wild. They remained good friends after the war. Courtesy of Brian Wild

was shot down by a *Luftwaffe* night fighter over Holland. Having been crewed up with Flight Lieutenant West in 256 Squadron and with two victories to his credit, he and his pilot had been transferred to 153 Squadron in October 1941. When it began to re-equip with the Beaufighter, Adams was undecided as to what he should do.

For some reason he was reluctant to apply to become an observer and as a result he was transferred to Bomber Command. After undergoing a conversion course he was posted to 405 Squadron (Royal Canadian Air Force) which had recently converted to the Halifax Mk II at Pocklington, near York. On the night of 29/30 June his aircraft was lost whilst attacking targets in Bremen and all the members of his crew perished. Despite the fact that he had been recommended for a decoration and a commission, in the end he did not receive either. Flight Sergeant Reginald Thomas Adams, the son of of William and Ethel of Marten in Wiltshire, was buried in Weststellingwerf (Noordwolds) Protestant churchyard, Plot G, Row 1, Grave 2.

CHAPTER-THIRTY

96 Squadron:
The End of an Era

At Wrexham 96 Squadron's conversion to the Beaufighter was not completed without further problems and Flying Officer Smith encountered some difficulties on landing during his first solo flight on 6 June. He found it very hard to judge the round out on the approach and he was forced to fly around in the circuit. Every time he tried to land he either came in too steeply or too flat and several times the aircraft bounced back into the air.

Squadron Leader Haines, who had taken Smith on his first flight in a Beaufighter prior to him going solo, came to the rescue with a portable VHF radio. He reassured Smith and talked him down, telling him 'Smithy … you can't stay up there all night because it's time for tea!' After a sortie lasting forty-five minutes Flying Officer Smith made a safe landing and he was greatly relieved to be back on 'Terra Firma' in one piece.

On 20 June Pilot Officer Hyam had problems taking-off and he failed to become airborne in T3414. The Beaufighter smashed through a hedge and crossed a main road before it burst into flames as it ended up in a pond. Sergeant Walker was one of several pilots who were in the flight hut at the time, so he and a few others quickly mounted their bicycles and were first on the scene. They found Hyam and his radio operator, Sergeant Busby, hidden behind a large tree, trying to keep out of the way of exploding ammunition.

The Beaufighter was a write-off and it was alleged that the accident was caused by Pilot Officer Hyam trying to take off with the propellers in course pitch. Sergeant Walker was involved in the subsequent investigation because he had flown the aircraft in the morning before Hyam had attempted to take off in the afternoon. Walker was accused of leaving the controls in the wrong setting, but it was something that he strongly denied. Even if he had, Pilot Officer Hyam should have noticed it during his cockpit checks. During the 1,844 hours which it took 96 Squadron to convert to the Beaufighter, there were many other minor and some more serious incidents.

On 16 July, even before it was declared fully operational on the Beaufighter IIf, 96 Squadron was given the task of detailing two aircraft to provide air cover during a royal visit. The King and Queen visited RAF High Ercall and the aircraft factory at Broughton near Chester, where they were given a guided tour by the General Manager, Mr Duncan. Four days after the visit 96 Squadron was finally declared fully operational on the Beaufighter.

Flying Officer Smith left the Squadron in August after being medically downgraded and taken off flying duties because he had suffered migraine and 'black outs'. His condition probably started after he banged his head on the instrument panel during the forced landing at Cranage earlier that year. The problem began to manifest itself in spells of blindness and on one occasion he very nearly walked into the tail of a Blenheim which was moving and preparing to take off. He was given the aircrew Medical Category A4 HBH which effectively meant he could fly as long as there was another pilot to accompany him. After leaving 96 Squadron he was given a number of jobs including a spell as the Commanding Officer of a gunnery range at Valley.

After being promoted, Flight Lieutenant Smith was appointed as a Permanent President to the Court of Inquiry in Training Command and he was based at Avening near Aston Down. His main duty was to investigate aircraft accidents involving 81 Group. One day something happened which reminded him of his accident at Cranage and since he had access to most of the Form 765 Accident Reports he decided to look it up.

What he found amazed him because the Accident Report had been written by Flying Officer Verity who had been the Acting Flight Commander of 'B' Flight at the time. Smith had been in 'A' Flight and technically Verity had no authority over him, but on the Form 765 he had claimed that the accident was the result of 'Pilot Error'. Verity stated that Smith had landed across wind without the use of flaps on a runway that was not in use and the Engineering Officer had added there were no technical defects.

At the time of the accident neither Verity nor the Engineering Officer had spoken to him about what had happened. As a result of what he found Smith's estimation of both of them went down a notch or two. Flight Lieutenant Smith still respected Verity as a pilot and for what he had done, but he thought the New Zealander was sometimes rather arrogant. As a reaction to what he found Smith very carefully cut out the 'endorsement' and removed every trace of it from his log book.

During September 96 Squadron was seven pilots below strength and flying was reduced to a bare minimum. One reason for the shortage was because some pilots had been injured but not necessarily in accidents involving flying. The unfortunate Pilot Officer Phoenix, who had already been hurt in October 1941 when he had escaped from a Defiant, was one of them. He fractured his leg in a motor-cycle accident and sustained a number of other serious injuries.

No. 96 Squadron was forced to leave Wrexham because the runway was in urgent need of repair so 'A' Flight moved out to Valley. Its crews took part in an air firing course and afterwards on 6 September the flight moved to Honiley in Warwickshire on detachment. On the same day there was a terrible accident involving Flying Officer Birbeck and Sergeant Nicholas who were taking off for Honiley in Beaufighter T3046. Almost as soon as the aircraft was airborne it began to behave strangely. It climbed into the air at a very steep angle before going into a stall and flattening out before crashing to the ground.

Amongst those who watched the Beaufighter take off were Leading Aircraftsman Tom Wilkinson and his friend Bob Gun. They watched in disbelief as the aircraft fell to earth very close to the spot where they were standing. Wilkinson said the Beaufighter 'pancaked' to the ground and exploded almost immediately, so they knew there was little chance that anyone could get out alive. One officer approached the wreckage on his motor-bike in a half-hearted rescue attempt, but it was more for effect than anything else. What stuck in Wilkinson's memory was a bicycle wheel sticking up out of the rear cockpit. It belonged to Sergeant Nicholas and Wilkinson claimed it made a macabre sight amongst the burnt out wreckage of the Beaufighter.

Flying Officer John Birbeck, the twenty-two year old son of Major Henry Anthony Birbeck, MC and Cybil Birbeck, was buried in West Acre churchyard, in Castle Acre, Norfolk. Twenty-nine-year-old Sergeant Dillwyn LLoyd Nicholas, the son of David and Mary Nicholas, was buried in Cwmavon (St. Michael) churchyard, Glamorganshire.

Although he did not hear about the death of his old friend straight away, Flight Lieutenant Smith was shocked when he found out. He had been quite close to Birbeck and on several occasions they had flown to Massingham and visited his parents' home. They used to 'buzz' the Birbeck family home, flying very low over the house and that was the signal for a car to be sent to Great Massingham to collect them.

Flight Lieutenant Smith had no more idea of what had happened than anyone else but in his capacity as an accident investigator, he later came across another accident involving a Beaufighter which had crashed in similar circumstances. He discovered that it was possible to connect the tail trim to one of two positions, and if the wrong end of the quadrant was connected, the tail trim was effectively reversed. That had been the cause of a crash which Flight Lieutenant Smith investigated but he had no evidence to prove that was what had happened to Birbeck's aircraft.

The Beaufighter had undergone extensive maintenance in the hangar at Wrexham, so it was possible that some adjustments had been made to the controls. Smith claimed that Flying Officer Birbeck was an excellent pilot and he would not have been foolish enough to overlook any of his preflight checks. The results of the court of inquiry were never made public and nobody on 96 Squadron ever heard what its finding were.

Sergeant Stan Walker at the controls of a Rapide at high Ercall during a detachment to 3 Delivery Flight in 1942. Like a number of others in 9 Group he was given a spell as a ferry pilot to broaden his experience and help move both aircraft and crews to other units. Courtesy of Stan Walker

Towards the end of September 96 Squadron re-equipped with the Beaufighter Mk. VI fitted with more powerful 1,650 hp Bristol Hercules engines. Most pilots were glad to get rid of the MkIIs. On 20 October the remainder of 96 Squadron moved to Honiley in Warwickshire but with regular detachments being sent to Tangmere and Ford on the south coast.

Sergeant Stanley Walker was posted to 3 Delivery Flight at High Ercall in November and began a six months tour ferrying and delivering aircraft. He often flew with the CO, Squadron Leader Brindon, in the flight's Dominie 'Doris'. The CO was a bit of an eccentric and always wore his trilby when they were taking off. Assisted by the 'Ferry Pilot's Notes' Sergeant Walker was to fly many different types of aircraft. On 18 April he flew Oxford HM 950 from Wrexham to Ballyhalbert with Sergeant Bennet and a Polish pilot, to pick up two Beaufighters, which were to be flown to Bicester. But for the luck of winning the toss of a coin it could have been his last flight.

Because Sergeant Walker had flown the Oxford to Ballyhalbert it was agreed that he and the Polish pilot would fly the Beaufighters while Sergeant Bennett would return in the Oxford. One of the aircraft was near the flight office, while the other was over the far side of the airfield. Sergeant Walker and the Pole tossed a coin to see who would fly which aircraft, agreeing that the winner would take the nearest and save themselves a long walk. Having won the toss, Sergeant Walker said that he would take-off and climb overhead, formate on the Oxford and wait for his colleague to join them.

All went to plan until the three aircraft were in the vicinity of the Calf of Man, when Sergeant Walker noticed that the other Beaufighter was slowly descending. He closed in on the Beaufighter and noticed that the Pole had his head held down and he did not respond to any messages or visual signals. The aircraft eventually crashed into the sea and Sergeant Walker maintained his station overhead while Sergeant Bennett alerted search and rescue. A ship left a convoy heading out of Liverpool and picked up the body of the Pole but by the time he was landed at Ramsay he was already dead.

Although he never found out what had happened to the other Beaufighter, Sergeant Walker thought that the Polish pilot must have been overwhelmed by toxic fumes of some kind. He considered himself to be very lucky in not getting that Beaufighter to fly back, but he also felt bad about what had happened. Two days later on 20 April he was posted to the OTU at Charter Hall near Berwick, prior to being posted overseas. There he crewed up with former 96 Squadron air gunner, Sergeant Willie Streeter and within a short while they flew out to Sicily and joined 255 Squadron.

At Honiley the black paint was removed from 96 Squadron's Beaufighters and every part and rivet was stripped down to the bare metal. Former LAC Tom Wilkinson recalled that he personally stripped and painted most of 'B' Flights aircraft helped only by a Corporal Ridley. The aircraft were taken into the hangar one by one and paint stripper was applied to aid the removal of the black paint. Then the aircraft was washed down before a deoxidisation agent was applied and the undercoat and the top coat were sprayed on. The aircraft were finished in the standard camouflage pattern, which unlike the overall black sceme made 96 Squadron's role as a night-fighter unit much less obvious.

The move to Honiley not only changed 96 Squadron's identity but ended its association with the North-West of England. As far as 96 Squadron is concerned Honiley was just another phase in the units history and some memories and anecdotes from its time there are worth recalling. LAC Tom Wilkinson had some happy times there and he remembered one night when everyone was busy on the flight lines and they left a young newly trained airman to answer the phone in the office. When it rang a voice at the other end said, 'Mother is resting – Babs is ill'.

This was a coded message from 9 Group HQ at Barton Hall, to inform the squadron that the air defences and balloon barrage were stood down. The young airman did not know that and when the others returned he seemed eager to tell them that he had had a phone call. He said someone had rang to say that his mother was well and having a good rest. The news about 'Babs' puzzled him, but eventually came to the conclusion that she must be the friend of his sister who had been unwell for some time!

On 7 November 96 Squadron lost a Beaufighter and its crew on a training flight after the aircraft's instruments failed. Flying Officer Tony Voller, with his navigator Sergeant Busby, had taken off in X7920 from Honiley at 2200 hours but within ten minutes they suffered a total failure of the air speed indicator, rate of climb indicator and the altimeter. The AI Radar also failed and there were anxious calls over the radio between Flying Officer Voller and those on the ground.

LAC Wilkinson was in the hangar finishing off painting one of the last Beaufighters and he heard much of the chatter over the R/T. As it was a lonely outpost he had arranged for one of the signals bods to fix up a radio so that he knew who was flying and what was going on. He recognised Flying Officer Voller's voice and there was a lot of talk about whether the pitot head cover had been left on. Eventually it all went quiet and he suspected the worst, although he did not find out what had happened until the next day.

The Beaufighter crashed two miles west of Wellesbourne at 2200 hours and it is possible that Flying Officer Voller was trying to land there. A signal requesting a searchlight canopy was sent immediately Voller got into difficulties but the ground radio operator was accused off failing to take action. At the court of inquiry it was stated that the signal arrived only minutes before the aircraft crashed and so it made little difference anyway.

Flying Officer William Edward Tony Voller was buried in Balsall Cemetery Warwickshire, South-East Corner, Row P, Grave 1. He was well liked and remembered by many for his youthful looks and brilliant blue eyes. The Commonwealth War Graves Commission records 'Sergeant' Busby as a pilot officer and so it seems that he had just been commissioned. He had previously escaped death on 20 June when his Beaufighter had crashed on take-off with Pilot Officer Hyam at the controls, but the second time around he was not so lucky. Pilot Officer Harold Edward Busby is buried in Bampton Cemetery near Witney in Oxfordshire in Grave 11B.

There was little excitement for the crews of 96 Squadron throughout the winter but on 20 February 1943 the unit celebrated Red Army Day with a fly-past over Birmingham. A number of crews were detached to Tangmere and there were other detachments to Ford. It was a time of uncertainty for aircrew and ground crews alike as rumours abounded about its future role.

In June 1943, Wing Commander Burns was posted out and replaced by Wing Commander Edward Crew, DFC. He was very much in the same mould as his predecessor and had served in 604 Squadron with the legendary John 'Cat's Eyes' Cunningham. Wing Commander Crew was posted to 96 Squadron from 85 Squadron, in which he had been a Flight Commander. At about the same time as he took over command, 96 Squadron was equipped with the Mosquito NF XII, although a number of Beaufighter Mk. VIs were retained. It was not known for where 96 Squadron was destined but rumours claimed that it was being sent to North Africa.

Some aircraft and crews were dispatched overseas and Flying Officer Maskell flew a Beaufighter out to Gibraltar but ran out of fuel. It was probably not his fault and the fuel endurance allowed little room for the slightest navigational error or bad weather. He could not make enough height to reach the runway at Gibraltar and crash landed on the wrong side of the Spanish border near Algeciras. Maskell was quite badly injured and although he was officially interned he was given good medical treatment and looked after by some nuns. When he was well enough he was taken to the border and allowed to slip back into Gibraltar, from where he was returned to the Home Establishment.

LAC Tom Wilkinson said that most of the airmen and senior NCOs on the squadron was sent to a holding camp at West Kirby, near Liverpool. Everyone could see the ship out in the Mersey, that they were told they would soon be boarding and everything was packed up ready to go. To keep them occupied airmen were drilled and given regular sessions of P.T. and there was also an evasion exercise. Airmen were dropped from a lorry some distance from the camp and had to find their own way back and avoid the police and guards, without money or ID cards. Despite that many airmen started to get restless and were keen to start their voyage to their unknown destination, wherever it may have been!

Then the word began to go around that the orders had been changed and they were staying in England after all! Within a few days a new posting was confirmed and in August 96 Squadron was sent north to Church Fenton. There it was equipped with the Beaufighter Mk. VI again, but the aircraft had been passed on from another squadron and were in a bad state of repair. There was a turnover in the squadron's personnel as well and Wing Commander Crew was one of the few officers to survive the move. The squadron

Wing Commander Crew's personal Mosquito 'ZJ – Y' after 96 Squadron re-equipped with the Mosquito NF XII in June 1943 at Honiley. Maintained and photographed by LAC Tom Wilkinson.
Courtesy of Tom Wilkinson

*Line up of 96 Squadron's Mosquito NFXIII at Ford in 1944. Much improved equipment over the
Defiant with which the unit had struggled at Cranage.* Courtesy of Tom Wilkinson

remained largely inactive at Church Fenton until it moved north to Drem on 2 September
1943, where it was to be re-equipped with the Mosquito NF XIII. Throughout its time at
Drem 96 Squadron had a number of aircraft detached to Peterhead and Sumburgh in the
Shetland Islands. The squadron moved south again to West Malling on 8 November 1943
and in January 1944 it scored its first victory since May 1941. On 2 January Flight
Lieutenant Head destroyed an FW 190 and on the 4th Wing Commander Crew destroyed
an Me 410 and damaged another. No. 96 Squadron was back in business and it was the
beginning of an upturn in its fortunes.

When the V1 weapon was launched against the south of England on 12 June 1944, none
of 9 Group's units were involved in the defensive operation. No. 96 Squadron was still a
night-fighter unit but by then it was part of 12 Group and based on the south coast at Ford.
It was equipped with the Mosquito NF XIII and still under the leadership of Wing
Commander Crew it took part in a number of Anti-diver operations against the V 1. In
June 1944 its crews destroyed 49 V 1s and during the course of the war accounted for a
grand total of 181. Up to the 12 December 1944, when 96 Squadron was disbanded from
its role in Fighter Command, it was credited with destroying a total of 26 enemy aircraft.

CHAPTER THIRTY-ONE

256 Squadron:
Woodvale and Beyond

Group Captain MacDonald had begun to make the arrangements for 256 to move just a short distance down the Lancashire coast to Woodvale, when he visited Squires Gate on 12 May. Over the next year or so Group Captain Somerled Douglas MacDonald would become a significant figure in 9 Group. He had only returned to the home establishment in 1941 after commanding a Bomber Command detachment in Iraq during the renowned Rachide Ali's revolt.

The forty-three-year-old group captain had served almost continuously overseas since 1924 when he had been posted to Egypt. He had spent many years in Sudan, Palestine, and Lebanon and served under various commands in various theatres of conflict. On his return he had been posted to the Speke Sector, but in October he was given command of the new Woodvale Sector.

During the group captain's visit in May it had been decided that 256 Squadron would initially only move its HQ and one flight to Woodvale. The other flight was to remain at Squires Gate for a short while so that the squadron could maintain its operational status. Just four days after the his visit, that decision was changed in favour of moving the whole squadron together, and the logistical arrangements began while training continued on the Beaufighter.

During the build-up, Squadron Leader Paul Rabone returned to 9 Group and was posted to 256 Squadron at Squires Gate. After leaving 96 Squadron in early 1941 he had gained considerable experience of night flying on 85 Squadron, flying Havocs from Hunsdon. From there he had been posted to 1528 Beam Approach Training Flight at Drem, and then to 29 Squadron. At West Malling he was found to be surplus to requirements and so in the middle of May he was posted to 9 Group and 256 Squadron. He was appointed the flight commander of 'A' Flight but mainly acted in the role of instructor.

Sergeant Wild was one of the pilots trained by Squadron Leader Rabone and he remembered the New Zealander as being friendly and helpful. He experienced his first flight in a Blenheim 19 May, when he flew in L6730, the first of its type to arrive at Squires Gate. Wild had an advantage over other pilots because he had already completed twenty hours on twin-engined Oxfords, but despite that he did not get his hands on the controls straight away. During the one-and-a-half hour flight he had to stand behind the squadron leader and listen to his commentary. The following day he flew a Blenheim solo for the first time, and completed an hour-long familiarization sortie.

Squadron Leader Rabone also trained Sergeant Wild to fly the Beaufighter and he had his first flight in X7651 on 31 May. The situation was the same as during his training on the Blenheim – during the twenty-minute flight he had to stand behind Rabone, listening and observing. However, when they landed Rabone allowed him to go solo straight away and on the eve of 256 Squadron's move to Woodvale, he completed an hour-long cross-country flight, which was a momentous occasion in his flying career.

No. 256 Squadron began the move to Woodvale on 24 May when two 3-ton trucks arrived at Squires Gate to transport as much equipment as could be spared in advance. Like the newly built airfield at Wrexham, Woodvale was built partly on a golf course, land which had belonged to the Liverpool Merchant Bank Club. The main runway was 4,816 ft. in length and had been built for convenience rather than practicality and it ran parallel to a railway line. Instead of heading into the direction of the prevailing westerly winds, the main runway ran north to south on bearings of 040/220. That did not help pilots who got into difficulties with engines or flaps. In fact the direction of the runway may have contributed to an accident on the first day that 256 Squadron flew into Woodvale.

On 1 June the new HQ was set up and within hours the first aircraft began to arrive, but Pilot Officer Johnson's Beaufighter crashed on the runway. The throttle control jammed and Johnson was forced to make a high-speed landing in a cross wind. He was taken to Weeton Hospital with multiple injuries to his head and legs but later made a full recovery.

256 Squadron aircrew gathered outside the officers' mess at Woodvale, displaying a Balkan Cross. Its origins are unknown but it might have been from the Ju 88 shot down by Flight Lieutenant Coleman and Sergeant Smith in October 1941. Photo features Pilot Officer Brian Wild (at rear with Mae West), Flight Lieutenant Don Toone (with hat) and Pilot Officer John Tweedale (far right). Pilot Officer Berry is in the doorway. Courtesy Brian Wild

Three days later A Flight moved to Woodvale and the first 100 airmen occupied the billets and messes. B Flight made the move on 6 June and Wing Commander Pinkerton, DFC, the CO of Woodvale inspected the airmens' huts. It was noted that the messing arrangements seemed exceptionally good and the accommodation satisfactory. However there was a lot of criticism about the accommodation from the airmen; many claimed the billets were too cramped.

At Woodvale new friendships were established between pilots and observers, generally of a different kind to those between pilots and air gunners. Most of the observers were commissioned officers who had been trained overseas and these technically educated airmen represented the new age of the RAF. Sergeant Wild crewed up with Flight Sergeant Ralph Gibbons, who was one of the few senior NCO aircrew on the squadron. Pilot Officer Berry crewed up with Pilot Officer Ian Watson from Newcastle and their partnership was to last through several exhausting campaigns.

Despite the fact that Sergeant Derek Hollindrake, a former professional footballer, had been posted out, there remained a strong football element in 256 Squadron. Pilot Officer Charles Ashton had played for the Corinthians before the war. He had also played cricket for Gloucestershire and his pilot and Flight Commander, Squadron Leader Winlaw was another all round sportsman and Cambridge Triple Blue. Sergeant Wild was a particularly good friend of Pilot Officer Ashton and they spent a lot of their spare time together, often in the company of Pilot Officers Joe Berry and Ian Watson.

Pilot Officer Berry was one of several pilots who had not been sent on the twin-engined conversion course and he spent the last few weeks at Squires Gate training on Airspeed

Flying Officer Bob Lamb (on left) and Flying Officer Don Toone standing outside officers' mess at Woodvale. The Balkan Cross from downed enemy aircraft appears again nailed to wall outside. Flight Lieutenant Don Toone was killed in February 1943 when his Beaufighter crashed into the sea during a hailstorm off the coast of Blackpool.

Oxfords. Together with his observer, Pilot Officer Watson, Berry flew a large number of map-reading exercises before he completed his first solo in a Blenheim during a return flight from Silloth on 2 June. Berry and Watson were one of the first crews of the A Flight contingent to move to Woodvale on 4 June.

Blenheims continued to be delivered to Woodvale for training purposes and on 19 June Pilot Officers Berry and Watson flew to Shawbury with Flight Lieutenant Hughes to collect one of them. Over the next month, Berry flew on repeated map-reading exercises and night-flying tests, practising dusk landings. Sometimes the crews doubled up and on 4 July Pilot Officer Watson made his first sortie in a Beaufighter with Sergeant Wild, accompanied by fellow radio operator, Flight Sergeant Gibbons. By 10 July, when they completed a cross-country flight to Valley and Wrexham, Berry and Watson were proficient and they began to practise more advanced operational procedures.

It was while 256 Squadron was settling in at Woodvale and working up on the Beaufighter that Sergeant Wild's name was put forward for a commission. Having joined the RAF in June 1940 he had trained in Canada and completed over a year of operational flying. He had seen many of his fellow sergeant pilots and friends like Joe Berry commissioned and the fact that officers and senior NCOs lived in different messes, affected their relationships. He was interviewed by the 9 Group AOC, Air Commodore Dickson, Group Captain McDonald, and the 256 Squadron CO, Wing Commander Adams. Despite being very nervous, everything went well and to his great satisfaction he was commissioned.

There were further amendments to Air Ministry orders in the summer of 1942 and the aircrew category of Observer (Radio) was changed to 'Navigator'. Some observers who had not been on astral navigation courses were sent for retraining and that further muddied the waters in what was already a complicated area. Because the observer's badge carried the letters 'RO' many airmen insisted that it stood for 'Radar Observer'. The change of title to 'Navigator' was unpopular with many observers who jealously guarded their role and badge. A concession was later made which allowed them to continue wearing their Observers wings, as long as they had been awarded before 3 September 1939.

No. 256 Squadron was declared operational with the Beaufighter on 23 July and its crews did not have long to wait until they got the opportunity to put their training into practice. On the night of 27 July there were a number of incursions into the North-West. That night Pilot Officer Wild flew his first operational scramble in a Beaufighter. His observer, Sergeant Gibbons, made visual contact with a Ju 88 near Liverpool but it was several thousand feet beneath them and travelling in the opposite direction.

Wild quickly turned around and closed in on the target, shortening the range from eight miles to four. Then the GCI controller said he had lost the contact and the interception had to be abandoned. The real reason might have been that a large number of aircraft from a Bomber Command OTU were operating over Cardigan Bay on an exercise. Their position was very close to the enemy aircraft and the risk of another friendly fire' incident was just too great. It was a disappointing night for Wild who flew two more operational sorties from Woodvale, but the element of danger and excitement was never far away.

Three nights later on 30 July there was more action over the Llyn Peninsula but it was the turn of Pilot Officer Wild's former unit, 456 Squadron, to be involved. A month earlier, on 26 June, it had suffered the embarrassment of having one of its Beaufighters

256 Squadron Beaufighter 'G', taken over Ballhalbert, Northern Ireland, in December 1942. It was taken from another Beaufighter by Pilot Officer Wild, who was posted overseas shortly afterwards.
Courtesy of Brian Wild

shot down by a lone Ju 88. Pilot Officer Day and Sergeant Mitchell survived but were left stranded in a dinghy, although they were rescued within a couple of hours.

Wing Commander Wolfe and his navigator, Pilot Officer Ashcroft, were out to avenge this loss and after take-off they were vectored on to an enemy aircraft but it managed to get away. Soon afterwards they had a visual sighting of an He 111 and after closing to a range of 250 yards they got in two short bursts. After jettisoning its bomb load the He 111 went into a steep dive and crashed on the beach at Pwllheli. Only two of the crew escaped. This was the last enemy aircraft to be shot down over North Wales.

Things became very quiet in all of 9 Group's sectors but there was still the occasional excitement. On the night of 24 October Pilot Officer Wild experienced some technical difficulties when one of the engines of Beaufighter R7644 suddenly seized up. The second engine also began to lose power and he struggled with the controls to keep the aircraft airborne. 'Lady Luck' smiled on him and he managed to reach Calveley in Cheshire where he made a difficult but safe isometric landing.

A few nights later, on 31 October, there was a much more serious incident involving a crew that was on a Bull's Eye exercise with aircraft from Bomber Command. The Flight Commander Squadron Leader Winlaw and his observer Pilot Officer Ashton were killed when their Beaufighter collided with a Wellington over Bangor. The two officers were very popular amongst airmen and officers alike and their loss badly affected not just those who knew them but the morale of everyone on the squadron.

In November there was so little operational flying that Flying Officer Berry, recently promoted, was temporarily detached to 1456 Gunnery Squadron. Much of the work involved towing drogues on air-to-air firing exercises which must have seemed terribly boring for a night-fighter pilot. On 7 December 256 Squadron was detached to Ballyhalbert in Northern Ireland for eight days. It provided a break and a change of scene from the endless routine of carrying out night flying tests at Woodvale. On their return to Woodvale some pilots were given the good news that they were about to be posted overseas.

In January 1943 Flying Officer Berry and Pilot Officer Wild, together with their navigators, were sent to the Bristol aircraft factory at Filton. On 9 January they collected two brand new Beaufighters and flew them to Lyneham where they carried out air tests. They then carried out vital fuel consumption tests, so they knew within reason how much petrol each engine used and the range of their aircraft. On 24 January 1943 they flew to Pitrith in Cornwall, where they refuelled before continuing to Gibraltar, Maison Blanche and finally Setiff in the Atlas Mountains. Having safely delivered their aircraft they joined the Pilot Pool at Maison Blanche and awaited notification of a posting to an operational squadron.

As a footnote to 256 Squadron's operations it is worth mentioning the fate that befell one of its air gunners, who happened to be one of its most popular characters. By late 1943 Flight Lieutenant Bob Lamb had been posted to 35 Squadron and was flying Halifax Mk IIIs from Gravely. On 20 December he and his crew were returning from Frankfurt, and at 1,200 ft, when the aircraft was approaching Gravely, it burst into flames. The pilot,

Former 256 Squadron air gunner, Flight Leutenant Bob Lamb (back row end left), with his crew on 35 Squadron at Gravely. His captain was Squadron Leader Julian Sale, D.F.C., (back row centre) who died in mysterious circumstances after they were shot down and taken as a prisoner of war by the Germans. Courtesy of Gordon Carter

Squadron Leader Sale, had ordered everybody out and he was about to abandon the aircraft when Flight Lieutenant Lamb appeared and told him he could not jump because his parachute had been burned.

The Halifax was full of smoke but the squadron leader was forced to perform a crash landing by sticking his head out of the window. As soon as they were down he and 'Sheep' Lamb, as he was known, ran for their lives. The aircraft exploded almost at once and was totally gutted but the air gunner and his skipper managed to escape and fight another day. For his action Squadron Leader Julian Sale was awarded a Bar to his DSO.

On 19 February 1945 on an operation to Leipzig they were not so fortunate and at 0243 Flight Lieutenant Lamb's Halifax, HX325, was shot down by a Ju 88 night fighter. Flight Lieutenant Lamb was captured along with the rest of his crew, but two of them later died of their injuries, including Squadron Leader Julian Sale, DSO and Bar, DFC. Lamb became PoW Number 2350 and was forced to sit out the rest of the war in Stalag Luft III at Sagan, the scene of the 'Great Escape'. He had plenty of time to ponder over his earlier days with 256 Squadron. He survived to return home at the end of the war.

No. 256 Squadron remained at Woodvale until April 1943 when, under the Command of Wing Commander Hayes, it moved south to Ford. Almost straight away it had some success when one of its crews shot down a Do 217 off the coast near Worthing. In May it began to convert to the Mosquito Mk XII in preparation for a move overseas and Wing Commander Park DFC, took over Command in June. A detachment was sent to Malta in July and by the 18th it had destroyed a total of twelve aircraft. The squadron remained overseas, in North Africa and Italy, for the remainder of the war and it was disbanded at Nicosia in Cyprus in September 1946.

Burned out remains of the Halifax from which Flight Leutenant Lamb escaped, after it caught fire and crashed at Gravely on 20 December 1943. Courtesy of Gordon Carter

CHAPTER THIRTY-TWO

After 9 Group:
Post-war RAF Preston

The structure of 9 Group began to change as early as August 1942 when Air Vice-Marshal McClaughry was posted to the Middle East and appointed as the Air Officer Commanding (AOC) Egypt. Air Commodore William Dickson, who had previously served as senior air staff officer (SASO) in Fighter Command took over as AOC and he already had significant experience of the tactics used by fighters.

Dickson arrived at Barton Hall when 9 Group's night-fighting role was finished and most of its units were redundant. Airfields such as Valley and Wrexham had fulfilled their original roles as fighter stations and other, more urgent, roles were required. Wrexham in particular was to play another vital role in the war effort and a meeting between the

Line up of airmen at R.A.F. Weeton with Wing Commander Pat Gibson (centre bottom row). Weeton became the parent station of Barton Hall in 1958 and Wing Commander Gibson was one of the last Commanding Officer's of R.A.F. Preston. He had connections with 9 Group and Squires Gate going back to 1941. Courtesy of Simon Gibson

Commander-in-Chief of Fighter Command, Air Marshal Sholto Douglas and Air Commodore Dickson on 3 October 1942 paved the way.

Wrexham became the Headquarters for 121 Wing which consisted of the three rocket-carrying, tank busting units and was made up of 19, 182 and 247 Squadrons. The HQ at Wrexham was the first of only two in the RAF and it was later to form part of the 2nd Tactical Air Force (TAF). A number of 9 Group's former Defiant pilots played a significant part in its operations and one of them went on to achieve great success and distinguish himself with the 2nd TAF during the Normandy landings.

In the autumn of 1942 Wing Commander F.T.K. Bullmore arrived at Preston to discuss the setting up of a Flying Control Liaison Section in 9 Group. Fighter Command was extremely concerned about the problems of controlling the large number of training aircraft flying over the Irish Sea, the busiest stretch of airspace in the country. The flying control system which originated in 10 Group had already been established in 11 and 13 Groups. It involved creating direct communications between the Air Sea Rescue units, the ROC and group controllers. A system of searchlights known as Sandra lights were installed on airfields to guide pilots home. The following year Wing Commander Bullmore moved to the Isle of Man and set up a much modified system which would make history.

Having been promoted in October, Air Vice Marshal W.F. Dickson, CB, DSO, OBE, AFC, handed over control of 9 Group to Air Commodore C. R. Steel, D.F.C. on 2 November. That 9 Group was being commanded by an officer of lower rank, could have been judged by some to be a result of its status in Fighter Command being diminished. That however might not have been the case and Steel was replaced only eight days later by Air Vice-Marshal Whitworth Jones, C.B. He was the A.O.C. of 9 Group when it was declared non operational on 15 April 1943 and he remained in office until the middle of the year.

No. 9 Group continued to exist but only in a training role and it retained command of 51 and 62 OTUs and a telecommunications flying unit. It was at this time that Flight Lieutenant Tom Smith arrived at Barton Hall because the work he had been doing in 81 Group on accident investigation was taken over by 9 Group. He was joined by Flight Lieutenant Dicky Martin, the legendary 'Prisoner of Luxemburg' who had flown in France with 73 Squadron. The two men who had met at Aston Down became good friends and drinking companions during Flight Lieutenant Smith's campaign to bribe and corrupt senior medical officers. As a result of being medically downgraded, Flight Lieutenant Smith was in his own words, trying to "Drink his way up the medical profession," in the hope of getting back to flying.

Not long after Smith arrived at Barton Hall he met Group Captain MacDonald in the Officers' Mess bar. MacDonald told Smith in no uncertain terms that he was drinking too much! The group captain had Flight Lieutenant Smith's bar bills in his hand and he said the drinking would have to stop. Not knowing quite who the group captain was, but respecting a senior officer anyway, Smith reluctantly agreed. MacDonald then called over the bar steward and told him that for the next month, he would receive Flight Lieutenant Smith's whisky ration. Smith was surprised but not too concerned and he had plenty of other 'watering holes' to go to. One of them was the Boar's Head public house just down the road in the village of Barton on the A6 and better known to RAF personnel as the 'Whore's Bed'. Smith had many happy times there but he remembered one particular

A group of officers from 9 Group H.Q. at Barton Hall on the wrong side of the recently erected fence which prevented easy access to the Boars Head public house. Flight Lieutenants Tom Smoth (on the right) and Dickie Martin, kneeling at front, described the security measures as turning Barton Hall into 'Oflag 9G' Courtesy Wing Commander Martin

night when a man with a moustache pencilled on his top lip appeared. He was dressed in cricket flannels and a sweater and rather annoyingly, he repeatedly knocked a cricket ball up in the air off his bat and refused to speak to anyone. He thought it was all quite strange until his friend Flight Lieutenant Dicky Martin walked in, wearing a pair of pyjamas. He explained that it was a fancy dress party and within a short while the place was full of many more weird and wonderfully dressed people.

The Boar's Head was at the back of Barton Hall, just a short walk across the fields, until the authorities decided it was too handy. At some point in 1943 a barbed wire fence was put up to prevent airmen getting to the pub without passing the guardroom. Smith and his colleagues thought that the fence was not erected as much for security issues but just to force officers to drink in the officers' mess. Those who visited the Boar's Head were faced with a long walk but that was still preferable to drinking in the official institutions.

Like most other young airmen Smith had an eye for the ladies and to obtain the affections of a young WAAF, he told her that if she ever wanted his help, all she had to do was to ask! The call came early on a Sunday morning when she was going home on leave and it was not what he had imagined. He and his colleague Flight Lieutenant Martin were called on to help with her horse and he said they must have looked a strange sight, trying to load the beast into a guards van on Preston Station.

The control of 9 Group changed hands several more times in 1943. On 6 July Air Vice-Marshal Hollinghurst, CB, OBE, DFC, took over as AOC but he only remained in the post until 11 October. Flight Lieutenant Smith remembered his leaving party very well because he and his colleague, Flight Lieutenant Martin, were billeted in Newsham House where it took place. The house was normally used only for accommodating senior officers, they were allowed to stay there because of the nature of their work.

On his last night as AOC of 9 Group Air Vice-Marshal Hollinghurst performed his party trick. He lay down on the floor. He then rested his full body weight on one arm and with the other arm in his trouser pocket he picked up a handkerchief with his teeth. The AOC has been described as being a 'Five By Five', which meant that he was short and stocky, so his build made his feat all the more remarkable. As the beer began to flow various officers tried to emulate the AOC's feat, but they all failed. As the night went on things got a bit rowdy and a number of officers were involved in some serious mischief.

Newsham House was owned by a Mr W. Smith who had purchased Barton Hall and three farms, which were part of the original estate, when they were put up for auction in June 1899. The property had been divided up by the late owner's widow Mrs Jacson, into seventy two lots and Mr Smith paid a total of £25,000 for some 395 acres of land and Barton Hall. Newsham House contained a number of antique items including some ornate clocks and valuable paintings. In the early hours of the morning some drunken engineering officers dismantled various clocks and then re-assembled them. The brass plates of the largest clock had been put back in the wrong pattern and the bell was fitted upside down, with an orange and a banana stuffed inside. The second clock was tampered with and instead of making a 'Tick Tock' noise, it sounded more like 'Tick Boom'. As a final insult a painting on the stairs was defaced with a glass. The incidents caused a great uproar and it cost some officers a lot of money to put things right, but more to the point it spoiled things and after that everyone had to be on their best behaviour.

Some months later Flight Lieutenant Smith's attempts at drinking himself up the medical branch finally paid off. Air Vice-Marshal Symons pronounced him fit to fly after nearly eighteen months of being earthbound. Smith had already decided he wanted to join 100 Group and so he was posted to 51 OTU at Cranfield where he learned to fly Mosquitoes. He was then sent to the Bomber Support Training Unit at Great Massingham for further training, where he crewed up with Flying Officer Arthur Cockayne. They were posted to 23 Squadron at Little Snoring and Flight Lieutenant Smith began flying again just as 9 Group was about to be disbanded.

Air Commodore Cecil Afred Stevens, CB, CBE, MC, took over command of 9 Group from Air Vice-Marshal Hollinghurst in October 1943. He had previously served as the SASO in Aden and he only stayed at Barton hall for two months before taking up another post in Burma. The third AOC of 9 Group to be appointed in five months was Air Vice-Marshal Donald Fasken Stevenson, CB, CBE, OBE, DSO, MC and Bar. He had started the war at the Air Ministry as Director of Home Operations, before moving on to Bomber Command where he was the AOC of 2 Group. He was then posted overseas and served in Burma and Bengal between 1942 and 1943. When he returned he took up a post at RAF

Northern Ireland. Stevenson held the post as AOC 9 Group until August 1944 when he became the High Commissioner of Romania.

In 1944 Group Captain MacDonald became the SASO in 9 Group. He had held a number of key positions including that of Woodvale Sector Commander and he temporarily took command of RAF Woodvale in late 1942. Having been involved with 9 Group's operations for over two years, it made sense that when his promotion came through, he should take over as the AOC. Air Commodore MacDonald became the final AOC of 9 Group on 15 August 1944 but his time in office was to be quite short.

No. 9 Group was completely disbanded on 18 September 1944. Its final tally was 36 enemy aircraft destroyed; ten probables; twenty-seven damaged. Despite this record it was the only Group in Fighter Command not to be awarded a badge; possibly because for the last seventeen months of its existence it had been non-operational. Although 9 Group's finest hour was undoubtably on the night of 7/8 May 1941, it reached its peak early in 1943 when it had ten operational units under its control, not including the merchant ship fighter units based at Speke.

Despite being run down, the final strength of personnel at 9 Group's HQ at Barton Hall was 102 officers; twenty-three WAAF officers; 216 airmen and 234 airwomen. The number of WAAFs alone was far more than the total staff at Barton Hall in September 1940, when there had been just 176 officers and airmen. There were many fond farewells and dances were held in the village of Broughton, just down the road from Barton Hall. When Wing Commander Rayner signed the final order winding up 9 Group on 17 September, a large proportion of the staff was posted to 12 Group, Fighter Command. Amongst them was Air Commodore MacDonald who took up the post of SASO in 12 Group.

Barton Hall reverted to being a filter unit and a station in 12 Group, as part of the Air Defence of Great Britain network, but there was little need for its services. On 1 November 1944, No. 4 Instructor's School (Educational & Vocational Training) moved in. The unit, which had up to 230 students at a time and was intended to provide education and resettlement for former servicemen after the war. The Instructor's School remained at Barton Hall until September 1945 when it was disbanded. After five years in the service of the RAF, Barton Hall was then closed down and temporarily put on a care and maintenance basis

In March 1943, after the Andreas Sector control room in Ramsey Grammar School on the Isle of Man closed down, it was taken over by Wing Commander F.T.K. Bullmore. Under his guidance and that of his assistant, Flight Lieutenant Hampson, MBE, it was converted to the Training Flying Control Centre Two hundred and thirty airmen and WAAFs were employed in what Bullmore described as the most novel set of Operations Rooms ever created.

The TFCC evolved into The Training Area Flying Control Centre during 1944 and the first area control system for air traffic control was created. The role of the Area Flying Control Centre was finally recognised in 1946 when it was visited by the Royal Family. On 17 July His Majesty King George VI and Queen Elizabeth unveiled a plaque to commemorate the occasion and the piece of aviation history that was created on the Isle of Man.

Loosely based on the RAF's sector control system, flying control centres provided a service to civil and military aircraft across the UK. Barton Hall was transferred from RAF Fighter Command to Technical Training Command and it was in at the beginning of the system which would shape aviation in the years to come. On 15 October 1947, it reopened as an area control centre and on 10 November its title was changed to Air Traffic Control Centre and Aeronautical Information Centre, Preston. On 24 June 1948 the Ministry of Civil Aviation assumed responsibility and RAF personnel were transferred to RAF Kirkam.

Preston was one of six such centres which were established under the control of the Ministry of Civil Aviation, to provide D/F (Direction Finding) navigational assistance, weather reports and a search and rescue service. The other flight safety regions were at Inverness, Prestwick, Watnall, Gloucester and Uxbridge. In September 1947 the number was reduced to five, and they were renamed flight information regions. The former 12 Group HQ at Watnall was absorbed into the air traffic control centre at Preston and history had turned full circle.

From June 1954 Preston was manned by civilian controllers who were assisted by their military counterparts. The centre at Barton Hall had close links with Northern Radar which was a Royal Naval facility based at Church Stretton. The naval air station provided civil controllers and military controllers at Preston with data and information from its extended Radar network.

By now RAF Weeton had become larger and more important than the run-down unit at Barton Hall and for several years it had been the HQ of No. 2 RAF Police District. It also housed a station hospital which had been established in 1940 and later became an independent unit. As a result of further changes in November 1958, RAF Weeton became the parent unit of RAF Warton and also took over the responsibility for the air traffic control centre at Barton Hall.

There was one other RAF and military facility at Preston so far not mentioned and it continued to remain independent of RAF Weeton. During the war RAF Preston expanded and a large bunker complex was built at Longley Lane, Goosnargh, just down the road from Barton Hall. One of only four such sites to be built, it consisted of a filter room bunker, communication room bunker and operations bunker. Each bunker was several hundred yards apart and capable of carrying out the role of the others. The RAF's Western Sector HQ was formed at Longley Lane in December 1950 and it controlled RAF operations such as those of 613 Squadron (City of Manchester) RAF Auxiliary from Ringway. The station flight of Western Sector HQ was based at Squires Gate and the unit was not disbanded until October 1957.

Longley Lane was also a Reserve Air Defence Operations Centre and the HQ of 21 Group, the ROC. One of the last men to serve there was Commandant Harry Sutton, a former Lancaster pilot who flew with 103 and 625 Squadrons. In the 1960s Longley Lane was a target for peace campaigners and CND protesters. Harry remembered being sent out to talk to them but he said they refused to listen to him, despite the fact that he told them Longley Lane did not control the V bombers or the nuclear deterrent. It did however play a crucial role during the Cold War and was an active part of Britain's defences until 1970.

In 1961 there was a debate about the location of ATCCs and in particular where the Oceanic ATCC, which controlled Trans-Atlantic traffic, should be based. At one point it was decided that the centre should be housed at Barton Hall but the plan was changed and the Apollo Computer was eventually installed at Prestwick, where the facilities for a Oceanic Centre already existed. In 1962 plans to build a new ATCC at Preston were shelved and that decision meant that its days as a major ATCC were numbered.

Many of those who served at Preston have happy memories of their time there and former RAF Bomber Command pilot and civilian air traffic controller Peter Perry, DFC, first arrived at Barton Hall in 1951. He said that during his three tours of duty there Barton Hall gradually fell into a state of bad repair and it was not economically viable to rewire the old building for the comptuter age. He remained based at Barton Hall until 30 January 1975 when the building, which dated back to 1786, was condemned and closed. The air traffic control facility was re-established at Manchester Airport, where Perry became the Senior Air Traffic Controller.

One of the last COs of RAF Preston was Wing Commander Pat Gibson, DFC, from Christchurch New Zealand. His background and experiences link wartime Blackpool with the more contemporary period of RAF Preston and some of the New Zealand airmen who served at Squires Gate. As a young man he sailed to England from Wellington on 7 April 1938 aboard the RMS *Rangitata*, as part of a group of eighteen air force cadets. By the end of 1941 he had already served for over two years on 210 Squadron and 95 Squadron, flying Sunderlands from Pembroke Dock and Oban.

Between 8 November and 13 December 1941 Flight Lieutenant Gibson was on a training course at 3 School of General Reconnaissance at Squires Gate where he met a number of airmen from 256 Squadron including Sergeants Jack Scott and Gordon Walden. The tragedy involving Sergeant Ellmers and Clifford was still fresh in everyone's mind and it was a regular topic of conversation, particularly amongst his fellow New Zealanders.

After leaving Blackpool Flight Lieutenant Gibson was posted to America and he did not return to the Home establishment until the end of 1943. He did a further tour with 210 Squadron before being posted to Gibraltar and in September 1945 he was seconded to BOAC. He also worked for an Argentinian airline called Dodero (ALFA), piloting Sandringham flying boats (converted Sunderlands) from England to South America.

Wing Commander Gibson shaking hands with a senior NCO as he prepared to leave R.A.F. Weeton on his retirement. Courtesy of Simon Gibson

Some time after the war he discovered that of those eighteen men who sailed with him to England in 1938, only one other had survived. His name was also Gibson: Johnny Gibson. He was not related.

Wing Commander Gibson was posted to RAF Preston in 1962 from RAF Uxbridge, where he had mainly worked as part of heathrow radar operations at London Airport. At Barton Hall he controlled the day-to-day affairs of the RAF's air traffic control facility from his office at RAF Preston's parent unit, Weeton. Shortly after he arrived his wife Mary and their daughter Cathy began to explore the Fylde area. The wing commander had probably told them about his time there during the war and of some of the incidents that took place there.

During one of their many walks they came across the grave of Sergeant Clifford buried in an isolated section of Lytham Park Cemetery. Cathy was quite upset at the fact that he was laid to rest some distance from his RAF colleagues and she began to visit the grave and lay flowers on it. In March 1977 when Wing Commander Gibson died the family decided that there was only place for him to be, alongside Sergeant Clifford 'to keep him company'. Wing Commander Thomas Patrick Gibson is buried in Roman Catholic Section 'D', Grave 514, while Sergeant Clifford's Grave was designated Grave 514 A.

In 1990 James Gibson, Wing Commander Gibson's brother, wrote a book called *Amongst The High Hills Of Canterbury* which was published in New Zealand. One of the chapters, *Two New Zealand Airmen*, describes the flying career of Wing Commander Gibson and the tragedy at Blackpool in which Sergeant Clifford was killed. James Gibson also wrote about Mrs Mary Gibson and says that over the years she 'weaved the two airmen's lives together' in her attempts to make contact with Sergeant Clifford's family.

Purely by chance the book was read by Sergeant Clifford's nephew, Dennis Clifford, who later made contact with Wing Commander Gibson's son, Simon. In 1995 Mary and Cathy Gibson's efforts were rewarded when Dennis Clifford visited England and his uncle's grave in Lytham Park Cemetery. That was the culmination of over thirty years research for Mary and Cathy Gibson. It united the two families and finally allowed them to let the two airmen from New Zealand rest in peace.

Very little has survived to remind the present generation about RAF Preston and 9 Group the role of its night-fighter units or its airfields. Cranage remained an active airfield throughout the war and during 1944 it was used by General Patton who had his HQ close by at Peover Hall near Knutsford. Cranage finally closed to flying operations in 1954 and it was handed over to the United States Air Force. It was used by a variety of USAF units including Number 1 Motor Transport Squadron, 7523 Support Squadron and a Special Investigations Wing. On 1 July 1957 it reverted to the control of the RAF but was shut down almost immediately, with the remaining RAF personnel being posted to RAF Sealand.

There has been an active campaign lead by local school teacher, Charlotte Peters Rock, to save what remains of the airfield at Cranage. Two wartime hangars and fourteen air raid shelters still remain but much of the former grass airfield was covered over many years ago by the M6 motorway. The greatest testimony to the presence of the RAF during the war is in St. John's Church Cemetery where lie the graves of eighteen airmen from Australia, Canada and New Zealand. The future of the former airfield is uncertain but as in the case of many other RAF stations the local church will always hold memories of Cranage's past.

RAF Valley, which is the long standing home of 4 Flight Training School, is the only former 9 Group and service airfield which remains operational. At the civilian establishments such as Squires Gate and Speke virtually all traces of their wartime roles have disappeared. Liverpool Airport has been rebuilt on a new site to the south of the original Speke Airport and there is a plaque on a wall in the terminal building to remind travellers of the airport's past role.

The plaque Commemorates the work carried out by the Merchant Ship Fighter Unit, which was formed in 9 Group at Speke on 5 May 1941. It was unveiled on 29 May 1993 by former MSFU pilot Air-Vice Marshal Lyne, CB, AFC, DL, (Retired). It records the actions of Flying Officer John Kendal who was the first MSFU pilot to destroy an enemy aircraft and who became the only pilot to die on operational service with the unit in May 1942. It also records that MSFU pilots carried out 175 sailings and destroyed seven enemy aircraft. Three MSFU pilots who were killed during flying accidents are also Commemorated and they are listed as Flight Lieutenant T.D.H. Davey; Pilot Officer R.B. McIntye and Pilot Officer E.R. Taylor.

CHAPTER THIRTY-THREE

Squadron Leader Rabone:
A Strange Coincidence

In August 1980 a dig was carried out at Rowlee's Pasture where Squadron Leader Rabone's Defiant had crashed and it was lead by author Ron Collier. A significant amount of wreckage from N1766 was excavated and the most interesting find was the Defiant's Rolls-Royce III engine. It was recovered almost intact and after being overhauled it was loaned to the Manchester Science and Industry Museum and displayed in the Air and Space Gallery.

Fifty years after the events which lead up to the aircraft's engine being buried in the ground, one of those who was involved in the recovery project had a chance meeting with a man who had been on duty the night the Defiant had crashed. Their meeting was a great coincidence and the former RAF officer was able to give his account of what happened that night in April 1941 and why Squadron Leader Rabone might have been forced to abandon his aircraft. It happened after the engine came under the control of a Mr Steve Hague who was involved with its renovation and, who then effectively became its curator. Several years ago Mr Hague was visiting RAF Manston in Kent to carry out some research when two elderly gentlemen walked by. One of them noticed that he had a Defiant badge on his overalls and he stopped and told Mr Hague that he had worked with Defiants during the war. The gentleman, who introduced himself as Mr Walter Chesher, began to recall a night in 1941 when he was on duty as a Sector Controller in 9 Group. He said that he had heard a pilot making repeated calls over the radio, declaring an emergency because his engine was failing.

He told Mr Hague that he was under strict orders not to answer such calls over the R/T because enemy aircraft were active in the area. There was a renewed threat of invasion and intelligence sources suspected that the *Luftwaffe* was monitoring radio frequencies used by the RAF. The authorities were concerned that if *Luftwaffe* crews became familar with airmen's terminology and the different code words that were being used, they might mimic them and make bogus calls to confuse the air defences.

Mr Chesher went on to say that he had often thought about the pilot and air gunner of that Defiant and he felt partly responsible for their deaths. Mr Hague suddenly realised that he was talking about the incident involving Flight Lieutenant Rabone and Flying Officer Ritchie in April 1941. Further questions confirmed this and Mr Hague was happy to inform Mr Chesher that both airmen had survived the incident. He told the former sector controller about the dig in 1980 and surprised him even further when he said that

Author, Ron Collier, with the engine from Squadron Leader Rabone's Defiant, which was recovered from the ground in August 1980. It was later exhibited at the Science and Industry Museum in Manchester and the Yorkshire Air Museum at Elvington.

he was the guardian of the Defiant's engine. As a result of what was a chance meeting at Manston, Mr Chesher walked away with his colleague a very happy man.

In June 1943 the subject of their conversation, Squadron Leader Paul Rabone, joined 23 Squadron and crewed up with Flying Officer Johns to operate on Mosquitoes. Based at Luqa in Malta, they flew together on numerous intruder sorties over Sicily and on 20 July 1943 they set a record for the distance flown on an intruder sortie. After taking off from Malta, Rabone and his navigator attacked targets north of Rome and damaged three seaplanes at Bracciano as well as destroying a convoy of lorries near Vitterbo. At the end of the year Squadron Leader Rabone returned to the home establishment and he was awarded the DFC. By then he had been officially credited with six enemy aircraft destroyed and for the next five months he was rested from operations and posted to 60 OTU as an instructor.

When they returned to operational flying during June 1944 Squadron Leader Rabone and his navigator were posted to 515 Squadron at Little Snoring. On 30 June they destroyed an He 111 and a JU 34, a twin-engined transport aircraft, but their Mosquito was hit by light flak in the starboard wing and Rabone was forced to abort the mission. Throughout July they continued to operate on day ranger sorties, attacking flak ships, railway bridges and other targets of opportunity. After another aborted sortie to Berlin on 10 July because of bad weather, Rabone and his navigator were given twelve days' leave.

Their former unit 23 Squadron had returned to the home establishment in May and on 24 July Squadron Leader Rabone and Flying Officer Johns were posted to it for the second time. On 24 July during their first sortie back with their old squadron they were shot down and killed while operating in the Schleswig-Holstein area of West Germany. It is understood that their Mosquito was badly shot up by a light flak battery and sustained severe damage to the rear fuselage. Both Rabone and Johns attempted to bale out but they were probably too low and the navigator's body was found with the parachute barely open. Flying Officer Frederick Charles Haver Johns was buried in Hannover War Cemetery, Grave 10, Plot E.

The 26 year old squadron leader was married and his widow, Pamela, did not discover that her husband's body had been found until 1995, when author Ron Collier contacted her. The information came from the renowned Dutch researcher, Mr Gerrie Zwananberg, MBE. His efforts were instrumental in finding out what had happened to Squadron Leader Rabone and where he had been buried. He discovered that the body of Squadron Leader Rabone had been washed up on Heligoland on 24 October 1944 and buried by the Germans in Heligoland Military Cemetery.

At some point after the war his body was exhumed by the Americans and reburied in the US Military Cemetery in the Ardennes. Then by the authority of the Air Ministry Squadron Leader Rabone's body was exhumed for a second time and he was finally laid to rest by the RAF in Hooton War Cemetery, Belguim. Squadron Leader Paul Wattling Rabone, DFC, is buried in Plot 11, Row C, Grave 8.

The engine of N1766 was moved from the Manchester Science and Industry Museum in 1996 and relocated at the Yorkshire Air Museum at Elvington, still under the care of Mr Hague. In 2002 it was moved again and at the time of publication it is on display at the South Yorkshire Air Museum in Doncaster.

CHAPTER THIRTY-FOUR

Of Those Who Served: The Airmen of 9 Group

On 4 January 1943, the former AOC of 9 Group, Air Vice-Marshal McClaughry, was killed in an accident involving a Lockheed Lodestar, which crashed while its pilot was trying to land at Heliopolis near Cairo. The twin-engined aircraft, EW986, had flown from Benina with a distinguished passenger, Lady Rosalinde Tedder, the wife of Air Chief Marshal Arthur William Tedder, who was then the AOC RAF Middle East, on board. Lady Tedder was committed to the welfare of airmen and she had been visiting an RAF hospital and some welfare centres in Cyrenica.

Other passengers included Wing Commander Gerard Basil Nicholas, DFC, Squadron Leader H. W. Cleland, Squadron Leader R. G. Chester, Flight Lieutenant Ritchie and Flying Officer Hawkins. After a four-and-a-half hour flight the Lodestar approached the airfield at Heliopolis and RAF Regiment Sergeant Burnard was one of many people who watched the Lodestar fly around the circuit quite low. Air Chief Marshal Tedder was also on the airfield waiting to greet his wife and he saw the aircraft disappear behind the sand hills and the great pall of smoke that was thrown up as it crashed at 1826 hours.

All eleven people on board the Lodestar were killed instantly and although the exact cause of the accident was never established, several factors were known to have contributed to the accident. One of them was that Air Vice-Marshal McClaughry had ordered the pilot, Flying Officer James, to take off from Benina, despite the fact that there were adverse weather conditions *en route*, including a sand storm at Heliopolis. Flying Officer James wanted to wait until the weather cleared and although he could have refused to fly, the AOC Egypt put pressure on him and exercised his authority.

There were other less controversial factors which might have caused the Lodestar to crash. It was found to have a very dirty windscreen, but that was hardly surprising as it had flown through a sand storm. A strong downdraft at Heliopolis might also have have played its part during the Lodestar's final moments in the air. Air Vice-Marshal Wilfred Ashton McClaughry, C.B., D.S.O., M.C., D.F.C., is buried in Heliopolis Cemetery, Plot 3, Row H, Grave 12. Lady Roasalinde Tedder was buried in Plot 3, Row G, Grave 10.

The burial parties were provided by the RAF Regiment and Sergeant Bernard recalled that someone decided the airmen should wear Best Blue uniforms. Many of those in the ranks of the Regiment had not worn RAF Blue for over a year, while those recruited from the army did not possess such a thing anyway. Moth eaten uniforms were recovered from storage while others were borrowed from a variety of sources. It made for a very sweaty and uncomfortable parade as those present paid their last respects to the victims of the air crash.

Air Vice-Marshal McClaughry lived a 'charmed' life during the First World War and he had survived being injured in flying accidents and wounded in action. While serving as a lieutenant with the 9th Australian Light Horse Brigade at Gallipoli, he had been shot in the left forearm and foot and evacuated to Egypt. He was taken to the Neaconessis Hospital in Alexandria, where he might have died twenty-eight years before the tragic events of 4 January 1943.

In 1934, just before he was promoted to group captain, he was appointed as the Commanding Officer of RAF Heliopolis. He had had a number of connections with Egypt over the years and it was in many ways ironic that fate determined it would be his final resting place. The AOC Egypt was married and his widow Angela was living at the time in St. John's Wood, London. It is not known whether he had any children or family other than his younger brother.

The original spelling of the family name was 'McCloughry' but for some unknown reason the older brother, Wilfred Ashton changed it. Edgar James kept the original spelling of the family name but added 'Kingston', to become Edgar James Kingston-McCloughry. At the time of Air Vice-Marshal Wilfred Ashton McClaughry's death his younger brother held the rank of air commodore and he was the AOC of 44 Group (Transport Command).

In early 1943 Air Commodore Kingston-McCloughry was actively involved in splitting up the organization which it had taken his late brother two years to create. His plan involved handing RAF Valley over to Transport Command and this was opposed by many senior officers in Fighter Command and 9 Group. The Commander-in-Chief of Fighter Command, Air Marshal Leigh Mallory delayed the plans but 44 Group finally took over Valley on 18 March 1944. Had Air Vice-Marshal Wilfred Ashton McClaughry survived, his brother's plans would undoubtably have been the source of heated debate and the only concession was that Trewan Sands GCI station remained under the control of 9 Group. The Valley Sector of 9 Group was absorbed into the Woodvale Sector and while some units were handed over to Coastal Command, Fighter Command's presence was reduced to that of a Lodger Unit.

Air Vice-Marshal Edgar James Kingston-McCloughry went on to become head planner for the AEAF and he was later appointed senior staff officer of the RAF's India Command. By 1947 he had been appointed as AOC of 18 Group but he later became the SASO Scotland. He then moved on to take up the post of Senior Air Officer of Fighter Command which he held from 1948 to 1950. At the time of his retirement in 1953 he was working in the Ministry of Defence as the Chief Air Defence Officer. He lived in Perthshire until his death in 1972.

Out in the Middle East the former 96 Squadron flight commander, Flight Lieutenant Victor Verity, continued to play an active role in operations. He was posted to 73 Squadron which, through the chain of command, came under the control of Air Vice-Marshal Wilfred Ashton McClaughry AOC Egypt. In September 1942 the AOC inspected 73 Squadron at LG 85 in the Western Desert and was photographed talking to some pilots. It is not known if he met Flight Lieutenant Verity, but if he did they might have had an interesting conversation about a certain night back in May 1941!

In November 1942 Verity was posted to an aircraft delivery unit but by 1943 had wangled his way back to operational flying and he was posted to 89 Squadron which flew

Beaufighters from Abu-Surir. He flew on numerous night-intruder sorties over Sicily and Italy and in the defence of Malta. While it was detached to Malta part of 89 Squadron became the nucleus for the formation of 108 Squadron. On 17 April 1943, with the help of his navigator, Warrant Officer Farquarson, Verity destroyed an He 111 to claim the new unit's first victory.

By the time Verity returned to the home establishment in July 1943 he had flown a total of 375 sorties. After some well-earned leave he was posted to Fighter Command HQ and became one of only three specialist controllers in 100 Group who targeted enemy night fighters on Bomber Command support operations. Verity yearned to return to flying duties, however, and in December 1943 he was posted to 650 Squadron, which was a target-towing unit based in a remote part of Cumberland, at Cark, near Grange-over-Sands.

Equipped initially with only Miles Martinets it was almost certainly not the posting that Verity would have wanted. The arrival of a small number of Hurricanes in April 1944 might have evoked memories of better days. When his promotion to squadron leader came through he was taken off flying duties again and posted to Ouston. His post as an instructor, teaching navigation, was the last one he held in the RAF and soon after arriving at Ouston he was demobbed.

After his discharge Verity returned to New Zealand and resumed his pre-war occupation as a farmer. In 1959, however, and for reasons that are not known, he returned to Britain. It is understood that he lived in the Northampton area and ran a roofing company. Not much is really known about this period of his life but he did finally return to New Zealand in 1969. He died at his home in Wellington during February 1979.

At the end of 1941, Sergeant McNair, the pilot who was responsible for 96 Squadron's first confirmed victory, was posted to a night-fighter OTU. He was later commissioned and posted to 87 Squadron which operated the Hurricane IIc from Charmy Down. The unit took part in air operations during the Dieppe raid on 19 August 1942. The following month he was awarded the DFC for his actions and for completing 110 sorties.

In December 1942 McNair was posted to 245 Squadron and having been promoted to flight lieutenant he became a flight commander. The unit, which was also based at Charmy Down, was equipped with rocket-firing Typhoons and McNair was one of the most able pilots to fly the aircraft. There were many problems with the Typhoon in the early days and it did not become operational as part of the 2nd TAF until March 1943. In January 1944 McNair was awarded a Bar to his DFC, and after attending the fighter leader's course, he was promoted to squadron leader and given the command of 247 Squadron. Equipped with the Typhoon IB and initially operating out of Hurn, it later flew from forward airfields in France.

Squadron Leader McNair flew on numerous Noball operations against V1 Flying Bomb sites and in July he took over as wing leader of 124 Wing. That month he was forced to crash land in Normandy; and the incident was caught on film by a newsreel cameraman. He was seen calmly walking around the field near his wrecked Typhoon, talking to soldiers and others who were on the scene. He went on to complete almost 500 sorties before he was taken off operations and posted to an administrative post in 12 Group concerned with training policy.

Squadron Leader McNair was demobilized in December 1945 and maintained his career in aviation. After a short spell at the Ministry of Aviation, in July 1946 he joined

British European Airways on its foundation working for the company in various capacities. He became the station superintendent at Frankfurt before moving to Geneva where he held the same post from 1948 to 1951. He later became the assistant commercial relations manager in Cyprus, before being appointed as sales and service manager. At the time of his retirement in 1979 he was the ground services manager for the south and west Europe region, of what was by then British Airways. Squadron Leader McNair, DFC and Bar, died in May 1996 aged 77 years.

Wing Commander Christopher Deanesly was posted in May 1944 as the Chief Flying Instructor to 107 OTU at Leicester East. Its main role was to train pilots to fly Dakotas on glider-towing operations and later he was posted to 575 Squadron, which operated in that role. He took over as the unit's CO but continued to fly and his last operational sortie was on 25 March 1945 when he flew a Dakota across the River Rhine as part of Operation Varsity.

He was finally released from the RAF in August 1945 and he returned to live in the Midlands, with his wife Kuni, whom he had met in 1941, when she was a WAAF officer at Warmwell. As a civilian he initially worked for a company engaged in brass foundering but he later started up his own business. He retired in 1971 and, with time to spare, the former wing commander was always willing to communicate and talk about his wartime experiences.

In 1976 his medals were stolen and he was absolutely devastated. A man later telephoned him to say that he had the medals but he had purchased them from reputable auction house and was reluctant to give them up. The wing commander tried to recover them by various means but it is understood that he failed. It was a bitter blow. He died on 19 February 1990.

Described by Wing Commander Deanesly as an 'Above Average' pilot, Flying Officer Joe Berry lived up to his former CO's expectations. Having flown to North Africa early in 1943, he and his friend Pilot Officer Brian Wild were posted to 153 Squadron. They were operational in 'A' Flight from 30 January and the units main role was to fly night patrols over British bases and provide fighter cover for Allied convoys. Amongst their colleagues and friends serving in 153 Squadron was Flying Officer Kenneth Rayment, DFC. Many years later he made the headlines for

Squadron Leader Joe Berry, D.F.C. and Two Bars, former Sergeant pilot on 256 Squadron. He later served with 153 and 255 Squadrons in the Mediterranean Theatre and in March 1944 he was awarded the D.F.C. During the summer of 1944 he was appointed as the Commanding Officer of 501 Squadron at Manston and before his death in October that year, he had destroyed the highest number of flying bombs. Courtesy of Joyce Berry

all the wrong reasons: he was one of the pilots involved in the Manchester United air disaster in 1958.

Flying Officer Berry's time in 153 Squadron was short, and he was soon posted to 255 Squadron, which was also operating Beaufighters in the Mediterranean theatre. For many months he did not have any success but on 9 September he shot down an Me 210 and that was followed by another over Salerno the next day. On 24 October he destroyed a Ju 88 but he and his navigator Flying Officer Watson had to abandon their aircraft when it was damaged during the combat. For Joe Berry it was the second time that he had had to abandon his aircraft but on this occasion both he and his navigator escaped unharmed.

Berry and Watson were tour-expired at the end of October 1943, and on 8 October they flew from Bo Rizzo in Sicily to El Aouna in Tunisia, cramped into a Beaufighter flown by a South African pilot, Pilot Officer Bob Spraag. In Tunisia they were to board the ship that would return them to England. Former 96 Squadron pilot, Warrant Officer Stan Walker was flying immediately behind their aircraft in another Beaufighter, carrying a second tour expired crew bound for the same ship.

When Walker approached to land he saw that the Beaufighter ahead of him had crashed and the airfield was a scene of total devastation. Pilot Officer Spraag's aircraft had

Former 96 and 256 Squadron aircrew, having moved to 255 Squadron in Sicily. Featuring Warrant Officer Willy Streeter (back row second from left) *and Warrant Officer Stan Walker* (back row fourth from left) *from 96 Squadron. From 256 Squadron there is Flying Officer Joe Berry* (front row second from left) *and his navigator Flying Officer Ian Watson* (second from right) *Other 255 Squadron personnel include the C.O., Squadron Leader Wells* (front row centre) *and Pilot Officer Bob Spraag* (front row end left). Courtesy of Stan Walker

undershot the runway and collided with the boundary fence. The Beaufighter had crashed into the ground and pieces of it were spread out all over the strip, so Walker was forced to make an unconventional landing, bouncing over the debris. He thought all four airmen on board were very lucky to escape death or serious injury. Fortunately, the accident did not delay Berry and Watson and they were able to board their ship and sail home as planned.

In March 1944 Flying Officer Berry was awarded the DFC for his contribution towards 255 Squadron's operations and the destruction of two enemy aircraft on successive nights in September. The citation also recognized the fact that on two occasion he had had to abandon his aircraft but had acted with coolness and courage. He was then sent on a course to Defford where various radio and radar projects created by the Telecommunications Establishment at Great Malvern were evaluated. Promotion followed rapidly at this point and in June Flight Lieutenant Berry was posted to the Fighter Interception Unit (FIU) at Ford.

While he was at the FIU, Berry flew a number of different types of aircraft, but possibly the most advanced was the Westland Welkin. The single-seat high-altitude fighter never entered RAF service and he was one of the few pilots to fly it. He was soon selected to join a special flight equipped with the Tempest, which was formed for a specific role to destroy the V1 flying bombs.

It was a task in which he excelled and Flight Lieutenant Berry became an expert in the destruction of the deadly weapon. Throughout July and August he flew on what were known as Diver Patrols over southern England and he destroyed his first V1 on the night of 28 June. On four occasions, the 6, 19 and 25 July and 7 August, he destroyed four flying bombs and then on two nights in succession, 3 and 5 August he downed five of them. On 16 August he was promoted to squadron leader and given command of 501 Squadron which was reforming at Manston with the Tempest. So serious was the situation that he was give personal orders from the the Prime Minister, Winston Churchill and the unit became operational with immediate effect.

Throughout the summer Berry continued to destroy an increasing number of flying bombs. In September 501 Squadron moved to Bradwell Bay. During the same month he was awarded a Bar to his DFC. It was from Bradwell Bay that he flew his last sortie when he took off at 0535 on 1 October. Together with two other pilots he was to take part in a ranger sortie and attack targets of opportunity in western Germany.

While flying very low over Holland in the vicinity of Veendam, his Tempest was hit by ground fire, probably from a German radar station called Gazzelle. In an attempt to save himself he climbed to 500 ft but a white vapour trail gave away the fact that the Glycol tank had been hit and the engine was rapidly overheating. He was heard by his fellow pilots, Flight Lieutenants Williams and Hanson to say, 'I've had it chaps....you go on!' The Tempest then crashed in flames at Kibbelgaarn, a small village 4½ miles from Scheemda.

Two local people, including the headmaster of a local school, ran out to see if they could do anything. They put out the fire and pulled Squadron Leader Berry from the Wreckage, but he was already dead. His identity tags were destroyed in the fire and so the only clues to who he was were in a small medicine box and a cigarette case with the initials 'JB' on it. The Germans arrived two hours later and Squadron Leader Berry was eventually buried in Scheemda, with just a plain wooden cross to mark his grave. On it was an inscription that said, 'Unknown RAF Pilot'. Squadron Leader Berry was awarded a second Bar to his DFC on 20 October 1946 backdated to 1944.

Another senior pilot from the early days of 96 Squadron was Flight Lieutenant Raphael, who went on to achieve great things. By late 1942 he had been promoted to wing commander and he took over the command of 85 Squadron. In April 1943 he was appointed as the CO of RAF Manston and it was a crucial period in the station's history. Raphael overlooked 617 Squadron's detachment when its crews were training for the 'Dams' raid at Reculver, and in 1944 the laying down of a permanent runway. After leaving Manston in September 1944 he was promoted to group captain and posted to the RAF Staff College.

It seemed that the young Canadian had a great future ahead of him but he was tragically killed on 10 April 1945 when the Spitfire he was flying collided with a C 46 American transport aircraft near Ashford. He had only recently married and his wife, Dorothy Pamela, was living in Bournemouth at the time. Twenty-eight-year-old Group Captain Gordon Learmouth Raphael DSO, DFC and Bar, was the son of Dr Howard and Pearl and he was buried in Cudham (St. Peter and Paul) Churchyard , in Grave 20.

Wing Commander Ronald Kellett, 96 Squadron's first charismatic CO, under whom Raphael served in 1941, later worked in the Air Ministry and went on to become an instructor at the Turkish Staff College. He continued to fly after the war and was the CO of 615 Squadron in the RAF Auxiliary Air Force from 1946 to 1949. He became a stockbroker and had a farm in Kent where he bred Charolais cattle and had his own private landing strip for his light aircraft. He continued to fly and lead an active life well into his twilight years. He was an authority on wine and claimed his cellar was stocked to last him until he died. That sad day arrived in November 1998 when he was eighty-nine years old.

The officer who succeeded Wing Commander Kellett, Squadron Leader Bobby Burns, ended the war as a group captain and CO of RAF Charter Hall at Berwick. The former 96 Squadron pilot, Flight Lieutenant Tom Smith, met him early in 1945 and Burns told him that he was not happy running a training unit and wanted to return to flying. That was unlikely to happen but he remained in the RAF and rose through the system to achieve air rank and a number of honours. Air Commodore Burns was awarded the CBE and after his retirement from the service he moved to Canada. In July 1979 he wrote to co-author Ron Collier describing how a fighter night operated.

The idea was to stop the AA down to say 15,000 ft over the target and pile the night-fighters on top of that at 500 ft intervals (on Aneroid altimeter setting). So the balloons forced the 'Huns' above 10,000 ft the AA forced them up to us and all we had to do was shoot them down, but without AI it was like looking for a needle in a haystack. But we got a few nevertheless.

Nothing was heard from him after that communication and his exact fate is not known.

Rather ironically, compared to the losses of Fighter Command units in the south of England, squadrons in 9 Group got away quite lightly; the north-west proved to be a safe place to operate. Relatively few pilots or aircrew were killed in action and it was training and other non-operational sorties which proved so costly in terms of the lives lost. Most of those killed in such circumstances have been forgotten but in this book they have been given their place in history. The young airmen who came from the Commonwealth and foreign shores and who died before they entered active service should not be forgotten.

There were a number of reunions after the war. In May 1977 Hans Muhlhann returned to thank the people of Nercws in North Wales for looking after him in May 1941. He met Tom Roberts, the man who had taken him prisoner and they exchanged gifts. Tom gave Hans his shoulder holster and signalling lamp back, which he had taken off him when he landed. Hans presented Tom with a beautiful genuine Stein beer mug. Then the two men visited the site where the Han's Heinkel had crashed and he met some of the other people who had helped him thirty-six years earlier. At this time Hans was living in Friedrichstadt and he had organized his visit through the North Wales Police who contacted many of those who were still alive.

In April 1988 there was another reunion at RAF Sealand involving Artur Weisemann, Walter Schaum, Heinrich Rodder and Heinz Kochy with Wing Commander Peter Ayerst, DFC, one of the pilot's who had shot them down in August 1940. The former enemies posed for a photograph besides a replica of a Spitfire before taking lunch in the Officers' Mess. It was a moving occasion for all those involved and it proved again, that those who were once old enemies could become good friends.

During the war Wing Commander Ayerst had a varied career in the RAF. After a tour in the Middle East he returned home and served with 124 Squadron, flying Spitfires from airfields in south-east England, at Bradwell Bay and Manston. In 1945 he became a test pilot and worked with Alex Henshaw, the chief test pilot of Vickers at Castle Bromwich. He continued in that role until the factory closed in July 1945; he was the last test pilot on the site.

After the war he left the RAF for a short while but by the end of 1949 he had joined up again. He later served in 5 and 16 Squadrons in Germany with distinction. In 1954 he was again under the command of former Wing Commander Hallings-Pott, with whom he had served at Hawarden in 1940. Now an air vice-marshal, Hallings-Pott was by this time the AOC of 2 Group in Germany. Squadron Leader McLean, the third pilot involved in the destruction of the Heinkel in august 1940, was promoted to group captain but he and Wing Commander Ayerst never met again after leaving Hawarden.

Wing Commander Ayerst's final posting was to Wattisham as the Deputy Station Commander. He retired from the RAF in April 1973. During his service career he had flown numerous types and variants of aircraft including the Hurricane, Lancaster, Vampire, Venom and Lightning. Of the band of brothers who served in France with 73 Squadron in 1939, Wing commander Peter Ayerst and Wing Commander Dicky Martin are the sole survivors.

Towards the end of the war 96 Squadron went through a number of changes and in December 1944 it was equipped with the Halifax Mk. III before converting to the Dakota in Transport Command. 256 Squadron kept its role as a night-fighter unit and in 1958, while it was based at Geilenkirchen in German, it was joined by 96 Squadron. Both squadrons were by then equipped with the Meteor N.F.11 and operated in the night-fighting role, just as they had when they were part of 9 Group in 1941. In 1958 both squadrons were renumbered with 96 Squadron becoming 3 Squadron and 256 becoming 11 Squadron. And so ended a period of history that stretched back to the First World War.

96 Squadron has an active Squadron Association and it still holds annual reunions. It publishes a regular newsletter and its Editor, Mr Dave Sanderson, has helped the authors to find former personnel like Tom Smith, Stan Walker and Tom Wilkinson. The bulk of its membership is made up of former airmen who served in RAF Germany, who worked

Caricatures of various members of 256 Squadron at Squires Gate drawn during the Summer of 1942 by Pat Rooney. It includes Squadron Leader Paul Rabone; Pilot Officer Joe Berry; Pilot Officer John Tweedale; Flying Officer Bob Lamb; Flying Officer Don Toone; Pilot Officer Leonard. It depicts a total of twenty-seven officers. Courtesy of Paul Tweedale

on or flew the Meteor, although there are still a small number of veterans from Second World War. 256 Squadron does not have an active association but Mr Russell Brown of Lytham is the unofficial keeper of its history. Mr Brown and other members of the Lancashire Aircraft Investigation Team have carried out extensive research into 256 Squadron and its operations from Squires Gate. The history of both units is entwined within that of the North-West of England generally and without such organisations, much of what is recorded in theses would have been lost forever.

Epilogue

During the research for this book we have managed to contact six former pilots and air gunners/navigators who have contributed to this account. Five of them are still alive and the survivors are Tom Smith, Brian Wild, John MacDonald, Stanley Walker, Eric Raybould, Stanley Sim. Former Sergeant air gunner Les Seales sadly died as the script was being processed for publication. Each one of them is, or was, unique and what they share is the common view that what they did in the war was nothing special and just a job.

Flight Lieutenant Tom Smith

On 22 August 1944 Flight Lieutenant Tom Smith followed in the footsteps of Squadron Leader Rabone when he joined 23 Squadron at Little Snoring. Throughout the autumn and winter of 1944 he flew on numerous intruder sorties over Europe but one incident in early 1945 brought his flying career to an abrupt end.

On 16 January Flight Lieutenant Smith and his observer, Flying Officer Arthur Cockayne, were patrolling an area west of Berlin. After seeing some aircraft take off from an airfield that he spotted through the cloud, they decided to attack it and see what damage they could do. Unfortunately Smith did not realize that the airfield was Fassburg, a very well-defended target. As he flew low over the airfield he passed between two flak towers and his Mosquito was badly damaged by the firepower aimed at them.

Smith stood little chance of keeping the aircraft in the air and had no option but to order his navigator out and make a crash landing in a forest. He was very badly injured, with burns to his face that caused him to go temporarily blind, and a broken leg that restricted his movement. Flying Officer Cockayne was less fortunate; he broke his neck and was killed after abandoning the stricken Mosquito.

The Germans took Flight Lieutenant Smith to the Dulag Luft PoW Transit camp near Frankfurt and for three months he was totally blind. He was given medical treatment, but was kept more or less in solitary confinement. Radar equipment found in the wreckage aroused the interest of the *Gestapo* and it wanted to interview him about it. He often asked about what had happened to Flying Officer Cockayne and

Caricature of Flight Lieutenant Tom Smith after he was posted to 23 Squadron at Little Snoring in 1944. Another drawing by artist Pat Rooney.
Courtesy of Tom Smith

The original grave (3rd right) of Flying Officer Arthur Clarence Cockayne of 23 Squadron, the navigator of Flight Lieutenant Tom Smith at Fassberg. Flight Lieutenant Smith was injured so badly that the Germans also dug a grave for him and the photo was later given to him by a German guard.
Courtesy Tom Smith

when his eyesight returned in one eye a guard showed him a photograph of his grave in a cemetery near the airfield at Fassburg. The guard pointed out that there was an open grave next to it and joked that everyone was so convinced that he would die, it had been dug for him.

Eventually Flight Lieutenant Smith was moved to a convent which acted as a hospital and he remembered the journey there on a tram, with just a single guard. In his condition there was not much chance he could escape but so that he would not be recognized as an RAF officer by German civilians he was given an old *Luftwaffe* great coat to put over his tattered uniform. He remained in the convent until the end of the war when he was eventually repatriated, although he still needed a lot of medical treatment.

Tom Smith continued to attend the hospitals at East Grinstead and Cosford where he received treatment for his burns and underwent plastic surgery. While he was in Cosford Hospital he was visited by William and Alice, the parents of his navigator, Flying Officer Cockayne. They told him that 'Cocky', as Tom called him, had plans to run a school after the war with his wife. He also discovered that his navigator was one of eight children and Tom realised there was a lot he did not know about the man with whom he had flown with for five months.

With 755 hours and 55 minutes in his log book Flight Lieutenant Smith's flying days were over. He was not demobbed immediately and as the RAF seemed reluctant to give him a permanent post he was sent from station to station trying to find a job. Eventually he had an interview with Air Vice-Marshal MacDonald whom he had met at Barton Hall when he was with 9 Group in 1943. MacDonald was by this time SASO of 12 Group but he was shortly to take up the post as AOC of 11 Group. The interview was a very casual affair, with MacDonald wearing his dressing gown while being served his breakfast. This time there was no mention of Flight Lieutenant Smith's drinking habits and AVM MacDonald offered him a job as a Staff Officer at Bentley Priory. It was the last post that he held in the RAF and soon afterwards he was discharged.

To begin with he was unable to work because of his medical condition but eventually he went to Glasgow University and studied engineering. After completing his course he was employed by Rolls-Royce at its shadow production factory at Hillington near Glasgow. Tom was involved in the construction of aero engines and became secretary of the Engine Handling Panel which controlled technical information relating to their use. When Hillington was threatened with closure he was told that he would have to move to Derby. He was not keen on that and although he had always dreamed of returning to flying, his career took a complete change of direction and he became a chartered accountant.

He retired at the age of 60 in 1980 and although he and his wife and former nurse, Joy, moved around, they later settled in Gloucestershire, close to his old friend Dicky Martin. After the war Dicky Martin had become an instructor at the Empire Test Pilots' School at Boscombe Down. He was later to become a test pilot for Gloster Aircraft and was the first pilot to fly the Javelin through the sound barrier. He later joined Avro as a Test Pilot and flew Vulcans from Woodford until he retired. After all this time their wives and families are still good friends. Flying is never very far away from their thoughts and they would happily do it all over again, if time would allow!

Flight Lieutenant Brian Wild
After being separated from his long term friend Flying Officer Joe Berry, Brian Wild was also promoted to flying officer and posted to 46 Squadron in Egypt. He flew various marks of Beaufighters from Idku near Alexandria and operated out of a number of airfields around the Mediterranean. The unit was involved in intruder operations over the Greek islands and also had a detachment based in Cyrpus.

On 14 November 1943 he shot down an He 111 off the island of Kos. The action was caught on the gun camera of the Beaufighter that was flying behind him and Flying Officer Wild's aircraft can be clearly identified in a photograph that he has kept of the incident. The enemy aircraft crashed on Kos and it turned out to be the only one that he shot down but there was no disputing whether it should be confirmed or not as the evidence was clear enough for all to see.

After being repatriated in April 1944 newly promoted Flight Lieutenant Wild was posted to 51 OTU at Cranfield as a flying instructor. Soon after he arrived he heard that his friend from 256 Squadron, Flight Lieutenant Derek Hollindrake, was to return to the home establishment. Wild put in an immediate request for him to be posted to Cranfield. Soon afterwards Hollindrake arrived and with further wrangling he became Wild's regular navigator.

Flight Lieutenant Wild was later posted to 25 Squadron flying Mosquito XVIIs from Coltishall, Castle Camps and Boxted. His partnership with Flight Lieutenant Hollindrake continued and he was also posted to 25 Squadron but was demobilized not long afterwards in early 1946. By that time Brian Wild was acting squadron commander and acting squadron leader, but as he has pointed out, still only on a flight lieutenant's pay. On leaving the service Brian returned to Bolton to live with a cousin.

Wild was always a keen sportsman and he regularly played cricket for his local team Farnworth. It turned out that the Bolton Wanderers captain, Billy Moirs, also played cricket for Farnworth and Brian got to know him quiet well. When Wild's cousin emigrated to Canada he had to go and live in digs, but word soon got around that he was not happy with his living arrangements. One evening Billy Moirs' wife told him that they had a room to spare and asked him if he wanted to move in. As a Bolton fan he was in his element and he stayed with the family for nearly a year until he began his training as a teacher.

In 1949 another chapter began in Wild's life when he met a girl called Bunty at a dance in Nottingham and a little while later they were married and went to live in Derbyshire. While they were on their honeymoon in the Scilly Isles Wild bumped into his former CO, Wing Commander Adams, and they had a good chat about old times. Wild remained a teacher for the rest of his working life and he retired as a Headmaster in 1983.

Over the years he kept in touch with some of his old friends and especially Derek Hollindrake, who had moved back north to Todmorden where he opened a chain of bookmakers' shops. Later he ran a successful hotel business. The former navigator invited Brian to be Godfather to his daughter, Jennifer. They met each other regularly and Wild was stunned by Derek's sudden death in 1993.

Although he has never been a man to dwell on the past, Brian Wild has always had a lot of respect for those who were less fortunate than himself. He has never forgotten his former air gunner, 'Ack' Greenwood, of whom he still talks about with great affection. He has visited Greenwood's grave at Hessle and his greatest regret is that his former friend and gunner died without getting the opportunity to use his skills, of which he was so proud, in action. Brian's family consists of a son and a daughter and he also regrets that Greenwood never had the chance to settle down and have a family.

As an amateur aviation artist Brian Wild has used his knowledge of aircraft and flying to paint some dramatic scenes from memory. He is a keen gardener and also enjoys visiting his daughter, who is the curator of a castle that is something of a national monument. Another popular pastime is playing bridge and one of their partners of Brian and his wife Bunty, is Joyce Berry, the widow of his old friend, Joe. She lives close by and they have a lot in common and enjoy each others company. They are amongst the survivors of a generation which lost a lot of close friends and family and they know just how lucky they are to be alive.

Squadron Leader John MacDonald

Former 256 Squadron pilot Sergeant John MacDonald was later commissioned while he was at Watchfield working as an instructor at the Beam Approach Training School. He was later appointed as a staff officer and worked in Whitehall, but he still occasionally got the opportunity to fly though mainly light communications aircraft for duties in France after D-Day. By the end of the war he had accumulated over 3,000 flying hours.

John MacDonald continued with his career in civil aviation and worked for many years as an air traffic controller. He gained his Commercial Pilot's License and flew both fixed

Sergeant John MacDonald of 256 Squadron sitting in a Defiant at Colerne before the move to Squires Gate. The senior N.C.O. pilot was one of the founder members of the unit and he was eventually commissioned after being posted as an instructor. Courtesy of Sqn. Ldr. MacDonald

wing aircraft and helicopters. By the time of his retirement he had risen to the top of his profession and had become the Deputy Director of Civil Aviation. He later turned his hand to writing and in 1981 John's book called, *Sheep and Actors* was published.

Sheep and Actors is a 'Factional' account of John's life, from his school days in Scotland to joining the RAF at the age of eighteen and training to become a pilot. The book recalls his experiences during training, when he lost a number of good friends and his time on 256 Squadron at Squires Gate. John knew many of those mentioned in this account and he shared a room with Sergeant Ellmers, while Flight Sergeant Walden was his air gunner. John has said that much of the tragic loss of life was caused by bad organisation and poor maintenance procedures, as well as pilots not being trained efficiently for night flying operations.

It was not until the final stages of completing the text for publication that Mr MacDonald was contacted and he has been extremely helpful. The information that he has provided has shed 'new light' on a number of incidents mentioned in this account and explained some things that were previously unknown. John Mcdonald lives in the south-west of England and in his retirement he enjoys skiing, walking and riding.

Warrant Officer Stanley Walker

Warrant Office Stanley Walker saw his former 96 Squadron colleague Warrant Officer Willie Streeter for the last time in November 1943. Many airmen in Sicily were suffering from Malaria and Streeter was hospitalized with what was suspected as a case of jaundice that could have been Malaria. The unit moved to Italy and continued to operate from Foggia Main and he had to crew up with another navigator.

Later in 1944 Walker was posted to the Mediterranean Coastal Air Force, a combined organization of British and American forces which was initially based in Algeria. He was attached to a communications flight which later moved to Naples, from where he spent a lot of time flying between Italy and North Africa in Ansons, Lockheed Hudsons and Beechcraft Expeditors. He remained overseas in the Mediterranean theatre until 1946. He has never forgotten his flight back to England, which turned to be the last one of his RAF service. In January 1946 he was instructed to fly as co-pilot on a B24 Liberator, from Capodichino near Naples to St Mawgan in England. The Liberator's final destination was Lichfield where it was to be handed over to civilian operator, Scottish Airways. Walker had never flown a Liberator before and he soon discovered that his South African captain only had twelve' hours experience on the type and no night-flying experience at all. They took off without a hitch, but as they tried to set course for England there were problems with the navigator and radio operator.

The navigator had the wrong charts and the radio operator seemed incapable of getting them a fix to confirm their position. It was becoming dark and things were not looking too good when Walker managed to contact Bordeaux. The controller gave him a magnetic bearing so they were able to obtain a fix and steer a course for St Mawgan. They were well behind schedule, and Customs Officers were waiting for them who demanded to search the Liberator.

They found nothing but when the navigator returned to the aircraft on his own, two RAF policeman quietly followed him. They hid and watched him unpacking something from a couple of parachutes and when they pounced, they discovered that the goods were watches, jewellery and money. The navigator was arrested, as was the radio operator soon afterwards when he was implicated by his partner. It later turned out that the two men were known to the RAF Police and had already served time at the Aircrew Correction Centre in Sheffield.

When Walker got back on board the Liberator he inspected it and found that the two miscreants had hidden the goods in his parachute and that of his fellow South African pilot. He felt a shiver run down his spine when he realized that they had been willing to risk the lives of their fellow crew, for what was probably a small personal gain. Walker was glad that the two airmen had been caught and he and the South African were only too happy to continue on to Lichfield without the aid of either of them.

After being demobbed Stan Walker returned to his previous employment in the steel industry. Just occasionally he bumped into some of his old colleagues from the RAF and in 1947 he met former 96 Squadron air gunner Freddie Wake. Freddie told Stan that he was working for Crawford's Biscuits but after a brief conversation recollecting their wartime experiences they wished each other well and never saw each other again.

Stan became president of the British Forging Association and in 1983 he was in Cologne for an International Conference of Forging Associations. While he was there he got talking to a former *Luftwaffe* night-fighter pilot called Ernst Holschmitt. They had seen each other at previous conferences but this time they talked about the war and after a while they found that they had met before in quite different circumstances.

It was probably on the night of 22/23 January 1944 when Walker was on patrol over the Anzio beachhead in Italy where he encountered a Ju 88 whose pilot was being very persistent. Despite the German's efforts however, Walker defended the beach and managed to chase him off, although he realized he was up against a skilful pilot. Ernst

Holschmitt was that pilot and it was quite a shock for both when they cross-checked and recalled their first meeting over the coast of Sicily fifty years before.

Walker lives in Wolverhampton quite close to the former Boulton & Paul factory and the museum which now houses a rebuilt Defiant. As a result he is able to maintain his associations with the aircraft that he flew many years ago. He is also a keen golfer and plays twice a week at his local club. He recalled that Laddie Lucas, with whom he trained in Canada, was also a keen golfer and a member of the pre-war Walker Cup Team. Out of the twenty-eight pilots that passed out from 11 EFS on 9 December 1940 Stan Walker is the only survivor.

Flight Lieutenant Eric Raybould

After transferring to 68 Squadron, former 256 squadron pilot Flight Lieutenant Eric Raybould claimed just a single victory when he shot down a Do 17 on the night of 29 July 1942. He remained in 68 Squadron until the end of 1942 when he was posted to 600 Squadron at Maison Blanche It was equipped with the Beaufighter Mk VI and it later moved to Luqa in Malta where he contracted a serious bout of TB.

After being ill for some time Raybloud was invalided out of the RAF in 1945. His condition continued to plague him and for a number of years it prevented him from working. Eventually he recovered enough take a degree course in Russian and German and he was later employed by ICI in personnel management. Although his work was based in the City of London, he travelled all over the country and became particularly fond of the south-west of England.

Despite the passing of time he has never forgotten a terrible night in 1941 when he lost a very dear friend, Jack Sharp. It shook him up badly and although he survived the war it made him think about his own vulnerability and future. After working for ICI for over twenty years he retired in the late 1970s and moved to Cornwall to pursue his hobby of boating. He settled for a tranquil life and the love of the sea and enjoying his retirement with his wife Valerie.

Squadron Leader Stanley Sim

Having left 96 Squadron on 6 May 1942, after training as a navigator (radar), Sergeant Stanley Sim was commissioned and posted to 153 Squadron in North Africa. Later he flew with a number of other units including 23 and 11 Squadrons and he is a link between the wartime era and the modern jet age. Having joined the RAF as an apprentice in 1938, he rose through the ranks and remained in the service after the war.

In May 1960, as a flight Lieutenant he was posted to 3 Squadron Geilenkirchen, in Germany, which was equipped with the all-weather fighter, the Gloster Javelin FAW4. It did not take him long to discover that 3 Squadron had been formed from 96 Squadron on 21 January 1959, when it was renumbered. In effect Flight Lieutenant Sim had rejoined his old unit and he felt very much at home as the unit was still in the night-fighting role.

Throughout the remainder of his flying career, during which he rose to the rank of Squadron Leader, he flew a variety of aircraft including the Canberra and he became a navigator/radar instructor. He continued to fly into his later years but, as is the way with the RAF, the ground tours got longer and the flying tours shorter. His final post before retiring from the RAF in 1975 was as officer commanding administration, RAF Northolt.

It was a fine way to end nearly thirty-eight years in the RAF on a station noted for its wartime connections with Fighter Command.

Warrant Officer Les Seales

None of the other six surviving airmen would deny that Les Seales was probably the most interesting and death-defying of them all. After leaving the RAF after the war he continued to lead a dangerous life and at the age of almost ninety he still flies, but not in the conventional sense. While any other person would be seated in an enclosed cabin, Les likes to stand on the wing exposed to the elements and face the perils of being a wing walker.

After leaving 96 Squadron in March 1942 Seales was posted to a detachment of 277 Squadron at Hawkinge which was an Air Sea Rescue unit. It was equipped with a variety of aircraft such as the Lysander, the Walrus and the Defiant which had been specially converted for the Air Sea Rescue (ASR) role. He later joined the main unit at Shoreham but in late 1943 he was posted to India and spent Christmas that year on the high seas. On his arrival in India he was posted to the newly formed 292 Squadron at Jessore in Ceylon. The unit flew the Walrus and Warwicks over the Bay of Bengal on Air Sea Rescue duties and he remained in Ceylon for the rest of the war. After his repatriation he was posted to Cirencester College where he took over the role of transport officer. He was demobbed in November 1945 and picked up on the exciting life he had left before the war. In the 1930s he and his team mate, Arthur Horton, were involved in motorcycle sidecar racing. It meant riding the side car just inches from the ground at breakneck speeds and they won the Swiss Grand Prix and were British Champions for three consecutive years.

In between riding motorcycles Les worked for a company which demonstrated earth moving equipment but in 1976 he lost a leg. The accident had nothing to do with his job or motorcycles and he was on foot at the time. He stepped off the kerb in London and was hit by a bus. Three years later he retired but after a while he began to yearn for some of the excitement and danger of his younger days.

Having heard about Les' wartime exploits and the incident involving Pilot Officer Phoenix, a friend suggested that he might like to take up wing walking and so he made all the arrangements for his first first flight. Much to the dismay of his wife, Joy, it was something that Les became quite fond of. Because he only had one leg, he had to be lifted into position by a fork-lift truck, but once he was in the air he enjoyed the freedom and fresh air. After completing his first wing walk Les assumed that he held the record for the oldest person in the world to do this, but he later discovered that an American gentleman held the title.

At the age of eighty-eight and having stolen the title from the American, Les was planning his next wing walk on his ninetieth Birthday. Sadly, Les never made it and after three weeks in hospital he died on 13 May 2004. His wife Joy said she was very sorry to lose him but he had had a good life! Les Seales will be truly missed by his family, friends and associates and there is no doubt that he was one of life's amazing characters. As a mark of respect, this account of Les Seales had been left in the Epilogue because it was already included in the original text.

Index

Main RAF Units:

Other RAF Units & Organisations: